Wicked Little Joe

ALSO BY JOSEPH HONE

FICTION
The Private Sector
The Sixth Directorate
The Paris Trap
The Flowers of the Forest
The Valley of the Fox
Summer Hill
Return to Summer Hill
Firesong

TRAVEL
The Dancing Waiters
Gone Tomorrow
Children of the Country: Coast to Coast Across Africa
Duck Soup in the Black Sea

Wicked Little Joe

A Tale of Childhood and Youth

Joseph Hone

THE LILLIPUT PRESS
DUBLIN

First published 2009 by
THE LILLIPUT PRESS
62–63 Sitric Road, Arbour Hill
Dublin 7, Ireland
www.lilliputpress.ie

ISBN 978 1 84351 147 2

1 3 5 7 9 10 8 6 4 2

The author gratefully acknowledges his several residencies at the
Tyrone Guthrie Centre at Annaghmakerrig whilst writing this memoir.

A CIP record for this title is available
from The British Library.

Set in 11 pt on 16 pt Caslon by Marsha Swan
Printed in England by Athenaeum Press Ltd, Tyne and Wear

In memory of SMB and HMB
and for our grandchildren – Harry, Cordelia and Jack

For the field is full of shadows as I near the
        Shadowy coast.
And a ghostly batsman plays to the bowling of
        A ghost.
And I look through my tears on a soundless-
        clapping host,
As the run-stealers flicker to and fro,
        To and fro –
O my Hornby and my Barlow long ago!

Francis Thompson

ONE

In the summer of 1939, as a two-year-old in London, I was given away by my parents to a Chelsea friend and taken on the Irish Mail to Dublin. On arrival she didn't abandon me in the Left Luggage. That, indeed, would have been carelessness. Instead I was deposited at my grandfather's house in Killiney next morning. He must have groaned at my arrival – he was prone to groan. With the arrival of my sister Geraldine and twin brothers, Antony and Camillus, landing on his doorstep in the two subsequent years, his groans must surely have become cries.

These babies became like time bombs for him, to be passed on as quickly as possible among equally alarmed friends and relations. My grandfather – (known as 'Old Joe', so that I became 'Little Joe') son of a respectable, well-to-do Dublin banking, merchant and artistic family, friend and biographer of Yeats and George Moore – was reduced to the status of a baby-hawker. Literally so, for when his 'Mary Poppins' friend, P.L. Travers, wanting to adopt a child, came to Dublin in 1940 to inspect the goods – in this case the twins – he said to her, 'Take two, they're small.'

How had all this come to pass?

Some years ago, after my foster parents Hubert and Peggy Butler died, I was told by Bernard Meehan, the archivist of Trinity College Library in

9

Dublin, that among literary and other papers which Hubert, the acclaimed Irish essayist and scholar, had sold to the College, there was a file about me. When I was next over I picked it up. Marked 'Little Joe', it was stuffed full of letters to Hubert and Peggy – with carbon copies of all Hubert's replies – from my real parents, Nat and Biddy, my grandparents, Old Joe and Vera, from my great-aunt Olive, from Peggy's theatre director brother Tony Guthrie, from Pamela Travers, from cousins, friends, headmasters, housemasters, a doctor-psychiatrist and others who had become involved in the seemingly all-absorbing cause of dealing with 'Little Joe', clearly an exceptional case, a real cracker in the difficult, troublesome boy department.

A glance through the file was enough. I saw the wispy heads of unhappy genies emerging, and firmly closed the bottle. I didn't want to revisit my childhood. Or at least the unhappy part of it, for it hadn't always been unhappy. In fact I had a very lucky and stimulating upbringing with the Butlers and the Guthries, in Maidenhall and at Annaghmakerrig, two lovely book-and-theatre-dominated country houses in County Kilkenny and County Monaghan, south and north in Ireland. But my origins, and being farmed out to strangers, my Dublin schooldays, my later meetings with my real parents – all this had certainly been trying. Let those bad genies rattle their chains in the bottle.

These days they would say I was 'in denial'; so be it. I see no good reason why one should uncork bad times, unless a later refusal to do this has formed a 'block', preventing one from getting on decently with one's life. And this has not, I think, been my case. Rather the opposite. The bad memories alone, when I touched on them – of a groaning, penny-pinching grandfather, of a sad grandmother, of irresponsible, drinky, unhappy-go-lucky parents, of my being moved from odd pillar to odder post among put-upon friends and relations; memories of a sadistic headmaster, of vomit-making school food and cold showers – all this long ago made me want to repress these shabby parts of my life, so freeing me to make something brighter of it.

To forget a past that was sometimes as unhappy as mine seemed to me then, and now, to be a very good idea. To deny is often to survive. To dwell on the shipwreck is likely to sink with the wreckage. Besides, as far as my schooldays went, every prep-school boarding boy of my generation, lonely, with parents inevitably absent, has a horror story – more likely a dozen – to tell. A commonplace experience then. And apart from sometimes speaking of the comic side of my family and schooldays – almost as a party piece – I have never wanted to think of, or trade upon, the sadder aspects of my early life. So I thought, let the no doubt troubled child I was then stay interred in the often-troubled tomb of youth.

On the other hand, having reached an age so distant from those times, and thus surely immune to any of its resurrected pains, I thought perhaps I owed it to myself, and as much to my minders – whose real purposes and actions I didn't understand then, or may have wilfully misunderstood or subsequently exaggerated – to take a proper look through the file. It might well have a purely archaeological interest now.

After all, it isn't everyone in their early seventies who discovers a fat file containing long-hidden secrets of their childhood, reflected in letters between various intelligent, well-meaning or irresponsible people who together, in thinking they were doing their best for me, made my early life more difficult than it was already.

But perhaps I'm wrong. Perhaps, marshalling the evidence in the file and in other family letters, I may come to see the good sense of their behaviour towards me. Or perhaps the file will justify my feelings that I was badly handled by all of them?

That's a thought. The proof of my pudding, like revenge, could well be a dish best relished cold, as all my minders are now. I can't hurt them. But perhaps, whether they were right or wrong in their behaviour towards me, in reading through the file and seeing their efforts on my behalf I may come to understand their confused supervision of me, as I was rarely able to do at the time.

So why not call up those spirits from the vasty deep – the dramatis personae of my early life – as witnesses for the prosecution, adding my own defence now? Why not resurrect the minders' view of me, and my own view of the child I was then, and how I was looked after, and see where the balance of judgment might lie?

So last year I opened the bottle and let the first genie out. And there he was, a wispy figure emerging, my grandfather, in a letter drawn out at random, written in 1951 to Hubert Butler, an old friend of his, who lived at Maidenhall in County Kilkenny and had been in effect my foster father since 1939:

Yes, it would be very nice for Little Joe if I could send him to Paris for a fortnight – if you could tell me how to find the money. £30 at least. But how?

1. To make it.
2. To save.
3. To borrow.
4. To beg.

1. My productive capacity has been about £50 p/a for the last six years. I wd. be delighted if you could suggest any means by which I could bring it up to a £100. Even tho' that wd. be but a few drops in the bucket out of which I'm pouring pints per annum. I have been spending 75% to 100% above my income. And over 20% of this has been on Little Joe's expenses and nearly another 15% has gone to Nat [my father]. This year with tax and increasing charges for Joe I am running at a rate of at least 150% above my income. My income earned is about £1000 after income tax and the rates on South Hill.

(I am speaking of Vera's money as well as mine.)

2. There are possibilities (I admit) here. I could save about £150 p/a by cutting out cigarettes, my sub. to the Kildare St Club and such hospitalities as we offer. We could do without a servant, until Vera broke down – another £150 I suppose. Vera and I could go into petit bourgeois lodgings and tell David he will have to fend for himself henceforth. But we did tell him (when times were better) that we could see him through the architectural course. We cd. cut off all aid to Nat. But the likely result of this is that Biddy who, with me, is his only visible means of support, would leave him, and he wd. return to my doorstep. Than having him here hanging about, I wd. much rather go into lodgings (I do not say Vera would) or die. And moreover the cost of keeping him with us wd. be as much as I give him now, so this is really ruled out. So what do you suggest in this line? Cigs, etc. We are quite old and haven't many small pleasures, and are not strong enough for golf or walks in the country.

3. Borrowing. I have been doing this for many years at a accelerated rate. This includes of course selling investments, since the bank has to be paid back from time to time. Counting Vera's little heritage, about a third of which has gone, she and I have enough to last us, say, eight years, without substantially altering our manner of life: this is assuming that values do not fall much further. Our capital has decreased on paper value by 15% at least in the last 4 months, since the socialists retired. And bills and taxes do not rise much further; also assuming that Little Joe is presently 'settled' and numerous other things. We cd. in short gamble on both being dead in eight years, for our only assets wd. then be the house we live in and the furniture. Do you advise us to resign ourselves to this course? It looks as if you were doing so. We have in the sense I have explained to you enough money to send Little Joe to Eton for 2 years. Neither of us has any expectations. I had one of £3000 but have anticipated it in purchasing this house.

4. To beg. Where? No doubt at the end of 8 years my brother and sister, who have always been most generous wd. not let us starve, if they live and have themselves anything left. I have laid my cards on the table.

He had indeed. Though perhaps he was hiding one or two under the table. When he died, eight years later (in that at least his forecast was correct) in 1959, he left an estate valued at nearly forty thousand pounds. Approaching half a million in today's values I imagine.

My grandfather's lengthy correspondence with the Butlers largely revolved around money: how much he was to pay for my keep with them, how much he had paid, or had overpaid, or how much he had forgotten to pay, or how much he would, or could not pay. Another letter, from 1944:

My dear Peggy
Did you get the letter from me with the cheque? I can't remember if I posted it. I had it in my pocket leaving here on Thursday and it was gone when I returned in the evening. I suppose I did post it but I can't recall the act.

My grandfather was a vague man.

He first drove a car – I was told by my aunt Sally – on a family holiday in the 1920s, all the way from Dublin to Galway without stopping. But this was only because he didn't know how to stop the car, which he did in the end by running straight into the hotel porch, demolishing a pillar or two and sending the porter flying.

Old Joe. And he always seemed very old to me. I see him writing, in one or other of the four attractive houses I knew him in, usually at the kitchen table, where there was heat from the stove and so no need to waste fuel on a fire for his wife Vera in the drawing-room. A tall, thin figure stooped over dip-pen, paper, and a cut-glass inkwell – and a tumbler of well-watered Mitchell's Green Spot whiskey to hand if it was after six o'clock. A high brow leading to a bald crown, but with streams of wispy white hair flowing out above his long ears, one or often two pairs of spectacles, one perched on wild eyebrows, the other against luminously pale-blue eyes. A tattered, ash-dusted, elbows-out pullover and befuddled tie, the trousers of an old suit hitched up by another tie, slippers where the heel-ends had long since been pushed down, embedded in the insoles; a forgotten cigarette drooping from thin lips, coughing slightly, or quietly humphing and sighing, or starting to groan when he took his cheque book stubs to the dilapidated drawing-room sofa after lunch, where the two smelly dachshunds, Gretel and Hilda, were already in somnolent residence.

Sitting at one end, he would settle his legs down over the dogs and start his count through the stubs. And then the groans. The dogs, disturbed, responded with their own moans and growls, so that soon the three of them had set up a dirge of throaty complaint, like notes from a diseased organ, each dog an organ pedal now, responding in a different plaintive key as he moved his legs here and there over them.

Most afternoons, having read the stock market prices in *The Irish Times* and dealt with his cheque stubs, he would settle himself to the grim task of making a tally, on the back of the cheque book or an old envelope, of all his worldly assets. First noting the cash in his pockets, perhaps a crumpled ten-shilling note and two sixpences; then making a column of his declining stocks and shares, his São Paulo Tramway stock particularly – this last producing a bad groan, a sudden movement of his thighs and loud yelps from the dogs. Clearly São Paulo trams were going down the tubes.

But there were other, firmer, assets to be cheered by – I saw the back of some of these cheque books and old envelopes later. They ran on the lines of: 'Two old Victorian dining-room chairs (not needed) – ten pounds? Old brass-headed double bedstead (hardly needed) – five pounds? Clothes horse: two pounds. A good desk (but one drawer missing) in basement – ten pounds. Old dress suit, starched shirt and dancing pumps (cert. not needed) – three pounds. Old shoes and hats – two pounds? Set of Hegel's works, (slightly foxed) – three pounds? (Possibly more).'

And then another column – 'This month's liabilities' and renewed groans: 'Sawyers Fish Mongers – one pound seventeen and sixpence. Smyths of the Green, groceries – three pounds, ten shillings and ninepence. Mitchell's, whiskey and cigs – two pounds fifteen shillings and tenpence. Kildare St Club sub – five pounds. School fees, Little Joe – seventeen pounds, ten shillings'. A sudden groan, anguished movement of the legs, dog yelping madly, a cacophony of outrage.

My grandfather was worried about money. In a letter to Peggy Butler, dated March 1945:

Dear Peggy

Hubert says he can't keep Little Joe at the price I am paying, and because I cause you annoyance by suggesting economies, as for instance having the child here for a few days when you went away.

I can't afford more. In fact I can expose my books and accounts which show that properly speaking I have never been able to afford anything, since all Little Joe's expenses come out of capital … I cannot take the child, here, except for occasional spells. I made this clear at the very beginning when the subject was brought before you by Pamela Travers. We were not then fitted to do so, and are now even less fitted, from the point of view of physical health and nerves alone, as any doctor would testify. These seem to be facts, and I suggest we should discuss what can be done with Little Joe in their light. I could, in the meanwhile, make an estimate of the total capital I could be prepared to put aside for Little Joe, say from this summer until he is 17 or 18, when he will have to make his own living. Getting into the merchant navy might be considered, as their career starts at 14, I think, and would therefore leave more over per annum …

Getting me off his hands and his bank balance at the earliest opportunity became a constant preoccupation of my grandfather's. There is no correspondence relating to it in the file, but I clearly remember seeing and then being told about the brochure and admission forms which my grandfather, in the light of this last letter, must have immediately requested. It was from a merchant navy training institution for orphaned or indigenous boys, not set on dry land but on an old ship of the line, the HMS *Conway*, moored in Colwyn Bay, North Wales, and thus a situation ideal from my grandfather's point of view, in that, apart from entry at fourteen, I would be well and truly off his hands, marooned offshore on the Napoleonic Wars hulk for several years. That I somehow escaped this fate must count as one of my earliest lucky breaks.

At the same time, this failure to transport me to Van Diemen's Land, as it were, resulted in ever more tortuous and argumentative letters between my grandfather and the Butlers; an increasingly contentious financial correspondence between them, as if they were Rothschilds and Warburgs arguing over millions rather than two quite well-off but rather miserly families disputing the toss over a few pounds, shillings and pence. An offended tone is there from the start in the first letter I have of my grandfather's, in 1942:

> Dear Peggy
> I'm enclosing Joe's keep in advance for September & October, £6.10.0. I don't know why you say I have been in arrears with payments. I have as a rule paid them in advance; once in the Kildare St Club I paid half a year in advance to Hubert. I was (in this payment) a few weeks early in paying, and now I will be a week or ten days late, with this unexpected 'taxi' bill. Please admit that you are wrong as to this, whatever you may think of my feelings.

Sometimes these letters, in his attempts to straighten things out, are reduced to pure financial farce. Another letter, later in 1942:

> Dear Peggy
> I am enclosing £5.15.0 on account of Joe's expenses to and from Ballingarry. I am not sure from yr. previous card whether I was to pay the whole £1 charged return fare from Bennettsbridge to Kilkenny, as you say the escort on the way back did not charge anything. On yr. account (or Hubert's) it would seem that he did charge; but that the other escort (outward journey) did not. I suppose the escort (return journey) was going to you anyway, so had the benefit of the car. I

16

am puzzled. So I send you both the account and the postcard. If I still owe you the 10/- I will add it to the November cheque. (I have paid the monthly sum for Oct. already.) Please return the account, as I keep a list of these expenses, so that my heirs, executors and assignees may see what a miser I was.

This is worthy of Kafka or Beckett. Who were the two mysterious 'escorts' on these outward and return journeys? – one who charged for his services, the other who didn't, and who 'had the benefit of the car'? Sam Beckett was an old friend of my grandfather's. I wonder if Sam got ideas for some of his more puzzling plays from Old Joe? – perhaps during the long walks they used to make together in the 1930s, up and down the Tipperary mountains. I can add that the one pound return rail fare charged to the Butlers, Bennettsbridge-Kilkenny, seems excessive for 1942, since the two stations were only five miles apart. These financial arrangements, with their consequent puzzlements and misunderstandings between my grandfather and the Butlers, are endless. They clearly absorbed a great deal of their time, which might have been better spent in writing their books and essays. Another letter, from November 1944:

> Dear Peggy
> I don't quite understand about the expense for Little Joe. I mean the '12½% boarding'. And the fee I take it is £5.5.0 for the three months. What will be the total cost? Could you let me know approximately? I mean within £2 or so, for his three month stay in Dublin. You know we think he is much better with you than in any other imaginable place. If I was endowed with £1,000 [he has crossed out £2,000] for his upbringing I could not think it better spent than you wd. spend it on him, and whatever happens we will always feel grateful to you for all you have done for him.
>
> Only as I have explained, I am not so endowed ... and have to consider, as far as can be possible, preserving enough money, so that my old age and Vera's will not be one of penury ... so you must not think me mean if I do 'talk of money' in connection with Little Joe.

Well, both parties went on with their 'talk of money'. It seems their lives, and certainly mine, clearly depended on this. And it was sometimes angry talk. From another cloudy letter to Hubert Butler, early in 1945:

Dear Hubert,

I was in bed when Vera got the telephone. She came up and said it was Peggy. 'Peggy says they are taking a holiday to friends, and Joe is invited. But before going Hubert said we'd better phone and consult the Hones about the cost of Joe's travelling.' I said 'Do you know what the cost will be?' And Vera returned to the phone and came back with the answer that she didn't know, but 'supposed about the same as the fare to Kilkenny'. I said 'All right but perhaps you'd better ask if there will be any motor sharings as well.' Peggy replied that 'There wd. be four motors for Joe to share in and also his part in any incidental expenses.' I said then 'We may as well have him here', as I thought at the time we'd have a servant in, and besides Vera wd. like to see him.

At this you Butlers got very angry – why I can't imagine, since you had at first invited me to make the decision. It was you I gathered who suggested I might like to make the little economy, and now you write as if I was trying to make the economy at your expense.

There are other things to discuss in regard to your letter, other grievances; but this I wd. like to clear up first, for if we can't clear up so simple a question, how can we clear up anything?

Quite so. My grandfather, in the light of his earlier letter querying the excessive return rail fare to Kilkenny, was understandably chary about lashing out another pound for a brief trip on Irish railways, especially since it might well include the mysterious 'escort' again, who this time, thinking he was onto a very good thing, might have charged the Butlers, and thereafter Old Joe, two pounds. And then there is the curious business of my 'sharing in the expenses of four motors'. One can hardly blame my grandfather for querying this. Four motors? Quite a cavalcade, in petrol-starved wartime Ireland – and surely, aged eight, I would only take up small room in one of the motors? And then the consequent 'incidental expenses'. My word! On such an apparently extravagant holiday these might be substantial, a Monte Carlo sum. I can imagine my grandfather in his nightcap, turning on his sick bed, groaning, seeing red for the next six months on his overdrawn bank account. Grievances indeed! And grievances taken onto a philosophical, even a religious plane in a further letter, to Peggy Butler, in May 1945:

My dear Peggy

The first thing to remember in this discussion is the obvious thing, that neither you nor I created this world. Little Joe was born under unfortunate auspices with no silver spoon in his mouth. This is not necessarily fatal to him. Many people so born have done well. But it is a fact to be remembered in discussion with me, as when you say my object is merely to save money. No, it is a question of what I can properly spend on him, having regard to my other obligations. So no doubt with you.

He is in fact in childhood at 'the caprice of the stock market' ... I can make no promises about him; nor can you. It can never be a question of more than six months or so ahead. Hubert's notion of calling in his parents is quite illusory, unless he believes in miracles, which he doesn't. He can write if he likes to them, but it will only waste the postage stamp.

'At the caprice of the stock market' indeed. Was my grandfather's meanness nature or nurture? Or was it not meanness at all, but simply understandable self-preservation? Certainly it was hardly nurture. His father, William Hone, retired early from the law, was well off. A family photograph, taken in what must have been the early 1920s in the garden of Palermo, his large Killiney house, when he would have been in his late seventies, shows him to be a short, stout, genial Victorian paterfamilias, moustached and watch-chained. He is surrounded by some of his extensive family, including my father Nat and my aunt Sally as children, sitting on the grass in front. William Hone's wife Sarah is not there. One of the seven beautiful Cooper sisters from Cooper Hill in County Limerick, she died at only twenty-nine, having given birth to my grandfather Joseph, and three others – my great-aunt Olive, and my two great-uncles Patrick and Christopher. Also in the picture is Maria, the formidable-looking housekeeper. There they all are, in rather stiff, outdated Edwardian clothes – a collection of quietly confident, high-bourgeois Dubliners.

No, it can't have been from his family that Old Joe got his terrible nervousness about money. It may have been due to the fact that throughout his life he rarely earned more than a guinea or so, for his lengthy book reviews for *The Irish Times*, *The London Mercury*, and *The Times Literary Supplement*, and lived off what was initially a substantial, but after the Great Depression in the

1930s an ever-reducing capital. And I, of course, came to be a major cause of this reduction: I and my first three siblings – Geraldine, Antony and Camillus – turning up on his doorstep, me as a toddler and the others in squirming bundles. This was surely a major factor in his miserliness.

In this anybody would have sympathy for him. He had paid expensively for the upbringing and education of his own three children – Nathaniel my father, my aunt Sally and my uncle David. To be landed with the financial and other responsibilities of looking after four more children, albeit his grandchildren, in his early old age, could well make the best of us feel put upon – and miserly. Besides, Old Joe, who was young once – though it was hard to credit this by the time I met him – was bad with children. The whole business of family and children, it seems, was quite alien to him. Beatty Glenavy (of whom more later), a great friend of my grandparents, once showed me a nicely wicked cartoon which my grandfather's friend Max Beerbohm had done of him and his wife Vera on their honeymoon night in Paris in about 1910: they were shown in a great canopied four-poster bed, Joe nervous in a pointy nightcap, Vera small and apprehensive, bedclothes up to her neck, with the caption, 'What do we do now, Vera?' I never saw the cartoon again. It must have disappeared into Beatty's estate when she died.

Yes, Vera, my grandmother. In age, the skin tight against her high cheekbones, the flesh retreating everywhere, leaving her teeth half bared; a skeletal, mournful expression, sometimes wide-eyed in horrified astonishment; put-upon, restless. Or motionless, sitting on a stool gazing into the fire, bony knees steeply raised, legs crossed and intertwined like a contortionist's, a cigarette in her long fine fingers, smoke curling round her head, gazing quizzically through the mist.

A woman who never found herself? Or never knew what she was looking for? Or who was admired so much in youth that her beauty may have seemed all-sufficient? For there is no doubt that Vera had been very beautiful. Dark-haired, large clear blue eyes, that wonderful bone structure, an innocent face; she wore anything with a sophisticated, easy grace. The face I have seen in some of William Orpen's several fine portraits of her: 'The Blue Hat' – sold for a fortune a few years ago – and 'The Roscommon Dragoon', where she's wearing a military uniform with unconscious panache. Orpen couldn't stop painting her when he and my grandparents were neighbours in Edwardian Dublin; dozens of sketches and several portraits. Orpen was certainly enticed by her beauty, and possibly by the hope of her as mistress? But that wasn't on. Vera was happily married at that point and of Puritan New England stock. Or was she? It may have been, as it was with me, uncertainty about her own family background that gave her that sometimes deeply mystified, perturbed look.

For with Vera there was not the long family tree of the Dublin Hones but one with the main branches missing. Little of her antecedents were ever revealed to me, so I assumed there was something to hide. Her family name was Brewster. I remember as a child hearing of the film, *The Brewster Millions*, and thinking that Vera must be part of these millions. I couldn't understand the penny-pinching so predominant in her household.

That Vera had a mother and father must be beyond dispute, but neither was ever spoken of in the family. She had been brought up in New York by her aunt Julia. This was freely admitted, because aunt Julia, taking the stage name of Julia Marlowe, was the foremost classical actress of her time in late-nineteenth-century America.

A 1940s reminiscence of aunt Julia, when she was at the height of her fame in the early 1900s, by the American playwright George Middleton describes her as having 'Loose black hair enfolding her pale face, the rich mouth and large wise eyes that looked out provocatively at me, when I was twenty-two, as she lay propped up in bed, with a crimson coverlet pulled up to the book of verse she was reading in that priceless voice of hers.'

She must have been a sensuous woman as well as a fine actress, a point at least partly confirmed by a studio photograph taken in 1897 when Julia, in her twenties, had just made her first great impact on the New York stage. It shows a biggish girl, staring straight to camera with shadowed, slumberous bedroom eyes, dark coiled tresses falling down over a wide décolleté, one bare arm, saucily at her hip, draped with a shawl. Yes, quite the temptress, except for the voluminous dress she's wearing – a heavy damask outfit, roped at the waist, a rope which then coils round her hips, falling away into a tassel of woolly bobbles. A bedspread, it seems. Not a great come-on, considering she was playing Juliet in the photograph.

This was a role she made so famous in America in her youth that, having married her older actor-manager Henry Southern, she played the love-lorn girl, with Henry as Romeo, until the two of them were at either end of their sixties. They toured America in their later years in these roles, in their own Pullman car, usually just playing the balcony scene – conclusive proof of the star-crossed lovers' deathless love, since both actors were now presumably quite long in the tooth and wrinkly round the gills. This didn't deter the audiences one bit. Southern and Marlowe brought the house down, from Albany to Albuquerque.

All this mummery made aunt Julia a very rich woman – the more so on the death of Henry, upon which she retired and spent the rest of her life in grand hotels, with a bevy of Pekinese dogs, in Switzerland, and every winter at the Cateract Hotel at Assuan in Upper Egypt. However, playing against type in their famous roles as lovers, they failed to have children. And so it was that aunt Julia took charge of Vera and her younger sister Grace, bringing them up and becoming their foster mother.

But who were their real parents? – there's the rub. The file and other family letters give no indication. Years ago I had some information on this, from Beatty Glenavy in Dublin. Beatty, née Beatrice Elvery, a fine painter who married Gordon, Lord Glenavy (and was mother to Paddy Campbell, the witty columnist and stammering TV panel-game star, and his younger brother Michael Campbell, the fine novelist). Beatty was a great friend of my grandfather's before and after he married. She told me how Joe and Vera had met in Paris in 1910. Aunt Julia had brought Vera over to Paris on a Grand Tour of sorts, staying at a grand hotel and buying her expensive hats and clothes in shops on the rue St Honoré. Here they met Old Joe (or Young Joe, as he must have been then) himself in Paris at the time with his friends Willie Yeats and John Synge.

Vera and Joe were smitten. They must have made an attractive and unusual pair, this American beauty and the tall, gauntly distinguished-looking Irishman. Marriage was proposed. This was not taken well by Joe's father in Dublin, who, Beatty told me, got the unlikely idea that Vera and her aunt were American fortune hunters out looking for a rich catch in Europe. *Au contraire*, Julia Marlowe was much richer than any of the Hones.

In the event, Joe and Vera had to get married secretly, in 1911, Beatty explained – with a week's notice, in a suburban church, by special licence from the Archbishop of Dublin, at eight in the morning, with Beatty and the church verger as the only witnesses – Beatty supplying the ring, a curtain ring, which she'd bought the previous day in a local haberdasher's.

Apart from retailing this drama, it was Beatty's view that Vera was possibly aunt Julia's illegitimate daughter, not her niece – aunt Julia's husband Henry Southern, Beatty implied, not being much of a Romeo in that department. But then who was the real father? Beatty didn't know.

Years later I had some further information from my uncle David in Dublin. It seems Vera's mother was aunt Julia's flighty younger sister who, having married conventionally (to a man of German extraction, called Burster, not Brewster) had given birth to Vera and her sister Grace, but had then abandoned husband and children and run off with a cad to Florida, never to surface again, either in reality or in the family annals. Everything was hushed up and aunt Julia then took charge of the two 'Orphans of the Storm' – a family embarrassment that repeated itself with me and my six brothers and sisters fifty years later. Which still leaves the question – what happened to the conventional husband, Mr Burster, father of my grandmother? He, too, has been erased from Vera's family record. In any event this difficult, cloudy background, rather like my own, may have had a lot to do with Vera's later sessions by the fire, on a stool, legs entwined; her puzzled, nervous look, gazing into the flames.

My grandparents were nervous people.

My aunt Sally once told me that the Hones were nervous people generally, a fact perhaps confirmed by my grandfather who, instead of living in his own lovely house, South Hill, overlooking Killiney Bay, leased it out in 1939 and lived the rest of his twenty years in leased accommodation: four houses in Ireland, in Dublin and the countryside, with earlier winters spent in rented houses in Provence and Italy.

These continual domestic upheavals suggest a certain nervous restlessness. Or perhaps that he wanted others to take the financial responsibility for the upkeep of the houses he lived in, and might avoid having to do the same with his own house? Certainly even as late as 1946, when he and Vera were in their seventies and apparently settled in Ballyorney House, a lovely if quite unsuitably isolated rented place beyond Enniskerry in the Wicklow mountains, he was still considering moving abroad.

In a letter to Hubert Butler, in the early 1950s, he writes:

> Vera and I may have to spend our declining years abroad, what with the cold (May, what a May) and the prices of houses in Ireland. I asked the landlord of Ballyorney for what price he would sell the house, and he suggested £7,000! The rent is £130 p/a and for £7,000 one can still get £240 a year in gilt edged securities, nearly twice as much; formerly it was the other way round.

I think Old Joe was nervous and miserly simply because he was totally unfitted for ordinary life, which he felt was going to ambush and bankrupt him at any moment, as indeed it nearly did with the arrival of all those babies on his doorstep. Apart from money, his mind moved on higher things: Swift's deeply pessimistic reflections, Berkeley's philosophic riddles, Nietzsche's deterministic superman, Yeats's ever-twirling gyres. Old Joe was a philosopher. He spent a good deal of his later years compiling a philosophical dictionary in a big red ledger with his equally philosophic friend, the writer Arland Ussher. At Joe's death they had reached the letter 'B'. Dealing properly with Aristotle, Aquinas and St Augustine had obviously taken up a good deal of their time.

Clearly, dealing with the world as it unfortunately is taxed Old Joe. In looking at an egg he was seeing something else – a rough beast inside, about to be born, before slouching towards Bethlehem. Or the egg was a potato. This he certainly thought, for on one of my grandmother's rare evenings out of the house, when they came to live in Dublin, she told him to boil himself an egg for supper in the kitchen. He put a new potato in the electric kettle, without water, turned it on, went away and forgot about it. The kettle had no automatic switch-off, so that it and part of the dresser were badly burnt on my grandmother's return.

My grandfather was a preoccupied man.

Apart from his various philosophic concerns, money and me, he had a fourth even more taxing problem to contend with – dealing with his son, and my father, and my mother Biddy. He writes to Hubert in June 1945:

There is nothing to say of Nat and Biddy. You always assume they can make 'moves', as you might, or I might. What moves can they make? I have never heard of them making a move in their lives, except for getting married.

And again, in September 1945:

We are faced with great difficulties as Nat may come back. Biddy is said to have left him definitely. Enough of that, but as you know it will be risky to have the child with us if Nat is here.

And again in June 1946:

I am afraid a hornet's nest has been stirred up by this planning for Little Joe. Nat arrived here Friday evening unannounced … He said he had come over to see about the child, in view of my letter … He had enquired in London about ordinary private schools … I suppose the vague idea was that he and Biddy cd. get some money into their fingers if any change was made … I am not giving him any money for Little Joe or for himself, beyond his fare back, which I must, as it is quite impossible here – he drives us all to distraction. I don't mean he is rowdy, but it is the utter sense of futility that is produced.

And again, with more anguish, in a letter to Peggy in March 1950:

Thank you for your kind letter abt. the child. May I write to you in two or three days' time? Nat is over here. I can't tell you the whole story in a letter – it is dreadful. But it is about Biddy and I am to pay the piper as usual, but this time not … He is talking about taking the child to England and putting him to work (Nat hasn't a penny or a job at the moment). This is of course to play on Vera's feelings abt. Little Joe, so as to induce us to part with money. It is hell – no amnesty for us in the Holy Year … I wish I could see you and Hubert but you could do nothing – no one can. I cannot write to you of Nat's visit, of all that was said and of all that we heard. I just have to give my memory of it a respite.

And with more anguish still, later that same month, to Peggy:

Of course you are quite right and it is obvious common sense to keep Little Joe here for the Easter holidays. Don't think we did not argue that. But Nat made it a point that the only chance of getting Biddy back was that he should be able to say Little Joe would come over … I did not bring Nat over here, and if you knew the pity, anger and dread with which he fills me when I see him, you would understand my weakness. It is our tempers that get frayed. Had he not got this conditional promise from me he wd. have stayed on here, and I could have gone mad. It was a disaster that he was able to borrow money to get here.

I have always felt, and think I've said it to you, that Nat was the tragic figure in all this history, not the children nor his wife tho' she had much to complain of … My conscience tortures me because when Nat showed the first signs of lack of conscience and disregard for others, coupled with bad habits, I did not insist that he should go out into the world and have no further dependence on us, and so perhaps realise that the world was not made for him. It was the only chance the poor fellow had, and I knew it, but I lacked the courage and was too indolent.

Yes, my father was a tragic figure.

TWO

If my grandfather was always writing at a kitchen table, Nat was always sitting at the end of a bar – alone with a pint of bitter, a packet of Players and *The Daily Telegraph* open at the crossword. I can hardly see him in any other position, usually at Peter's Montpellier Bar in Cheltenham, where he and my mother Biddy had unaccountably come to live when they left London in the late 1940s.

Nat spent most of the pub's opening hours here, his thin dark hair slicked down with water, a faraway expression set off, alarmingly, by the same startling pale-blue eyes as his father, always wearing the same sick-coloured tweed jacket, carefully creased pre-war flannels, brown shoes of a similar age, holes in the soles, but carefully tended, polished every morning. And always – his proudest possession I think – the same faded lightning-striped Royal Air Force Volunteer Reserve tie. A tie so long used that the beery pub airs had acted on it like starch, and I saw it once in his bedroom practically standing up by itself against the back of a chair.

Nat was as much part of the fixtures and fittings of Peter's Bar as the slate shove-ha'penny board (a game he played so often in pubs that he never lost), the beer-pull labels for Bass and Worthington Pale Ale and the stale sandwiches under a glass dome. I see him querying the odd crossword clue with Peter the landlord, a big, bear-like, bearded nautical man who had sunk a few German pocket battleships, I gathered, in the war.

Here Nat would eke out his languid, gentlemanly days, fingering his top lip, carefully pacing his cigarettes and pints of bitter, one of each every forty-five minutes or thereabouts, so that his money allocated for that morning would last from twelve until the two-thirty closing time. Then he would go home to a snack of strongly soused herrings and onions, prepared the previous day for him by my mother, with heels of white bread, before drowsing the afternoon away in bed, reading 'tec novels.

At six he would stroll out again, down the faded Georgian glories of Landsdowne Crescent where they had a third-floor cold-water flat, buying the *Cheltenham Echo* at the Montpellier corner for the racing results to see what he might have won or lost, for he was a passionate follower of the turf, not at any racecourse (that would have been too costly) but via the racing pages and the bookie's runner who came into Peter's Bar every morning. Now I think of it he may have chosen to leave London and live in Cheltenham for its great racing traditions and its excellent off-course betting and credit facilities, in the shape of its many bookie's runners, with their hot tips for the two-thirty.

At half past six my mother would meet him at Peter's Bar, having finished work as a filing clerk at Walker Crossweller, a firm that made bathroom fittings in the Cheltenham suburbs. He would buy her a pint of bitter – with her money. For, as I soon learnt, all his beer and cigarettes and racing debts – along with the food and rent for the flat – were paid for out of my mother's wages packet, handed over to him every Friday when they met at Peter's Bar. I remember the exact sums she got – nine pounds a week to start with, then ten pounds after a few years and finally, before she left the firm ten years later, eleven pounds a week. She would keep only a pound or two for herself.

Apart from being paid for delivering flyers around Cheltenham for the local Tory party at election time, the only money my father received was from his father in Dublin – meagre, most unwilling cheques which soon dried up, and afterwards secret cheques from his loving mother, Vera, which he cashed with Peter, so allowing himself a pint and a cigarette every thirty minutes instead of forty-five – and some rash bets on outsiders at the races. Though Old Joe was sometimes prepared to give money to Nat in kind. On his being asked by my mother for cash to buy Nat a pair of shoes – winter coming on, his one other pair down to their last – my uncle David remembers being told to look under Old Joe's bed, where he found a pair of cracked Edwardian dancing pumps, which were laboriously parcelled up and sent, second class, to Cheltenham.

My father, since he was strictly a one-outfit man, had trouble with his clothes. After the war, he came on one of his visits to dun money from his parents, then living at Ballyorney House beyond Enniskerry in the Wicklow mountains. At that time they employed a smiling, round-faced, mischievous, lank-haired little dwarf of a man, Johnny, as chef and general factotum. My grandfather – always anxious to get rid of his son as soon as possible – gave Johnny cash for Nat's ticket on the mailboat back to England, and charged him with making sure Nat got on it. A mistake, for Johnny was as partial to the drink as Nat. The two of them drank away the ticket money in Dun Laoghaire bars so that penniless now and fearing – or unable – to return home, they put up for the night in a boarding house. But with no money for the bill next morning, Johnny set out with Nat's suit, overcoat and shoes, hocked them and returned with the money to settle the account.

It can't have occurred to them in their befuddled state that Nat, apart from his shirt and socks (for some reason he never wore underclothes – penury, bravado, hygiene?), had now been left almost naked, trapped in the boarding house. A blanket and a taxi were negotiated. They got home. History doesn't relate my grandfather's reaction on their return. But it can well be imagined.

My father was the mother of all remittance men.

But considering he was good-looking, charming, intelligent, had been to Radley and (briefly) to New College, Oxford and had been left ten thousand pounds when he was twenty-one by a rich bachelor cousin, William Hone, whose fortune had come to him as a bookmaker (discreetly no doubt since he lived in one of London's most elegantly respectable addresses, at Albany, Picadilly), one may wonder at Nat's later come-down. Or not wonder. Such a silver-spoon-in-the-mouth background, in a wilful, suddenly rich, free-spending young man-about-London-and-Dublin in the 1930s would seem a good recipe for a possible fall. And so it was for Nat.

How had all this come about? Well, that Nat had his glory days there is no doubt, though of what exactly he got up to in those days I learnt only a few details, then or after he died in 1959 aged forty-six. These matters were never spoken of by my grandparents or the Butlers. A pall – an appalled pall – of silence surrounded Nat's doings in young adult life. I heard only vague accounts from my uncle David and from friends of Nat who I met years later. One friend of his (who later became a director of the Shell Oil Company) was a student with him at New College in the early 1930s. He told me how Nat was often absent from the college, taking a hire car to London to restaurants and nightclubs several evenings a week and climbing over the high college wall on his return, for which he was soon sent down. Though not before he had run over someone in Oxford on his motorcycle, resulting in serious injuries to both, with Nat breaking his jaw in several places, which must have accounted for the unnerving, palpitating movement of one cheek like a stranded fish when he was annoyed.

These Oxford high jinks might be seen as par for the course among the gilded youth at the University between the wars, except that Nat had some demon in him that always pushed him a mad stage farther. On returning to Dublin in the mid-thirties, when General O'Duffy's Nazi-inclined Blueshirts were out and about recruiting, Nat became a camp follower of the movement, patrolling the Dublin cocktail bars carrying a loaded .45 revolver under his coat, where he once blasted the tops off the brandy and Benedictine bottles in the Wicklow Hotel; target practice for the real thing in the Spanish Civil War to fight for Franco, a campaign frustrated when the plane he was piloting never made it beyond Biarritz, where he and the others of his bibulous Irish Brigade spent a few days attacking the Champagne at the Imperial Palace Hotel instead of the Republicans.

Yes, some devil came to possess my father. But in one crucial matter at least I should thank this demon in him, for without his irresponsible behaviour I would never have come to write this book – since I wouldn't have been abandoned as a child, or have taken all the great advantages I did from the Butler family, and there would have been none of all these concerned letters from my minders and I would probably have led a pretty awful life with my parents.

Nat's sad demons probably started with his good looks and his great charm; though when I came to know him there was little enough of this latter left. Several people described it to me later as a 'fatal charm'. The cliché in his case proved to be almost literally true. Nat had always got what he wanted, with the usual whims and tantrums of childhood indulged by nannies and servants in the household of his parents who, it's clear from the Beerbohm cartoon, knew little or nothing about either conceiving or bringing up children.

Nat was partly brought up by my grandfather's elder sister, my great-aunt Olive, who lived at Lime Hill, a lovely parkland Georgian house near Malahide outside Dublin. Olive was a most kindly, motherly, well-off woman, who, childless herself, took Nat under her wing. He spent a lot of his childhood with her and her stockbroker husband, George Symes. Here, as surrogate son to Olive, he found loving affection and no doubt traded on this. So for him there was initially a 'farming out', as there later was for me more formally with the Butlers – and so no doubt a feeling of parental abandonment that, mixed with his quick intellect and charm and a great whack of money too soon in his life, led him around to those Dublin cocktail bars with a loaded .45 revolver.

And afterwards, in 1936, to a meeting with my mother Biddy, Bridget Anthony, and marriage to her on 30 August of that year – at the registry office in Plymouth of all inexplicable places, since they had no connections with the town. And since I was born in the following February 1937, Biddy was three months' pregnant when she married Nat. A shotgun marriage, in order to legitimize my birth? A holiday in Cornwall and spur-of-the-moment decision to confirm their love affair? Possibly both.

In any case my mother Biddy would have gone along with anything Nat suggested. She was gentle and yielding by nature. And in this, and her clear skin and fine hands, long delicate fingers and country-blue eyes, she was an attractive woman. Her mind was intuitive, untutored, but with veins of a strong native intelligence running through it. A free and independent spirit showed few traces of what must have been an impoverished Catholic upbringing and education in the wilds of 1920s rural Ireland. She had an innate sense of style, a quiet charm, an ability to get on with literally anyone. She was her own woman, except with Nat, who in many ways was her undoing.

Her gentleness, delicacy and non-confrontational character played into his hands. He came to use her. She became a put-upon woman. So in the end her marriage with Nat defeated her and, in her last years when she was still only in her forties, she took to drink and sad confusions.

Nat met Biddy in the King's Head and Eight Bells, a Chelsea pub on the river. Meetings anywhere else than in a pub were a sore trial for Nat. Biddy was about twenty, studying to be a nurse in London at the time. She was from a widespread family of Anthonys in south Kilkenny (a cousin ran the large inn on the main road through the village of Piltown). She was the second-oldest of some dozen or more children. I'm not certain of the exact number or how many survived, for several died early and I met very few of them. Certainly, a great number of children – aunts and uncles to me, but difficult to keep track of afterwards. My maternal grandparents were clearly better at the family game than my paternal grandparents.

My mother's Anthonys lived in a small whitewashed cottage outside the village. It must have been crowded. My mother's father, from what little I knew of him, for I can't remember ever meeting him, did little if any work. (I heard years afterwards from my sister Geraldine that he suffered from serious depression – which didn't stop him fathering a dozen or more children). My grandfather writes of him to Hubert in 1955 in the light of the Hone family having 'very varied temperaments':

> And then there is Joe's mother's family to be taken into consideration. I understand that Mr Anthony, the grandfather, has leant entirely for material support upon his wife and children for many years. Oh dear, oh dear, it is frightful. If Little Joe can't help himself who is going to help him?

It seems there was a tendency on both sides of my family for the men to rely entirely on the women.

I visited the Anthony cottage only twice, with my mother when I was about eleven. I found the visits embarrassing. I didn't know what to do with myself. I helped out once at the inn, filling bottles with porter from a barrel and a semi-automatic filler, six weighted spigots and a corking machine. On another occasion I went out shooting with a cousin with a .22 rifle. On another day, my mother and I and an older and well-off Scots friend of hers, Ian McCorkadale (who I learnt years later had been her lover) went to the Commercial Hotel in Clonmel, where all three of us spent the afternoon in the lounge, gin and tonics for them, the local cider for me.

That's all I remember. Or want to remember?

The discreditable fact is that I looked down on the Anthonys, their small cottage and generally impoverished set-up. All were light years from the people, the large country houses and gracious vistas, the maids and gardeners, the libraries and theatre goings-on of my other homes – with the Butlers and the Guthries at Maidenhall (which was only thirty miles up the road from Piltown), at Annaghmakerrig and at Old Joe's successive attractive houses in and around Dublin.

I was a child of two utterly different worlds, and never the twain did meet. Except by that initial chance meeting between my parents in the King's Head and Eight Bells in 1936.

For Nat and Biddy this meeting was the start of what seems to me to have been either a lifelong love affair between them or a union based on poverty-stricken inertia. A bit of both probably. I can see no other reasons for my mother sticking with Nat, for their practical life together was unhappy and one of almost continual crises. True, my mother left Nat several times, as is clear from my grandfather's letter to the Butlers in which I was used as a decoy by my father to lure Biddy back. And she left him again in 1950, for there is a letter from my great-aunt Olive to Hubert dated 1 May of that year:

> Nat came over here in a great state about Biddy having left him and wanting still to get her back, and you have to admit that if there is to be any prospect of a home for the children in the future it would have to be with their parents, who are considerably younger than myself or Joe or Vera … Nat said 'He had better come over to me, and it may influence Biddy to return to me.' … I went out to Enniskerry the next day and heard there that Nat had pressed the (same) point with his father, as his only hope.

On one or other, or all of these occasions, I think my mother took up with her older married Scots friend, Ian McCorkadale, for on the first occasion there is a letter from her to Hubert from a prep school in Perthshire where she was housekeeping. In any event she returned to Nat. Ian's wife may have caused trouble. Or did Biddy come to feel guilty about leaving Nat, knowing he would not survive without her? Nat certainly needed her. And perhaps poverty made sex their one certain joy, which might help explain the seven children they had in almost successive years from 1937 onwards. Their penury, their endless struggle for survival, left them nothing reliable except each other.

For whatever reason, for my mother it was a remarkable attachment. Nat must often have been an impossibly difficult husband – using her, financially and emotionally; depressed, work-shy, a failure, the gilded youth become a very black sheep. And though he repressed all this, in Peter's Bar, with slow pints of bitter, the *Telegraph* crossword puzzle, the racing pages, shove ha'penny, soused herrings and 'tec novels, my mother must have been well aware of, and suffered from, his bitter disquiet. It's clear that with Nat she was a loving and tenacious woman.

But what of us, the seven children, born and farmed out every year? Not much loving tenacity in my mother there. Or were the children forced on her by my father? Or the produce of drinky nights together? Or the result of my mother's Catholic upbringing and ignorance of family planning? Hardly. She was a student nurse and rarely went to church. And one of her younger brothers was a salesman for the London Rubber Company – in short, for Durex contraceptives.

I imagine the reason for each of us seven children was a mix of all these factors, and perhaps I have no right to criticize here. Procreative urges are many and varied, the concern only of the couple. But to farm the product out, one after the other, abandoning each child to unhappiness, among strangers, mewling bundles thrown out, orphans of the storm – that's another matter.

Orphans of the storm … On one level my whole family business has something of the air of a wicked fairy story, the babies cursed at birth, so that they had to be abandoned in the Evil Forest. But on another level it can only be seen as sheer crass irresponsibility on the part of our parents.

Perhaps there's some way for reason in between? Well, there is one reason – chronic poverty. Which would seem a very good reason for not having so many children.

However, there was one blameless circumstance in my father's life which may help explain his decline and fall. A year before the war he got tuberculosis, which led to isolation wards in England, a stay in a Swiss mountain sanatorium in 1940 (arranged and paid for by aunt Julia, then living in a grand hotel in Lausanne with her bevy of Pekinese dogs) and an operation to remove half of one of his lungs. This incapacity must have been a major factor in curtailing his boisterous golden youth, and equally a reason for his sad depressive life afterwards. But it was a disease that didn't deter his sexual potency. (It may indeed have increased it, as evidenced by the four subsequent children he fathered, year in, year out, from 1940 onwards.)

But to be fair Nat's problems of nature and nurture, with which he might have come to live reasonably, included the destruction of the hopes he surely had by this tuberculosis; the then general fatality of the disease had given him a death sentence in 1939, so that he lived the rest of his short life on death row. And so it's perhaps insensitive of me to be too critical of my father's behaviour. I've not taken proper account of the medical and psychological horrors he must have undergone in the long twenty-year course of his disease before he died of it (and cancer) in 1959. Did my grandfather take these horrors into account in dealing with his son? He must have done; he was an intelligent and sensitive man. But his way of dealing with Nat's continuous health problems and difficult behaviour was to retreat, to protect himself behind a show of fatalistic irony. And that's understandable. We protect ourselves from hurt and the insoluble in whatever way we can. This distancing stance which my grandfather came to take about Nat is well evidenced – is curtly summed up – in a letter to Peggy Butler, in April 1942:

> I hope all's well with you. Someone told me Hubert was in Cork. Biddy had another child, a boy. Nat had a bad go of bronchitis (probably pneumonic) and lost his job in the brewery. We had to lend them money, a good deal, to tide them over. I hope it will.

Biddy has another child. (The boy was Michael, as I learnt years afterwards, who, born in 1941, died eighteen months later. A mystery boy, of whom more later.)

Meanwhile the pub-haunting Nat found a job with a brewery – work which, given his drinky character, was surely a bad career move. A touch of comedy. But then pneumonic bronchitis disconnects him from the brewery, and yet my grandfather no doubt has to sell a good whack of that São Paulo Tramway stock to keep my parents afloat. The letter reflects a typical episode in the Hone family tragicomedy. But more tragedy than comedy. I can only read this letter with sadness, for my grandfather, my father, mother and children.

Now it's time for the two major players in my early life to make their proper entrance: Hubert and Peggy Butler, of Maidenhall, County Kilkenny. Hubert was from the old Anglo-Irish Butler family, 'minor gentry' as he described his family, but distantly related to the Dukes of Ormonde, who had lived for hundreds of years in splendour at Kilkenny Castle. Hubert's grandfather was a local rector and his own father, a retiring conservative country gentleman, farmed some five hundred acres six miles south of the city, near the village of Bennettsbridge.

But Hubert was very different from his conventional family – a questioning boy, with great academic gifts who went to Charterhouse and, in 1918, on a scholarship, to St John's, Oxford, reading first Maths and then Classics: a young man in the early 1920s of liberal views – indeed heretical views as far as his Unionist family was concerned – including support for Irish nationalism; a man who, as the historian Roy Foster said of him years later, '… could not see a boat safely moored without wanting to rock it'.

This tendency to rock the boat – not at home or socially, for he was very conventional in these fields – led him throughout his long life, in his journalism, essays and letters to the papers, to ferret out awkward truths, political, historical and religious, in Ireland and elsewhere in Europe. He became a lie hunter, successfully exposing the liars. And of course this did him no good at all with right-thinking people everywhere, especially in Ireland, concerned with avoiding 'trouble', quite happy to be accomplices with the liars, and indeed with murderers and war criminals. For having gone to Vienna after the Anschluss, there with the Quakers to help get Jews out of the country, he came particularly to sympathize with their subsequent fate and that of other European minorities. He made it his business after the war to search out some of their persecutors, war criminals who had gone to ground, most notably in Yugoslavia where from Zagreb in the late 1940s he followed the trail of Artukovic, the brutal Home Affairs Minister in Pavelic's Nazi puppet regime in Croatia; Artukovic, who, with priests and prelates in the Catholic Church, had been responsible for the forced conversion and more often murder of some 750,000 Orthodox Serbs in Croatia during the war.

It was a trail that led him to Ireland, where Artukovic, with the help of a Vatican escape line, had found sanctuary in a Galway monastery, and afterwards lived comfortably with his family in a Dublin suburb for a year, before getting a visa for America.

Hubert was the first to publicize this religious holocaust outside Yugoslavia in articles and letters to the papers – and he made a very public exposure of it all in 1951 at a meeting of the Irish Foreign Affairs Society in Dublin at which, unknown to Hubert, the Irish Papal Nuncio was present. Hubert began to speak of how appallingly the Catholic Church had behaved in wartime Croatia. The Nuncio, naturally enough, got up and left. There was a front page scandal about it all in the Irish papers next day: INSULT TO NUNCIO!

These truths, as they were, did not go down at all well in the Holy Catholic Ireland of the early 1950s. Hubert was ostracized by his community, kicked out of the Kilkenny Archaeological Society (which he had re-established in 1940 after a lapse of over fifty years), denied milk by the local creamery and libelously condemned by a drunken member of the Kilkenny City Council as being a disgrace to the County of Kilkenny and a Red to boot.

The Irish Special Branch took an interest; the local village sergeant was asked to get on his bike and keep a watch on the front gates of Maidenhall. It was thought Hubert might do a runner to Moscow. Years later, when the Special Branch papers on the investigation somehow leaked out, a memo from one of the detectives to the head of the service said there was no communist taint in the man at all, that he was simply an apple grower, bee keeper and market gardener.

As indeed he was. And it was as 'market gardener' that he described himself on identity forms. And it was as this and bee keeper and apple grower that I knew him in my early years at Maidenhall, and not as a latter-day Orwell and Swift with whom he was later compared when his forgotten essays in small magazines were published as books, in Ireland, by Antony Farrell's adventurous Lilliput Press, in the last decade of his life.

All this came years later. For me – I see the natural man, at home in Maidenhall, moving through the seasons, far from the terrible lies and murderers. A morning in late summer, perhaps, fifty years ago: he sees the warm day coming up outside, no wind. Ideal for his purposes. And a few hours later I see him again, a tall, slightly awkward figure, an old pair of flannels, belted with an older tweed tie, a ragged honey-smeared green flannel shirt buttoned to the wrists, gloves, smoker bellows in hand, a felt hat and bee veil. He's dabbing furiously at one of the dozen beehives below the front lawn.

The sun is hot, the bees angry. I can hear their distant outraged hum from the safety of the porch. And half an hour later Hubert is digging out the small square honeycombs from their waxy beds in the hive, and the larger frames in the other hives.

And then it's the next day and the frames are in the oak-barreled honey separator in the pantry, the handle turning. The honey is spinning out inside, the whole room dripping with honey. And I have the smell – the thick sweet smell. Hubert's turning the handle, I'm turning it, we're all turning it throughout the day, and the next day bottling it.

And as the year, that particular year, begins to turn, falling into September, it's apple time. The risen fruit – red-cheeked, yellow, orange, brown. The early Worcesters and James Grieve, the Conference pears in the walled garden, the Coxes in the high orchard. The chip baskets to get ready in the basement, the pickers to pick, me to be persuaded to join in. I can smell those Maidenhall apples now, the tart-sweet odours, a day taken out of time, where he lives again, and is about to storm the orchard.

Winter. The drawing-room. He is in the high-back red chair by the fire. Legs crossed, slippers, winter. He's older now. The face longer, thinner, sculpted, eyes a paler blue. Gazing at the fire a moment. Returning to his book. A book on the Irish Saints. His face like one.

And in an earlier winter – I'm about twelve. The two of us are out in the yard stables, with the big cross-cut saw. Hubert is feeling suddenly energetic and I've been press-ganged again. There's been a gale, trees down in the wood. There's a big pile of wet branches behind us. We start off at quite a pace. But soon the teeth are getting stuck in the wet wood. The saw wrenched out – fumbled in again, and stuck again. I say 'It's pretty useless, isn't it? Let's stop.' The rain is pelting down outside. But there is his annoyed determination then. 'No, let's go on.' Another minute or two. The cross-cut sticks again. Another five minutes and we pack it in. Rain. Rain and wind. Hubert returns to the drawing-room fire, to a journal in Serbo-Croat, then switches to a text in Gaelic, a commentary on the Irish Saints. I go and get the tea. Peggy is away. The house is empty. No TV then, or radio. No electricity. Lamplight. And after the tea Hubert switches his reading again, reaching for a long shelf of French books to his left. Picks one out at random, starts to read it straightaway. I see the spine. It's Maupassant's *La Maison Tellier*.

He glides through the three very different languages so deftly that they might all be the one to him. He hears Archbishop Stepinac, Saint Columcille and the chatter of the girls in Madame Tellier's establishment – all in their original tongues. Where most of us see through a glass darkly in other languages, Hubert sees the light clearly in more than half a dozen of them.

Another winter. We children are up on the top floor playroom, at lessons – of a vague sort – with Miss Goulding, the awful ogreish yellow-haired governess. There is a big red felt screen by the door. Suddenly, heavy footsteps charge up the stairs. The door flies open, the screen falls with a great crash. And Hubert is there, thundering in stage left, vengeful, fire-breathing, a figure in a pantomime come to save the hero and heroine from the wicked witch. 'How dare you tell the children not to speak to the maids, Miss Goulding! How dare you say it was vulgar to speak to them! You will take your notice immediately!'

Uproar! Joy! No more lessons. Miss Goulding leaves that afternoon. Hubert has promoted his liberal ethic in a most palpable way.

Spring, years later. I've come into the drawing-room. Hubert is sitting at the desk by the window. But he's not writing. He's lost to the world, gazing down over the lawn, the valley, across the river to the mountains beyond, the Blackstairs and Mount Leinster half hidden in cloud. Hearing me he gets up suddenly, energetic again. It's spring, and it's daffodil-picking time, lush gold carpets of them, all over the lower lawn, but planted in various patterns, circles or huge letters spelling out people's initials. Picked, they must be counted and bunched in dozens for the country market in Kilkenny. 'Joe, we need help with the daffodils.' I am not too keen. The stalks, greasy with sap, will get my hands all sticky and why not leave the daffodils nicely on the lawn where they are? 'Oh, Joe, do stop talking rot.'

Spring turning to summer, and Hubert abandons Archbishop Stepinac, Saint Columcille and Madame Tellier. For the bees and their hives are to be loaded onto a lorry and taken up to the gorse and wild flowers on the mountains across the valley.

And another summer and we're all out on the upper lawn, having tea under the big maple tree by the swing and the tennis court. Hubert, with his felt hat – which he wore in the most unnecessary circumstances and lost when it was needed – is leaning across the table looking at some papers which James Delahanty, the very literate Kilkenny ironmonger, has passed to him. Peggy and her daughter Julia are poised on chairs, in summer dresses, talking to the novelist Ben Kiely. The scene is frozen suddenly. The papers stay halfway up in Hubert's hand, the voices are unheard. The dappled sunlit patterns through the maple leaves are stilled. It's high summer, set in amber now, at Maidenhall under the maple tree, by the swing next to the tennis court.

Autumn and rumours of fruit once more, and Hubert is togged out again in his old flannels, felt hat and bee veil, a cloud of furious bees about his head, and there is the smell of burning corrugated paper from the bellows smoker. And the oak-barrelled honey separator must be got up from the basement once more. And now he's turning the handle, and I'm turning it, the honey spinning out. And a week later there are autumn storms, and Hubert is happy as ever with nature – a few more trees fallen by the river, more wet wood to be cut for the winter. He'll be looking for me again with that damn great cross-cut saw.

I was often an unwilling participant in the natural life of Maidenhall. So, too, as it turns out, was Hubert in his early years there. I learnt afterwards of how he fell out with his family, his formidable mother particularly and elder sister, and in later years blamed this on his feelings of being 'dumped' as he put it, aged eight, at Bigshotte Reyles, a prep school in Berkshire. He was devastated, thinking his parents had given him away. So it's strange that he didn't forecast or afterwards seem to notice my own unhappiness at the dreadful Sandford Park School in Dublin, where I was dumped, aged eight, in 1945. Hubert would have had influence with my grandfather in removing me from it. But by then he and my grandfather were absorbed with the financial aspects of my upbringing rather than with my feelings.

It's likely that both men, like many other men of their generation, were emotionally maimed by their prep schools, as I very nearly was. Hubert (like my grandfather) wrote very little about his childhood, or his personal feelings generally. It was as if both of them, as a result of their early boarding-school horrors, feared to unearth that sort or any sort of emotional problem in their later lives. Something awful had happened to them behind the bicycle shed or in the housemaster's study which had frozen their hearts, so that afterwards in their lives they concentrated on philosophical dictionaries, apple growing and the fate of the orthodox Serbs in wartime Croatia.

But for Hubert, at least, going up to St John's College, Oxford in 1918 was clearly an academic and social liberation, in that he met his match intellectually, and, in Tony Guthrie, a fellow student at the College, his first mature friend. And more importantly a year or two later he met Tony's sister, Peggy Guthrie, visiting her brother from their home in Tunbridge Wells. Peggy, though she was only sixteen, took to Hubert at once, and forever after, though they didn't marry until 1930. It was a lifelong love for her and, in a different way, for Hubert – for they were very different people. Yet in their lives together they convincingly proved that the chalk and the cheese can get along fine, if they come to understand why they are both very different, and appreciate that, and take strength from it.

If Hubert was very unorthodox intellectual chalk, Peggy was intuitive, a whole cheeseboard of different flavours. Yeats spoke well of the sort of love I think they shared: 'In wise love each divines the high secret self of the other, and, refusing to believe in the mere daily self, creates a mirror where the lover or beloved sees an image to copy in daily life.' On a more mundane level – and perhaps a more important ingredient in a long and, on most levels, a happy marriage – they never ceased to 'pull together', for their own and even more for the common good. 'Are you pulling with me, or against me?' the hero asks the heroine at the end of Mary Webb's *Precious Bane*. This was a question neither of them, I think, ever had to ask.

Although they were very different people in character, they were equally unconventional – Hubert intellectually, in his rocking of every comfy boat, Peggy intuitively, in her whole attitude to life as it was and should not be. It was the key to her character, her impatience with the expected in a character that was always unexpected, without ever this being a shallow showy-off business. No time, for this fine, sharp-featured, six-foot-tall, vigorous commanding woman, for show in this most serious and exciting business of living.

And here is another key to her: her attack; her energy; in and for life and with people. She was quite exceptional in this. A tremendous getter-on with things, no footling about, an endless organizer, a real touch of the dictator. She could be ruthless – she played tennis in a quite merciless manner. But she could as quickly switch into a Victorian Mad Hatter's tea-party mode, as on picnics by the river when we were children at Maidenhall, where things were turned on their head and moral lessons given: virtues made of horseflies, rain, forgetting the butter. She once said to me, when I was about nine and complained of the latter: 'What a treat for you, Joe – bread with no butter!'

And in her latter years, in her eighties, when she was often wheel-chair-bound, she never ceased her original and busy approach to her many schemes. For her, as for her brother Tony Guthrie in his theatre work, it was ever a matter of 'Rise above! On, on …'

Like her brother, Peggy was dramatic, and sometimes explosively so, in word and deed. So that being with her could be a hair-raising experience, as it was equally for outsiders, even total strangers, usually public servants and such like, who had no idea that there was a real thunderflash in the post for them or coming down the telephone – that they were shortly to be at the cutting edge of her performance, her anger risen at some ignorant, fatuous or self-serving behaviour of theirs. Though she was absolutely no fool, she made a habit of rushing in where angels would never have dared tread. Like

Hubert, but in a different abrasively verbal way, she was a great upsetter of applecarts so that her friends – and enemies, for she had quite a few – came to keep such vehicles well off the road and out of her way.

She was the enemy of every sort of 'humbug' – a favourite word of hers – old-fashioned, smacking of Tunbridge Wells and the Edwardian era into which she was born, both town and period equally hated. It was another part of her originality that, coming from this stuffy formal Empire background (and no doubt in reaction to it) she was passionately pro-Ireland and the Irish; sometimes rashly so. I doubt there was ever a better example of someone being 'More Irish than the Irish themselves'.

She was equally modern in her other views: artistic, social and moral; always taking surprisingly advanced positions whether the matter was personal, among her family, with friends or in the public domain. She could be cruel in this way, with servants or with others who couldn't or wouldn't deign to reply. But her intuitive realism about people could hit the nail right on the head. Once, in a rather long-winded account of troubles I was having with a woman, she cut my cackle and said simply 'Joe, if you are blackmailable – you will be blackmailed.'

Some of us, if we're lucky, mellow with age. More usually we move from vivid youthful left to grumpy-grey right. Peggy did neither. She was always 'advanced'. Age seemed only to sharpen her critical claws against the fuddy-duddies. For her it was always the new, right up to the end. I read her an Anita Brookner novel some months before she died. She admired things in it, but found it generally too formal and 'expected'. She would have preferred *Trainspotting* I felt.

Of course she had a youthful background in this modernity, in the London of the 1920s where she studied painting at the Regent Street Polytechnic, and, in many of her oils and drawings of that period and later, showed herself to be a painter of great talent and technical ability. Indeed it's clear that she could have made a successful career, as her brother did in theatre, as an artist or designer. She was intensely cosmopolitan, loved the concerts, art galleries, theatres and cinemas of big-city life.

She largely gave up these big-city stimulations and any of her own possible careers when she and Hubert came to live at Maidenhall in 1941. It was a real sacrifice for her; and a great benefit for Hubert, who was tone deaf and barely interested in the arts. Peggy, in the rural peace of Maidenhall, organized the household and became the anchor for his work. And if Hubert benefited so did the local community, for whom she did many fine things – helping organize the Country Market in Kilkenny in the 1950s, creating the Butler modern art gallery in the castle and getting the Kilkenny Arts Week going. None of which would have happened, given the reactionary nature of Irish rural officials at the time, without her tweaking innumerable council, corporate and clerical beards.

There was no element of do-goodery in her involvement in these local affairs. She, like Hubert, simply brought the virtue of what one might call Protestant private judgment to these neighbourhood matters.

And I was a beneficiary of Hubert and Peggy's unorthodoxies and fearless outspeaking – and their scoldings. Of course I suffered these, in rows with Hubert over the cross-cut saw, and with Peggy, often enough – for example on my once cooking an omelette with butter, not margarine. 'Joe, what extravagance! You either have it this way, or not at all.'

But even fighting over the cooker I benefited, for I would not have dared to reply to her thus but for her constant forthright and candid example. I got that sturdy, if sometimes abrasive, attitude from Peggy.

More importantly, I also got wonderful gifts of language from her, in her dramatic readings to us as children and from her own vividly descriptive, laconic and original use of words – the idea that words, if you adventured with them, were magic weapons, could be powerfully evocative, hilarious or killing things. And that to be unorthodox and creative with them was the road to salvation. To be a painter, as she was, or a novelist as I became, though not of course something to be made anything of in public, was of the essence.

Peggy gave me the excitement of words and some of the bare-faced confidence to write books. Peggy had a great deal of bare-faced confidence. She could put people's backs up very quickly. But some of us emerged from the encounter with stronger backs. It was sink or swim with Peggy.

But there was another, largely hidden side to her. At heart she was a hugely understanding person. The sympathy of real concern – immediately in heartfelt words, or later down a telephone or in a letter. It was her greatest quality – the quick and genuine interest she took in people of every sort and background, their lives, problems. Her advice, when she gave it, was usually right and sometimes extreme. She could be coldly dispassionate here, in a manner that could be daunting.

However, if she could be dryly objective, she was far more a woman of intense emotion. This was cramped, 'bitten back', largely for lack of that channel of artistic expression through which her brother Tony so vividly expressed himself in theatre. Her own frustrated gifts and emotions led now and then to outbursts of cruelty, her talent twisted and hurtful. High-handed, imperious, naturally gifted, psychologically astute, fearless – and to be feared. A treader-on-toes.

Because one knew how often she was treading on her own toes, in frustration or unhappiness, you could understand the arrogance and scoldings and know of her great warmth beneath the cold. Impatient, inspiring and infuriating – she was all of a piece.

Peggy was an extraordinary mother to be landed with. How different from my real mother Biddy, in her transparency, simplicity and gentleness. And Hubert, with his high-minded pondering of ancient Serbo-Croatian texts light years away from my father's mental efforts: studying the *Telegraph* crossword puzzle, the racing forecasts and playing shove-ha'penny in Peter's Bar.

So here – apart from the minor players of headmasters, housemasters, a doctor-psychiatrist, uncles and aunts, well-meaning friends and acquaintances of my grandparents and the Butlers – here are the major players, all of them: stars, spear carriers, understudies, seemingly anxious to shine in the melodrama, 'The Saving of Little Joe', that real cracker of a play.

THREE

Since I was the first parcel in the Pass the Parcel game that my parents forced on their children, my grandfather, unaware of the other babies to follow on his doorstep, moved me on fairly carefully. In 1939, aged two-and-a-half, I was lucky to land up with Peggy and Hubert Butler, who wanted a companion for their daughter Julia, eighteen months older than me.

The Butlers then looked after me, with a small board fee of fifteen shillings a week paid by my grandfather. Initially Peggy would have liked to adopt me legally, but my parents wouldn't agree to this. So the matter of my status with the Butlers was left in abeyance for a year or two. But as I grew up, it understandably became a vital issue for Peggy and Hubert and thus a main bone of contention between them, my parents and grandparents: which of the trio was to have authority over me? And was I meanwhile to be just a paying guest with the Butlers (as other children were at Maidenhall then and later), or a full member of the family, as I was clearly becoming with every month that passed? The matter was never resolved. And my betwixt-and-between position with the Butlers and my own family was to continue indefinitely, to the detriment of all concerned.

For of course my parents never took me back. They didn't have the money to support themselves, let alone me or the six other children who followed. And my grandparents, Joe and Vera, were too old and infirm to deal with me on a permanent basis. So the Butlers were left holding the baby, though by now the baby was growing into a difficult, obstreperous little boy.

Nat, with Biddy on the sidelines in wartime London at that point, did nothing to help resolve this issue of my future. From the evidence in the file Nat wasn't in any direct touch with his parents or the Butlers during the war (except for one notably fraught occasion when Hubert went to see them in London in 1942, of which more later) and he simply didn't reply to any letters on the subject of my future. One reason for this, I think, was that having spent all his cousin's ten-thousand-pound legacy on high living, and then having contracted tuberculosis just before the war and lost half a lung, my father was a semi-invalid and saw the welfare of his progeny as a secondary issue. Realizing that he was going to need Biddy to look after him, he was anxious not to have her dilute her efforts in this by having to care for any of their children.

But for me, at that point, there were the beginnings of a life in two very different worlds. Since Hubert Butler's father was still alive – as a somewhat disturbed old man living at Maidenhall in the south – I was first taken north with the Butlers to live an Annaghmakerrig in County Monaghan. This was the family house of Peggy's mother, Norah Power, before she married Dr Guthrie, an Edinburgh physician who had moved his practice to Tunbridge Wells. But on his early death in 1929, Mrs Guthrie, partly blind, returned to live at Annaghmakerrig. Peggy and Tony had spent their childhood holidays here, and loved the place, and after their father died the house in Tunbridge Wells was sold and Annaghmakerrig became the Guthrie family home.

By the time I arrived there, late in 1939, old Mrs Guthrie – Mrs G as she was always called – lived there with her tiny tidy Yorkshire nurse-companion, Miss Worby, known as Bunty, with a fair deal of help inside and outside the big house, in those days also a working farm and forestry estate.

Annaghmakerrig is a lovely, winding-corridored, secret-cubby-holed, mid-Victorian house, with many variously angled roofs and rounded gable ends in the Dutch manner, set on a hill in rhododendron-blooming grounds, overlooking a big lake, and surrounded by pine forests. A touch of Bavaria.

In winter one expected snow and glittering ice on the lake. Indeed that is my first memory of Annaghmakerrig, during the icy snowbound winter of 1940: a horse pulling a big wooden sleigh drawing up at the front door steps; and being pushed about, with other children, on nursery chairs over the frozen lake, while the adults skated around us. And later summers there, playing in a wooden Wendy house on the front lawn under the big sycamore tree – a little house called Rosebud.

Afterwards, living at Maidenhall, we children only went to Annaghmakerrig for Christmas and summer holidays, so we especially looked forward to our visits there. I'm a little surprised at this, for Annaghmakerrig then was a household where a formal order prevailed, very different from the informal, workaday world I came to know later at Maidenhall. At Annaghmakerrig there was a precise Victorian manner of things, a nineteenth-century air and ethos, serenely but strictly maintained in the house and on the estate – an almost feudal world, which continued there for fifty years after Queen Victoria had died. The house and its inhabitants were imbued with things and thoughts Victorian: the heavy drapes and furnishings, red-and-gilt bound copies of Punch and the *Illustrated London News* in the morning room, paintings of farm animals and bewhiskered nineteenth-century military ancestors; an impression permeated especially by the Protestant work ethic, where pleasure was always to be earned, where it was not merely incidental, chanced-on in pursuit of some much more serious goal.

And yet the pleasure for us children there was often incidental and unearned. It lay all around us – through the winding corridors, endless rooms and attics of the house and about the wider estate. And when Bob Burns, Mrs G's chauffeur, met us at Newbliss off the Dundalk train in the immaculate leather-smelling green Austin 12 and the house finally reared up across the lake over the last hill, I always felt a thrill of pleasure, thinking of the impending adventures and surprises.

I was lucky indeed, living there in my early years and afterwards at Maidenhall, unaware of my real background, of my grandfather in Dublin coming to fear every knock on the door; the postman as stork, delivering another baby; of my mother, an office slave, filing papers nine to five, and of my father holding up four ale bars in London and Cheltenham.

Annaghmakerrig, moated by lakes, remotely distant beyond its three avenues, inviolate behind its fir-clad hills, boggy fields and small brackish canals, was a dream kingdom, a view of the exotic over that last hill. Once up the steps and into the big hall, the smell of Aladdin oil lamps and candle wax for this was the only form of lighting in the house until the 1950s.

Settled and secure, the house offered both mystery and comfort – the soft-carpeted, lamplit rooms warmed by log fires, where pools of rose-gold light ran away into shadowy spaces, down long corridors into ghost-haunted nooks and crannies, hidden rooms filled with novelties, secrets. In winter the house was clearly divided between light and dark, just as the seasons of our visits were equally extreme, divided into either midwinter or midsummer holidays. We children never knew the place in its rehearsal seasons of spring and autumn. For us the curtain was always about to rise on Christmas or the summer play was in full swing.

Winter was the more obviously exciting, with its central drama of Christmas. But the teasing prelude was almost as good. Dumb Crambo and charades – getting dressed up in the hall from boxes of Victorian finery and tat. Children's parties: musical chairs to the dance of 'The Dashing White Sergeant' from the cabinet gramophone; 'Oranges and Lemons say the Bells of Saint Clements', the procession through a pair of arched arms where you were trapped on the last words of 'Here comes a candle to light you to bed, here – comes – a – chopper – to – chop – off – YOUR HEAD!'

And then the long woolly stocking at the end of the bed on Christmas morning, waking early in the dark, the thrill of touching its bulky folds, but resisting until dawn; simple wartime stocking fillers, with pencils and sharpeners, a notebook, a torch, an apple in the toe. The thrill was in the earlier unknowing. And later the opening of the proper presents, that evening round the tall fir tree in the study at the end of the hall, the magic of the candles all over it, the intoxicating smell of melting wax and warmed fir needles. And finally the heart-stopping moment when the labelled brown-paper parcels – the presents piled round the tree – could be set upon and fiercely unwrapped. The brown paper and every bit of string had to be kept, afterwards to be folded and the string wound up in balls, by Mrs Guthrie.

If Christmas at Annaghmakerrig, with its silks of Araby in the charades, its décor of tinsel and coloured streamers, its warm perfumes of wax, fir and almond-cake icing, had a touch of *A Thousand and One Nights*, our summer holidays were straight out of *Swallows and Amazons*. The drama moved from the house to the lake – a windblown watery theatre: boating, bathing, fishing, picnicking.

There were two heavy rowing boats and big crayfish under the stones in the shallow water by the boathouse. To avoid what I understood to be their fierce pincers I soon learnt to swim, surging away as quickly as possible into deeper waters. Again, the spaces of the lake, like those of the house, always beckoned: an equal invitation to promote our fantasies. For the lake was silent and private then, a water which we children could make over entirely in our own adventurous images, living Ransome's book in reality, or creating our own fictions, as explorers and cartographers, making for secret waters, compassing the island on stakes, the prow of the boat pushing through a carpet of water lilies there; or daringly swimming beneath them, seeing the tangle of their long slimy stems sinking from the sunlit surface into the greeny-black depths – the sudden fear of sinking too far, of drowning in the forested underworld, those realms of the big fish that had snatched at the legs of Jeremy Fisher.

Life at Annaghmakerrig made the heart beat faster. My own real family, or what little I knew of it, faded into the background. Instead, at Maidenhall and Annaghmakerrig, I found two much more engaging families. And in Tony Guthrie, a father figure.

By the time I arrived at Annaghmakerrig late in 1939 Tony was the well-known theatre producer and administrator of the Old Vic and Sadler's Wells in London. And during the next few years, up on holidays from Maidenhall, Tony and his wife Judy would come over from London for a few days, and always at Christmas, and then there would be the real drama, for me and the other children staying in the house.

Dressed up for charades, waiting in the hall before making our entrances into the drawing-room – Tony or Peggy or her great friend Ailish Fitzsimon directing us, to see that we made our entrances at exactly the right moment. And although we children knew nothing of real theatre then, there was a theatrical heightening of reality, a mood of sudden invention flooding the staid Victorian house, with Tony master of the revels, alchemist in the dross-to-gold department.

Tony was a transforming influence for me. It was from him, over the next few years at Annaghmakerrig, that I had the first intimations that life need not be unhappy, dull, difficult, penny-pinching; that in the stage setting of the house with its Victorian props and costumes, life could be 'produced' to show a much more significant, exciting side; that in Tony's inventive hands it could be transformed into all sorts of magic, when the workaday would be banished in the cause of illusion. And just as importantly I came to see that all this make-believe world was valid (which other grown-ups were wont to deny – 'Don't tell lies, Joe!') since the fun and games were promoted by this scion of the family, this giant visiting uncle.

Tony was pushing six-foot-six in his socks. He towered over everything. Eyes narrowed in the smoke from a dangling cigarette, pondering some dramatic plan – anything, as I see it now, which would kick ordinary life in the pants, or celebrate it, or alter it entirely. There wasn't a moment to waste in this transformation of the mundane, nothing of life that couldn't be tinkered with, fashioned by his vital spirit into something unexpected, astonishing, spectacular. Everything was prey to his inventions. Evenings, taking to the soft-toned Blüthner piano in the drawing-room, he would sing in his high voice old ballads with exaggerated relish, a Thomas Moore melody or 'The Skye Boat Song'. Or just as suddenly, in his quick military way, he would go to the cabinet gramophone, wind it up, put on a record and bring forth *The Pirates of Penzance*, annotating the songs mischievously, taking different roles, counterpointing the words in a *basso profundo* or an exaggeratedly high tenor voice.

He was a man overcome with endless schemes, and fits of energetic, creative or sometimes destructive fever, whether directing us in our charades or in leading an attack on the garden scrub, with bonfires, the whole household commandeered, the grown-ups issued with bow-saws, scythes and choppers, we children the lesser spear-carriers, as the wilderness rapidly diminished, the whole tiresome business made fun, produced as vivid spectacle, like the mob scene in *Coriolanus*.

'On, on!' he would shout, rising up suddenly from behind a bush like a Jack-in-the-Box, with a mock-fierce smile, urging us on, prophet-like, to smite the nettles and brambles – storming the barricades of convention, in life as in theatre, gathering up every sort of hungry cat and setting them among the complacent pigeons, to propose and often to achieve the unlikely or the impossible. Like Peggy, his sister, he was another very unconventional figure from whom I took courage in my own dumb feelings of being an outsider. I was lucky. Life at Annaghmakerrig became a repertory theatre for me, a cabinet of curiosities filled with surprises that I could pick and finger and possess. A time of gifts indeed.

On the death of Hubert's father in 1941 the Butlers, with me, all moved south to the workaday world of Maidenhall. Though there was nothing grim or grinding about life in Maidenhall, in a house as attractive in its way as the holiday home in the north.

If Annaghmakerrig had rumours of Victorian neo-gothic, Maidenhall was minor Irish Georgian classic. Set on another hill, the four-square, lime-washed house lay, and still lies, beyond two white gates on a rook-clamorous, tree-covered ridge overlooking sloping lawns, beehives, a chestnut-and-beech-filled parkland bordered by a tree-arched byroad, with water meadows and the river Nore beyond. On the other side of the valley sits a ruined sixteenth-century Norman castle and a much earlier Celtic round tower before the land rises again in gorse-covered green hills and distant blue mountains.

I still see it in this way – perhaps because this was the first view I remember when I arrived at Maidenhall, seen from high up in the old nursery on the top floor, as I looked out of a small low window, wondering where I was.

Years of the same view, through the seasons, from the same nursery window that became the playroom and then the schoolroom. Yellow daffodil springs, lush-green chestnut summers, orange autumns, dark rain-stormed winters, snow-powdered New Years. I spent a lot of time by the nursery window. This room was my world, my centre, the start of governess schooling shared with Julia and the Mosse girls, Pam and Berry, nieces of the village mill owner; and the two Fitzsimon boys, Christopher and Nicky, who sometimes stayed at Maidenhall to take lessons with us – from a succession of governesses – high up, where the rest of the house was barely known territory to me.

Morning, noon and night – and sometimes best when it was getting dark, in the autumn, winter rushing in, a blowy wind rattling the windows, the other children gone, Julia and I roasting chestnuts in the ashes of the fire beneath the small Victorian iron grate. And then there were words in the evening from children's books or poems, read by Peggy or by Ailish Fitzsimon, both in wonderfully clear, dark-dramatic voices:

> Up the airy mountain
>   Down the rushy glen,
> We daren't go a-hunting
>   For fear of little men;
> Wee folk, good folk,
>   Trooping altogether;
> Green jacket, red cap,
>   And white owl's feather …

Or *Young Lochinvar*, who came out of the west; or Nesbit's *The Phoenix and the Carpet*, the first proper book I remember, with the petulant Phoenix breaking from its egg in the ashes of a suburban London fireplace, so that I tried to repeat the trick in the playroom fireplace with an egg stolen from the larder, with messy, disappointing results.

Or getting to play with the strange machine found in the playroom cupboard – a mahogany, brass-cornered box which, when you opened it, displayed on the inside of the lid groups of pink, flimsy-winged piping cherubs, gliding up towards a blue empyrean – on their way to God, I was sure. A musical box with a large selection of indented metal discs, which you pressed down onto a comb of metal bars of different musical notes, then wound the machine up and listened to the tinkly, ethereal music. 'Ave Maria' and 'In a Monastery Garden' I remember. And another disc, which played just the opposite sort of music, martial airs, military marches and 'Goodbye Dolly Gray'. I found this machine potently evocative of something I knew not what; looking at the cherubs, hearing the music, I was carried away with these fat little infants on the wings of song.

But the greatest thrill of all was a magic lantern, with its coloured glass slides pushed across a beam of oil light onto a sheet in the nursery-playroom, showing one heart-stopping scene after another, the progress of Little Red Riding Hood towards her awful nemesis with the Big Bad Wolf. Another collection of slides showed Royal Occasions – Queen Victoria 'Reviewing the Fleet at Spithead', her Diamond Jubilee and such like.

Vision, words, music, roasted chestnuts, the nursery-playroom held everything I needed, and more. If I'd been abandoned by my real parents I never knew it. I'd been given the company of young Lochinvar, of Nesbit's Bastable family, of Barbar on his travels and of Red Riding Hood in those eye-popping images, seen at the end of a smoky light cast by a magic eye shining on the wall of the playroom. And with this a dozen other secret rooms and attics at Annaghmakerrig and Maidenhall, full of novelties and surprises, opening into or out of life. In any case I don't remember ever feeling that I'd been abandoned by my parents, or wondering where I was. Maidenhall was home and that was that.

At some point I moved from the nursery-playroom to a small bedroom on the first floor. But my world was still bounded by the orbit of the house and grounds. I had no conception of a wider world beyond the gorsey blue mountains. Apart from the supplies from the local grocer, Mr Hennessy, who came down a back lane every week with a cob and a trap with a delivery of candles, tea, sugar, matches, Brasso, starch and so on, almost everything needed in the household was supplied from the small dairy farm and market garden. Fruit and vegetables, milk, cream and butter from the basement dairy with its Alfa-Laval separating machine, big oak churn, grooved butter pats and rollers, where I helped turn the whirring, pinging separator every evening with Mrs Kennedy from the village, rapt at the miracle of cream from one spout, thin milk from the other. Hams and black puddings from the pigs in the back yard, snuffling through the vegetable waste that was cooked up for them every week in a vast iron cauldron in the back yard with a bonfire beneath. Electricity from an erratic windcharger on a nearby hill, water from a deep well hidden in the woods and pumped up by a tub-thumping Croxley diesel engine.

There was an old Morris 12 car (CMU 716) abandoned without petrol during the war, set on bricks in one of the garages, but all our transport was in the corduroy-upholstered trap, pulled by Pat the pony. A trap that, when we were older, took Julia and me rain or shine (and mostly the former) to junior school at Kilkenny College five miles north, the reins held in the gnarled fingers of Joe Devine, the elderly Maidenhall coachman with Hubert's father, asked out of retirement, whose wind-scoured red nose always had a lengthening drip at the end which we watched intently, waiting for it to drop.

We had a wireless in the sitting-room, but the acid batteries leaked so that it rarely worked. Entertainments at Maidenhall were almost entirely familial and non-mechanical. Arthur Ransome was the most modern author read aloud to us children every evening, from a greater store of Victorian and Edwardian children's classics. Nesbit again, *The Wouldbegoods*, *Five Children and It*, and R.M. Ballantyne's *Coral Island* – a book that, just writing the title here, gives me a tingle up the spine: seeing again those sun-struck, distant, coral waters, my living again with the three so totally liberated boys; above all diving with Peterkin in his stomach-turning free fall – hundreds of feet off the cliff into the blue lagoon – an image renewed mint fresh for me, sixty years later, and in so doing experiencing again that reading in the drawing-room and the very moment of that high-diving fall.

Then the traditional card and board games on the round sitting-room table: Beggar-my-Neighbour and Old Maid (Peggy, to us children beforehand: 'Make sure Miss Doughty [a pernickety house guest] isn't left holding the Old Maid card'); and a board game, Cargoes, played with dice, each player pushing a little lead steamer round the oceans of the world from dot to dot, landing on hazards in ports which were not part of the Empire: ('Coolies at Shanghai refuse to load cargo, miss a turn'), attacked by pirates lurking in seas not patrolled by the Royal Navy ('Go back to Singapore'); the little ships racing across the Pacific, facing a hurricane rounding Terra del Fuego ('Make for shelter at Port Stanley, miss a turn'), then across the Atlantic ('Delayed at Madeira for repairs, miss two turns'), before being the first (or last) to end up at the final haven of Tilbury Docks.

And older, reading to myself now from the store of other boys' adventure books at Maidenhall or Annaghmakerrig – dusty, empire-glorying books from attics and playroom shelves; seduced by the covers, the gilt and gaudy pictorial boards with their Union Jacks and blood-red images of der-ring-do. Dusting them off so that the young lieutenant's scarlet tunic, white pouch belt and pith helmet on the cover of Captain Brereton's *With Wolseley to Kumasi* shone mint fresh, as the intrepid officer pushed through an evil mangrove swamp, service Webley at the ready. And the same author seeking revenge against the lesser breeds in his *The Grip of the Mullah*.

I went in search of Prester John, too, and rose over the animal-choked plains of East Africa with Jules Verne for six weeks in his balloon, and went with him to the vast mysterious caverns in his *Journey to the Centre of the Earth*.

Above all I went with Allan Quartermain to *King Solomon's Mines*. And Gagool the Witchfinder afterwards was never truly dead for me. She lurked, half crushed, half alive, in a dark corner of the old laundry at Annaghmak-errig where there was a malign Victorian device, a thundering linen press that worked on huge rollers, pressed down by a moving coffin-like half-ton weight, a mangle that had caught the hideous sorceress in its rolling jaws but had not quite extinguished her evil flame.

The magic lantern, with its thrills of Little Red Riding Hood and staid views of Queen Victoria's Diamond Jubilee; the musical box, cherubs with pipes and lyres rising heavenwards to the tune of 'Goodbye Dolly Gray'; the Cargoes game, where it was clear that Britannia actually did rule the waves – these were vivid Victorian worlds that kept the real world at bay for me, and the world of my real family whom I knew barely anything about.

But as I see it now from letters in the file they and the Butlers were hard at work behind my back arguing between themselves, all of them at cross purposes with only one thing in common, it seems – to do their best for Little Joe by thinking up a future of schools and other unpleasant schemes. Knowledge of this unhappy reality, with my real family in Dublin and Cheltenham, lay in wait for me beyond the happy isles of Maidenhall and Annaghmakerrig.

FOUR

Long before I actually experienced my parents' and grandparents' sad lives in Cheltenham and Dublin there were the ever-unresolved arguments between them and the Butlers about who was to have the authority for my upbringing. And of course, even more unresolved, who was to pay: who was now paying unwillingly, who should be paying and wasn't, who wouldn't pay or hadn't, who one day might pay or be made to pay, or who would certainly never pay. Arguments as confused and long-winded as a Vatican conclave.

As to who should have this clear-cut responsibility for my upbringing there is an early letter from Hubert Butler, early in 1942, to my parents:

Dear Nat and Biddy

Little Joe has been with us for two years now and both for his sake and Peggy's, and to a less extent Julia and mine, it would be better if there was more security in the relationship. He is getting to an age when sudden changes wd. be bad for him. And Peggy is becoming too fond of him and used to him, to part with him readily. A decision one way or the other should be come to soon. We do not want to adopt him ... but to offer him a home for a certain period of his boyhood, and if he has to be taken away in a year or two, frankly I would prefer for Peggy's sake that he went now. There is no question of Nat's father or mother being able to bring him up; apart from any question of money, they would not be equal to it. But they are prepared to contribute, as long as they can, to his support with us.

I think you will agree therefore that it is better for him to continue with us, especially as Biddy has the two children in England to look after? Our proposal does not mean that you could not see him or have him with you at times, tho' while the war continues this is not likely to be feasible.

This all sounds very reasonable. And indeed my parents agreed to Hubert's suggestion that I should live with the Butlers as a member of the family for three years, and there is a letter of agreement to this effect signed by all four of them dated 1 March 1942, when I was now five:

This is an agreement between Hubert and Peggy Butler and Nat and Biddy Hone.

Hubert and Peggy Butler will take charge of Joe Hone for the next three years for the weekly payment of 15/- to be paid by Nat and Biddy Hone, in addition to the 15/6 weekly, plus expenses for sundries at present paid by Joe Hone (senior). If at any time, Joe Hone (senior) should be unwilling to pay his sum, Nat and Biddy will do their best to make up the amount.

Hubert and Peggy Butler undertake in return to take charge of Joe Hone as a member of their family during the period stated, and at any time during this period to send him back to Nat and Biddy. They hope that Nat and Biddy will give them as long notice for this as possible.

Signed: Hubert Butler

S M Butler

Nat Hone

Biddy Hone

This agreement is made without prejudice to and notwithstanding the agreement made by Nat Hone and Joe Hone (senior) that he (JH senior) would be responsible for the keep of the child while in charge of Hubert Butler.

This agreement, too, seems reasonable enough, if my parents had stuck to their financial side of it – which of course they didn't. So that later in the summer of 1942 Hubert went to London, among other things to deal with Nat and Biddy face to face. Clearly, when Hubert eventually ran them to earth in the Holborn bar, it was going to be an unhappy meeting, as it was suggested by a letter from Hubert to Biddy, written to her from his hotel before they finally met:

Dear Biddy

I have never been so annoyed or offended in my life. One of the reasons I came over to London was to talk to you and Nat about your son Joe – as I imagine that, though you completely ignore his existence, you still have some sort of affection for him.

I wrote to you the moment I arrived, and when I was extremely busy I went round enquiring of Nat at the High Commissioner's office, the Free French HQ, etc. Only this morning, when I was leaving for Oxford, did I get your card. I gave up all idea of leaving and my room at the hotel, so that now I must look for another one. My friends who were expecting me had to be disappointed. At 3.30 I rang you up. I waited 'til 3.45 and rang you again. I rang five times until I was finally rewarded by the manageress of the Holborn bar and told to ring up 'The same time tomorrow'! I'll see you and Nat damned first!! I consider it the most disgracefully impertinent and inconsiderate piece of cheek I have ever heard of.

We have given your son a home for two years in our house. He has been obstreperous, difficult and often ill. My wife has sat up with him when he was ill and never spared herself looking after him. We have given him affection and care and constant thought. In return we have had 15/- a week (£1 less than we were getting for the other children we boarded). We looked after him because we were sorry for him, and counted on a certain measure of gratitude and understanding from you and Nat. (At one time you promised me cash, too, but we were not surprised, nor did we complain, when this did not turn up). Now you can't even bother to see me, but I must telephone and wait about during an afternoon which I kept specially for you, by your own instructions.

Well, I have never wanted to adopt Joe, but I had thought the present situation so unsatisfactory, where we had all the worry and expense, and none of the authority, that we might come to some arrangement by which Peggy and I became Joe's guardians till he was of an age to look after himself. Now I do not believe that with anyone so inconsiderate as you appear to be, any such agreement would be the least binding or satisfactory.

We anticipate that you will ask for Joe to be sent back to you just whenever it suits your caprice, quite irrespective of his health or happiness. It is on his account mainly that we were anxious for a fixed settlement. He is a very difficult, nervous child – and any feeling of insecurity or sense of 'belonging to nobody' would be very injurious to him. None the less I do not intend that Peggy's happiness should be sacrificed to his. I must have some definite agreement with you about him or else I intend to treat it as a business matter.

I learnt from the solicitors, when a question of guardianship arose, that though there was no legal guardianship or adoption in Ireland, parents could be sued for the repayment of money expended on their child.

I can't tell you how painful and disappointing it is to me to write all this. I had looked forward to a friendly meeting with you and Nat at which Joe's future could be discussed without rancour. I may add that Mrs Symes [my great-aunt Olive] and Nat's parents are in full agreement with Peggy and me about this question of Joe's guardianship. All the same Peggy and I have always thought of you both as people on your own, and have not taken other people's views of you, which are often harsh. We very greatly wished to be on friendly terms with you both.

That is why I feel so angry and hurt now.

Yours sincerely,
Hubert Butler.

PS: I am going down to the Holborn bar now and I hope I shall find you there and not have to deliver this letter.

There is no reply to this justifiably hurt, yet ultimately generous letter. It's possible that Hubert finally ran them to earth in the Holborn bar and never delivered it. But whatever transpired, or, as it happened, didn't transpire, between the three of them on Hubert's trip to London, it's certain that as far as anyone in my own family was concerned no definite arrangements for my future were made.

Once again, towards the end of 1942, Hubert tries to solve this issue. He writes to my grandparents, in another very fair letter:

My dear Joe and Vera,
How nice to see you again. I loved my time with you. I wish you didn't live so far away or that petrol was more plentiful. I got back and found all the family very well. It's turned out very cold and the old gent who drives the children to the Kilkenny school still bears up and we hope he'll hold out 'till Xmas.

Joe now has a College cap, which he can't bear to take off, even at meals, and expects very frequent appreciative comments.

I suppose some day we'll have to tackle the question of Little Joe's future. But, as the decision rests with neither of us, it's difficult and awkward and one naturally shrinks from those rather fruitless debates. I told Nat that our relationship with Joe must be a commercial one (as it isn't now), if we weren't to be authorised guardians. I'm still ready to undertake the guardianship, but present uncertainty can't be continued much longer. It is, I am sure, bad for Little Joe, as well as for us.

He is old enough to feel a sense of insecurity and this reacts on his development – and may be responsible for certain little bad habits of his which occasionally alarm us. We have not noticed them in all the other children with secure backgrounds, of whom at various times we have had charge. Joe is far more gifted than most of them, but he is so extraordinarily impressionable and plastic that I can easily see all his talents going bad on him. I don't believe even an intelligent school wd. cure him of this, if he has no stability at home. I hope he feels he will always have a home here. We've never let him have even a hint of any other impression, but soon he'll be asking questions. Frankly, if he passed to Nat & Biddy – though we shd. not cease to have a strong interest in him – we shd. feel worried abt. the future relationship. We are very fond of him and would hate to break it off, but he shows no sign of loyalty or responsibility and an absolutely dazzling precocity of charm and talent. A sort of male Biddy on the fringes of our family, yet not under our control, might be a real menace …

If there's no word from Nat & Biddy about their intentions by the new year, I'll make fresh suggestions – there's nothing to be done 'till then. It seems fair, though, to tell you what's on our mind. We are so very fond of Little Joe that I'm sure you won't resent this candour. If he turns out badly and not a genius the world will say it's our fault; by offering to be his guardian I'm taking that risk.

> Much love to you both.
> Yrs, Hubert

There is no reply from Old Joe in the file to this letter either, though it seems Hubert and my grandparents may have talked of my future, as appears from Hubert's next letter in which he has another try at getting things straight about me.

Dear Joe and Vera,

I daresay I can make myself clearer in writing than talking so I am sending you this letter. It's about Little Joe … I think both for his sake and Peggy's, and to a lesser extent Julia's and mine, it would be better if there was some sort of security about the relationship. He is getting to an age when sudden changes would be bad for him, and Peggy is getting fond of him and used to him. I do not want her to start planning for his future and then to find that his future is somewhere else and out of her hands. Nor do I want to adopt him, or any child for that matter. I think we can offer him a completely satisfying home as Joe Hone who lives with the Butlers, and one which he will ultimately prefer, as he is already very sensitive and proud of having special relations of his own.

What I am going to suggest is that you and Vera adopt him and that we should on our own part undertake to look after him 'till he was able to look after himself. Do you think Nat and Biddy would agree to this? They would understand that we don't intend any slight to them by this suggestion. We hardly know them and have no grounds for any but friendly feelings towards them. But naturally it is easier for us to take over responsibility for Joe from you and Vera, than from his parents whom we hardly know and never see. We could never be sure what their intentions were (about him) supposing their circumstances changed. On the other hand we seem to understand each other well …

If you adopted Joe it would be your business of course to decide on what terms it was done. We shd. not wish to usurp Nat & Biddy's place as parents, so long as they have no rights over him. He always talks of us as 'Peggy and Hubert' and of them as 'Mummy and Daddy' who because of the war could not bring him up, and we shd. always speak well of them to him.

You wd. not by the adoption be taking on any fresh responsibility. We shd. expect you, as long as you were able, to pay as you have been doing for Joe's keep, but our engagement to look after him wd. be independent of this. The money side is not the important one. If you got richer and we poorer and vice versa, contributions cd. be altered to suit. We would apply our means test without quarrelling …

You'll understand why I consider the question an urgent one now. The nursery struggles are over for Peggy, when Joe was a very difficult unmanageable child; he still is but not so bad. The planning stage has begun and Peggy must know whether it is safe to begin planning for him. Otherwise there are bound to be bruised feelings on one side or the other. She has either to be rather callous and indifferent about him, or rather maternal and possessive and she must know which it is to be.

Yrs, Hubert

Again, there is no reply in the file about my grandparents adopting me. In any case they didn't. Instead Old Joe resumes his financial invoices, queries, misunderstandings and manoeuvrings with Peggy and Hubert. A letter dated 7 April 1943:

Dear Hubert

Thank you for your letter. I am enclosing cheque for £3.5.0 for his keep this month, as follows:

Clothes, from Jan 1942	5.	12.	0
Dancing Classes	4.	8.	2
For April 1943	3.	5.	0
Less one week spent with us		16.	0
For his savings account		2.	6
	£12.	11.	8

I add 2/6 to his savings account. My sister (Olive Symes) started a small savings a/c for him long ago. Perhaps it could be amalgamated with yours? I will ask her. You say in yr. letter – lessons to 15th April, 17 weeks from 1st Jan brings us up to May 1st. I have now therefore paid for lessons to 1st May. Will you make a note of this?

But Old Joe has got his figures wrong, so that Peggy writes to him later:

Dear Joe,

Thanks for the cheque but I think it's simpler to return as it's not quite right. The total bill for last year's incidentals was £22.8.3. On 12th Oct you sent me £5. On 27th Oct you sent me £10. The difference between them is £7.8.3. That's right, isn't it? I'm keeping your letter so let me hear from you at once in case I've overlooked a cheque since 27th Oct. I got the new suit for Joe as Vera requested and enclose bill for £4.00. Please wait and send cheque when I let you know rail fares to Dublin and then please make it a complete payment up to date as otherwise we get muddled.

Old Joe retaliates with an ambiguous letter, some of it indecipherable:

Dear Peggy

I am enclosing cheque for £10 further on Little Joe's account. I think when I paid the cheque for £26 in April for his sojourn in Dublin you … wrote a letter … the cheque … I'd like now to go back to the 12½% query for Park House School …

In this financial joust he has succeeded in making things more muddled still – something he continues to do in his next letter:

Dear Peggy,

Here is Joe's book of coupons. He hasn't used any. I suppose the expense for the kindergarten, if summer terms only, will be about a third of £10, (£3.6.8). But I don't know how the terms are arranged at the Kilkenny school. And the transport about 5/- weekly; Joe's share – say 10 weeks in term – £2.10.0. A total charge of about £6. You might let me know if that is what you calculate approx.

There are more letters in the same financial vein – in the permanent matter of Old Joe's settling, and not settling, his accounts with the Butlers. Matters to do with new gumboots, my transport and train fares (always, since the matter of the paid 'escort', a touchy subject with my grandfather), dentist's fees, and notably a disagreement about a tube of Kolynos toothpaste bought for me, at one shilling and ninepence, which my grandfather seems to have thought he'd paid for twice. But soon the letters move on to (or in fact back to) weightier financial matters, the old theme of who will pay for my general board and lodging with the Butlers, and devolving from this who will have clear authority over me now that the earlier agreement, between my parents in London and the Butlers, had run its three-year term – an agreement which, of course, in its financial requirements from my parents, they never kept. Hubert thus writes a memorandum of the present situation for the local Income Tax Inspector, since it seems that Old Joe (more canny in such matters) had told him he could claim the unpaid cost of my upkeep (due from my father) as an expense which he has had to pay and could therefore put against his tax:

Joseph Hone, aged 7 on 25th Feb last, has been in our charge since his mother left him with us 27th November 1939. During that period we have had sole responsibility for his upbringing, though he has paid occasional visits to his grandparents, Mr & Mrs J M Hone in Dublin.

Mr J M Hone has paid us 15/- a week for his maintenance; they have also paid for doctor's bills and clothes. Except for a few occasional extras paid by us. We have not heard from his parents, Mr & Mrs Nat Hone, for a very long time. But we learnt at Xmas that they are still alive and living, I believe, in Edinburgh. Because of illness, poverty and other causes they have been unable to look after any of their six children and have taken no interest at all in Joe since he has been with us.

In March 1942 I managed to get in touch with Nat Hone in London and to extract a promise from him that he would pay a supplement weekly for Joe's board and education. I agreed to accept 15/- a week more, as the matter was not on a business footing. Normally, when we have had charge of children, they have paid us £2.10.0 a week. No payment whatever has, however, been sent. It is now out of the question that any will be paid, as I learn that he (Mr Nat Hone) is still penniless.

Any necessary confirmation can be given of the above facts. I have not until now sought income-tax rebate for the past five years, when he was with us, simply from inexperience. The 15/- a week granted [*by my grandfather*] has naturally been totally inadequate to cover his maintenance and our responsibility.

I should mention, perhaps that our reasons for taking charge of Joe Hone has been our friendship with Mr & Mrs J M Hone and our willingness to bring up another child with our own. [*Crossed out*] our wish that our own child should have companionship because we only have one child of our own.

> Hubert Butler
> Susan Butler

Whether Hubert received any income-tax rebate is not recorded. He probably didn't, so that in his next letter to my grandfather he returns to the fray – the possibility, nay the miracle, that he might still get some of my unpaid upkeep paid by Nat:

Dear Joe
I had better have Nat's address so that later he cannot say that silence gives consent. I agree with you that the miracle of his paying me is unlikely. But if

financial miracles are to happen to him, I can try and make sure that one of the first will be with me.

It is not our fault that the arrangement with Little Joe, apart from our affection for him, became largely a commercial one. I offered him (Nat) the alternative of guardianship (either ours or through you). He refused. And the agreement, which he never observed and has now expired, was made. You were not concerned in the matter as you had no authority about the guardianship and it was from Nat that I wished the balance of Joe's upkeep to come.

Peggy and I wish to do our best for Little Joe, but the present arrangements cannot continue and are good for nobody. If he is to keep up his association with us he must go to a good school (I don't mean an expensive school but one where he will be properly looked after). He would then come to us for his holidays.

From the time of his return to Maidenhall I will tell Nat that our charge for looking after him will be two and a half [*this is then crossed out*] three guineas a week. This is extremely reasonable, as we were being paid at the rate of two and a half guineas before the war, and with the shortage of everything we should be fully justified in charging four guineas.

We recognize that the obligation is Nat's more than yours, but I hope you will be able to increase the actual payment to 30/-. As regards Income Tax allowance, our shares would be in proportion to what was paid of the three guineas …

I'm truly sorry I have to be so commercially minded abt. Little Joe, but things are not easy for us and we can't afford to be out of pocket. Also Peggy is finding the uncertainty about his future schooling very worrying.

Yrs ever,

Hubert.

Then out of the blue, at the end of the war in 1945, my mother made a surprise entrance on the stage, a coup de theatre. She arrived in Ireland, in Piltown, south Kilkenny, at the little cottage of her parents, Mr and Mrs Anthony. She would have liked to have seen me but, perhaps remembering the contretemps with Hubert three years before at the bar in Holborn, she didn't contact the Butlers. Instead she told my grandparents in Dublin of her arrival; they told Hubert. Hubert, it seems from his subsequent letter to my mother, appeared in two minds over his feelings about my future

– whether to encourage Biddy to take me away from Maidenhall or to discourage her from doing this:

Dear Biddy

I have heard from the Hones that you are in Piltown and would like to see Joe. Peggy and the two children will be at Annaghmakerrig on 17th July, so if you wished to see him you would have to come before then. Would that suit and would you give us a ring?

I was very much surprised not to hear from you or Nat all these years, after our conversation (in London), but it did not seem that I would gain anything by writing. We have told Joe that his father and mother have been in England and that they are very occupied because of the war, etc. At one time this puzzled him but he has not asked for some time.

He is a fine healthy and intelligent boy, but has a very suggestible and possibly corruptible temperament. He goes to school in September and we hope that the discipline and the companionship of many other boys will be good for him. We are naturally worried about his future, as he is a child who would suffer greatly from an unstable or insecure background ... We have always, for his sake, tried to make him feel that he has a home here and avoided any unsettling ideas. I mean, for example, that he was only temporarily a member of our family.

I assume you will be pleased with him, if you come. He will naturally ask us many questions and we will naturally answer them in as reassuring a way as possible.

Please do not think we intend to be in the very least bit possessive about Joe. For some time Peggy and I have felt that Joe needed more discipline than we are giving him here and we felt that until we had seen what effect school was having on him, we would not decide whether it was in his interests or ours that he should go on living with us ...

If a change was to be made we intended to do it very slowly, as I think the sudden realisation that a place which he had regarded as his home almost as long as he could remember, was not really his home – might have a bad effect on his nervous disposition.

We shan't mention a word to Joe about your visit until we know that you are coming. We would be glad to put you up for the night here as soon as we hear your plans. The situation is a difficult one for you as for us and we will do our best not to make it harder. I understand you are over here for a short visit only. You could tell him (Little Joe), what I understand is the case, that Nat is not well and you have to be in England looking after him. Peggy is rather fussed with visitors or she would write. She sends greetings to Mrs Anthony.

Yrs, Hubert Butler.

Another fair and, in the circumstances, a very hospitable letter. But my mother didn't turn up at Maidenhall. At least I have no memory of her doing so, while I have a very clear memory of my first meeting with my parents, in London, the following year. Meanwhile there is the matter, as Hubert intimates in the letter, of my proper schooling. And here my grandfather must have taken a crucial hand, for in the autumn of 1945, aged eight, I was packed off (and the phrase is literal: bags and baggage for someone who had no idea that trunks, tuck boxes, and the other bits and pieces necessary for prep school life, were, in fact, to be the chattels of exile) – packed off to a day and boarding school, Sandford Park, in Ranelagh, at that time largely a genteel late-Victorian inner suburb of south Dublin. And I was sent there, as I learnt later, quite simply because Old Joe had played cricket years before with the now elderly headmaster, A.D. Cordner, a passionate cricketer who had once played wicket keeper several times for the Gentlemen of Ireland and also, surprisingly, for Canada, though he was an upstanding Irish Protestant, so far as I know. Very upstanding, at well over six feet and large generally, so that he was known as 'The Bull'. Though the novelist William Trevor, a pupil at Sandford Park earlier, says in an essay about the school that he was called The Bull because of the way he roared at one of the boys, called Boland.

In the first instance my kindly great-aunt Olive (with only one leg, the other amputated as a young woman after a serious fall from an apple tree) who lived at Lime Hill, a lovely house in the north Dublin countryside near Malahide with her stockbroker husband George Symes, went to Sandford Park on a reconnaissance mission with Vera. She writes to Peggy Butler in the spring of 1945:

Dear Peggy
I saw Sandford Park school with Vera, but as I missed the bus into town I was too late to go all over it. However, Vera liked the dormitories and the whole

place seemed well kept – surprisingly country-like for its situation and a very grand air. There is a very fine big playground so the boys have every chance to learn games, especially as the headmaster is very keen on them. He played cricket against Uncle Pat in Canada. Rather odd. I just cannot remember his name at the moment. I don't think he has a wife. The matron gave us tea and seemed a pleasant person and we were favourably impressed altogether; more than that it's hard to say without more knowledge. But a friend of mine tells me that it's very well thought of and nice boys go there. They take about 16 boarders, the rest day boys – 60 in all I think.

I know Joe understood you wanted Little Joe to go in September – and I hear from Sally [*my aunt*] that he is taking David [*my uncle*] away from St Columba's at Christmas. I suppose he can't manage both sets of fees. I think it's a terrible pity to take David away so young, and if you think Little Joe could wait until the spring I might be able to induce Joe senior to leave David at St Columba's. I will talk it over with him when we next meet. I'm glad Little Joe is settling down with you well. I hope you are both well. My love to the children.

Yrs. ever,

Olive Symes.

If it was odd that the headmaster should have been playing cricket against Pat Hone (my grandfather's younger brother) in Canada, it seems equally odd that my grandfather, for the sake of saving a little money (the fees at Columba's then were about a hundred pounds a year, at Sandford Park about half that) should be taking his son David away from his prestigious public school in the Dublin mountains in order to finance me at the little suburban school of Sandford Park – odd in that, as he had written earlier to Hubert, his first duty was to see his daughter Sally and son David properly launched on the world, before considering me. And quite right, too. But here, it seems, he is about to deny David his later education in order to give me one. I wonder if David may have been leaving St Columba's in any case? Or was it, as I fear more likely, that Old Joe saw that by taking David out of his school early he would thus make a saving of about fifty pounds a year when he came to pay for mine?

The other interesting point, in the light of what happened in Sandford Park a year after I arrived there, is how far it fell from great-aunt Olive's and my grandmother Vera's good impressions of it. Certainly, for as long as the elderly, very decent, cricket-mad Bull Cordner was in charge, they were right to think well of it. It was a good school. Founded in 1922 as the first inter-denominational school in Dublin, Sandford Park had produced fine sports teams and academic results – and some very notable old boys, like Owen Sheey Skeffington (the famously liberal and outspoken Senator and Trinity College Professor of French), William Trevor and Conor Cruise O'Brien.

It's true that under Bull Cordner's benign and rather lax wartime regime the school had declined academically, if not in cricket. The Bull had no academic qualifications whatsoever and it was his view that all a boy needed to know was how to play cricket well and spell properly. So in his classes he conducted lengthy spelling bees and in the afternoons, indeed at every spare moment of the summer day, he would get all the boys togged out in their whites and onto the cricket pitch and into the nets. I remember, on my first summer term, his asking me 'How is your cricket, Hone?' (as though everyone had a 'cricket' on them, as a natural adjunct, like an arm or a leg). He was in his study overlooking the park, watching a house match. I said I had played French cricket at home with the girls at Maidenhall. 'Oh, no, Hone,' he said gravely. 'Real cricket, we play real cricket here.' He turned and looked out the window, gazing lovingly at the game, murmuring, 'Ah, the boys in their whites, their summer whites …' I did come to play real cricket at Sandford Park and became quite good at it. Bull Cordner was a kind man, surely the most important educational qualification for a teacher.

The main school building was (and indeed still is, for the school survives today in a vastly improved form) a late Victorian house, rather in the mode of a grand, south-coast resort villa residence that made forceful attempts to imitate previous architectural glories in the Tudor and neo-Gothic modes. There was false half-timbering, oriel windows, stained glass in the front rooms, a false moat round the basement and various doodles and excrescences in relief wherever the architect's imagination had got out of hand. It had been built in the 1890s by a rich Dublin builder, James Pile, as something of a country retreat. But between the wars a crop of pebbledash suburbs had grown up around it, so that it became isolated in ten acres of parkland, fine chestnut and beech trees behind barbed wire and granite walls.

With its steep roofs, ornate eaves, spiky adornments, loud red brick and coloured windows, a big pond in front bordered by pampas grass and bulrushes with a Giverny bridge over to a bushy willow-tree island, there was a degree of fantasy about the place and its many trees, exotic shrubs and a laurel drive ending with a Gothic gate lodge. Beyond lay Ranelagh Road – a busy and forbidden main road, with shops, buses and real people. The Catholic Irish. For Sandford Park, despite its original interdenominational intents, was, apart from several Jewish boys, entirely Protestant. And so at that time in the 1940s, whether the headmaster and staff knew it or liked it or not, the school was implicitly involved in sustaining the faith of the British oppressor, along with imperial notions of class, clubs, good form and so on. More than any English counterpart the school was isolated in time and place, administrating the last rites of the faith to a small Dublin Protestant minority – in the midst of a Catholic nation that had suffered more than any from the Imperial cause. Politics and geography, more than Common Entrance, threatened the school's existence. Dr Arnold's lofty zeal, together with the whole muscular-Protestant-colonial ethic, had come full circle here, and the school was waging a last battle against an imagined Catholic horde, pressing forwards just outside the gates. We boys were the unknowing foot soldiers in the coming siege, potential cannon fodder, victims of a beleaguered officer belief in the efficacy of the Bible and the Birch, so that, with this carrot and stick, we would stand firm to the very last.

I was eight when I went there. And despite the kindly Bull Cordner, who seemed merely to preside over the school as an honorary presence, like God, I was appalled, desolate, in the weeks after my arrival. I couldn't understand what had happened to me, except that I'd been unaccountably abandoned, simply given away like a box of apples by the Butlers, for I barely knew anything of my grandparents then and nothing of my parents. I arrived in the winter term, and in my memory of those first few years it seemed to be always winter there. The heating was minimal, with no hot water, and only a sheet and a thin blue blanket covered me on the junior dorm iron bed. I was perished with the sort of cold that not only chapped my hands permanently, made my ears blue and my nose run like an oil can, but was like a Lord of the Frost, coming inside me and making a frozen core that never thawed. I must have been literally numb, in body and spirit. My faculties seized up, a defence mechanism no doubt against the chill and loneliness, the only feelings I had then, with what was left of my mind running savagely to and fro over the unbelievable fact that I had been abandoned in this hell of utter discomfort, and was not at home in Maidenhall or Annaghmakerrig.

I spent all my free time crowding the red-hot pot-bellied stove in the assembly hall, the old ballroom, vainly trying to push my way into the circle of larger boys who spat on the throbbing metal at intervals, creating sizzling globules, small explosions of saliva – a performance which I looked on then, not with disgust, but as an envied pastime, symbolic of good fellowship and warmth.

Of course I see now how such physical horrors were commonplace in most boarding schools of the time – the cold and the dirt were the same in hundreds of other similar institutions. The dank, dripping washrooms in the back yard, miles away from the dormitories in the main house, where one skidded about over decades of congealed soap and human detritus; the yellowed margarine less than a varnish on the curled-up bread slices, porridge that dripped glutinously from the spoon like catarrh, the daily meat stew that was indistinguishable from vomit, the dried excrement on the lavatory seats.

A child has few civilized standards and can make fewer comparisons. He quickly comes to believe that this is how things are everywhere in the world outside his home. It wasn't until I was older at the school that I discovered how the headmaster and staff lived in quite a different manner, with their own food, bathrooms and oil heaters in their bedrooms. And this discovery was for me the beginning of a cunning and a passion for revolt that formed my real education at school.

At the end of my first year, Bull Cordner died suddenly overnight in his bed in his tiny room next to our junior dormitory. It was quite unreal, like the end of a chapter in a childrens' story. We had seen him the day before, but now, for some fictional reason, we would not see him again. There was to be a new chapter, a new headmaster. We juniors waited expectantly for the story to continue.

What followed was a reign of terror that lasted five years – a period in my life that marked me more conclusively than any other, forcing my character abruptly and completely into ways it would never naturally have taken. The school for us boarders became an enemy-occupied country; the pupils collaborators, resisters, victims.

The new head, Hal Dudgeon, was the science master. He'd been a skilled boxer and had fought professionally apparently, so he was known as the 'Battling Bottle Brush'. He was a brute. But then he would have appeared to an outsider, a parent, no more than a reasoned disciplinarian, intent on sharpening things up in a school that had become somewhat lax. A school inspector would surely have commended his scrupulous attitude here; a good education demanded no less. How then could he be guilty of anything? He resorted only to the usual violence of such places at the time: he beat me with sudden impromptu severity, at the least excuse, and slowly pulled up the hair on the nape of my neck in class, as if such torture would force me to admit the three properties of water, of which I was ignorant.

But this was only the beginning of his cruelties. We feared him because his real punishments were much more subtle. He presented an awful threat. He had that rare quality of sinister omnipresence, seen or unseen. He was fearsome in his insights and prophecies. In the way of transgression he knew what you had done, by divination, and what you were going to do before you did it. With him retribution didn't catch up with you, it never left your side. His malign gifts were those of a Gestapo interrogator who convinces you that your friend in the resistance network has told all an hour before and that you are there merely to confirm what he has said. He used this and other methods with me and the boys – playing one boy off against another, placing informers and bribing potential Fifth Columnists – a Himmler running a network in an occupied country. So that in the next four years of his reign at the school I became adept in all the arts of concealment, subterfuge and espionage – a secret agent, the school a foreign country where I had been placed before the war, ever alert, disguised.

Dudgeon was a very ordinary-looking man – sadists often are. Tall, thin, grey-faced, grey-suited, thin grey hair flattened down over his scalp, thin and grey and bloodless all over. But his eyes were the worst, cold blue, unmoving when he looked at you, and his rare smile was as bad, a small movement of grey flesh about the cheeks that always boded ill. He was fanatically neat in everything. In his study, while gazing at you he would slowly marshall pins on his desk as if their disruption threatened the balance of the world. He seemed to have been constructed like a machine, bit by bit, according to some perfect blueprint. It was impossible to imagine him naked or washing or even eating – for he never ate with the staff or the boys, and was, in fact, never seen in the open except on some precise school business. He knew the importance of withholding himself, knew that the unfamiliar is half the fright in fear – knew how, when you swooped on a boy, you had to do it fast and silently, from behind. He wore rubber-soled shoes and I can hear the sudden squeaks even now, as he made his final run in for me, diving out of the sun or from the darkness of the laurel drive when he would take me like a hawk by the back of your neck.

Most boys gave up any idea of learning in the school, for we lived night and day in fear and enmity. All our behaviour was dictated by the possibility of Dudgeon's sudden presence and his eyes hungry to punish someone. So we learnt to scan minutely any area of the school before we moved into it, never to sit in a room with only one exit, take up any exposed position, or round a corner without first peeking round it, always have an alibi. To survive was to continually dissemble. And because of this fearful atmosphere I formed no close friendships in the school then – no more than an agent will risk betrayal by making his real identity known to another spy in the network.

The boys, thus separated from each other, were left to their lonely devices after lights out in the junior dorm, or took comfort in inanimate objects, in the secrets of their lockers or tuck boxes. Above all we found solace in the forbidden life of the suburban high street that lay beyond the laurel drive. This drab thoroughfare of sweetshops, newsagents and fruiterers full of damp cabbages was freedom for us, a glittering country over the border for which we often risked everything. It became a matter of honour to creep down the drive, usually in the late afternoon before first prep, showing ourselves like heroes under the misty street lights, before darting into a shop for some small article which we carried back as proof of time spent in a free world.

Sometimes one or two of us boarders would try and filter into the crowd of day boys who left every afternoon at half past three. We were like desperate men in a prison break. We knew the risk. For at just that time Dudgeon would start to move hungrily about the bow window of his study that gave onto the drive, his gaze like a swivelling beam of light on the barbed wire, searching for just such hapless fools. One could be lucky and get out during an interval of his attention. But more usually the attempt ended in a scene which I was later to become familiar with in various POW Colditz movies. Dudgeon would open and shout from his window. One of the staff or a senior boy would be dispatched, chasing down the drive, and the miscreant would be dragged back by the ear, disappearing into Dudgeon's study, a fly returned to the spider.

William Trevor, an earlier pupil at Sandford Park, has written of Dudgeon as 'the most appalling man I've ever met'. And I have often asked myself since why the very liberal Butlers and my grandfather, who was not liberal but was capable of odd bouts of feeling, allowed me to stay in this juvenile prison camp. And I can come up with no very good answer. Of course I couldn't have written home about the horrors, since our weekly letter home was censored by Dudgeon or the duty master. But surely I must at some point in the holidays, have spoken to Peggy and Hubert of these continual cruelties? Perhaps I didn't. Or perhaps I did and nothing was done about it. There are no family letters in the file showing evidence or knowledge of Dudgeon's cruel behaviour or of the dreadful conditions in the school generally. It seems that, completely isolated as I was (except for those few heroic escapes down Ranelagh Road), I, like most schoolboys then, must simply have accepted the school and Dudgeon's monstrous regime as the way things were everywhere outside my home.

FIVE

No doubt as a reaction against the horrors of Sandford Park and Dudgeon and my feelings of having being abandoned by the Butlers (as I'd not felt with my parents, never having known them), I started a sly process of thieving money from Peggy and my grandmother in the next year, during weekends at Ballorney, my grandparents' house in the Wicklow mountains, and at home in Maidenhall. At first it was small sums, pennies taken from my grandmother's handbag, and then more from Peggy's – threepenny bits, sixpences, shillings; then, gradually more daring, florins and finally the ultimate in coined wealth, big shiny Irish half-crowns with that lovely prancing horse on them – keeping the money in a wooden pencil box I'd been given for school and hiding it under my bed.

Ten shillings, a pound, two pounds – after a few months I had a wonderful silver hoard of money that I took out and counted every so often and gloated over like a miser – like my grandfather, I suppose, as I saw him in later years, doing the daily tot of all his worldly assets on the sofa after lunch with the two smelly dachshunds.

It was a good feeling, this careful counting-house business in the secrecy of my bedroom. But an even better feeling was the power I felt now, a hidden power over all the abandoners, footlers and forbidders as I saw them, in my own family and the Butlers, along with the ogre Dudgeon and my other tormentors among the bully boys and some of the masters at school.

So that, with this money, when I was back at Sandford Park again, during the next winter term, I made up for the unhappiness of it all by sneaking out of bounds in the afternoons, down the laurel drive, and out onto Ranelagh Road to the Sandford Sweeteries with their liquorice twists and bulls' eyes, then past the drab fruiterers and down to The Elm stationers where they sold the 'Dandy', 'Beano' and 'The Champion'. Now I could buy everything I wanted: a big double slice of vanilla ice cream at fourpence, whole bags of gob stoppers at the Sweeteries, all three comics – everything that had been beyond my reach with the ninepence pocket money I was allowed each week, pretty useless money for any extravagance since a third of it had to be kept for the collection at Sandford Church each Sunday. Before, I had sixpence a week left for any extras. Now I had silver pounds in my pocket.

Of course the whole business was one of unconscious revenge on all the people who had arranged for my unhappy circumstances at school. Yet the stealing was motivated by something else just as important to me – a need to please my grandmother Vera, and most especially placate the mother figure in my life, Peggy. For I soon started buying them presents in the Ranelagh shops with their money, cigarettes and perfume, without realizing that this could be my undoing. It wasn't, in the event, though these gifts aroused suspicions. What ended my successful career as a thief was that, as with so many thieves, I became overconfident.

I had a bicycle by then, bought second hand with money I'd found, three pound notes, in the lion house on a visit to the Dublin Zoo with the Butlers – which, unclaimed after three months, I was allowed to keep. Although second hand, it seemed a splendid machine, a slightly drop-handle-barred black Humber. But it needed a few extras. A pump, a puncture repair outfit, a little saddle bag and a bell. Very conveniently a bicycle repair shop had just opened in Bennettsbridge, the village a mile away from Maidenhall. Why spend my good money (Peggy's good money in fact) on buying these extras? I could simply take these items from the shop in the village. Conveniently again, my bicycle sprang a leak in one of the tyres on my next holiday at Maidenhall. So I wheeled it down to the repair shop straight away.

Before I got there I knew just what I had to do – ask the rather surly new man (he wasn't a local villager) if he could mend the puncture and, while he was away in the back of the shop, I'd help myself to the various items I needed on the shelves.

In retrospect I can see that I had no qualms whatever about my behaviour. I wasn't going to be caught – I had proved that already in my many robbings of the handbags – and in any case I felt it entirely natural behaviour, given my circumstances. It was in the necessary order of things for me. I somehow knew that it was sink or swim in my life, and I was swimming. I was 'morally blind' as Hubert described me in a subsequent letter to a doctor-psychiatrist in Dublin.

At the bicycle shop all went exactly to plan. The man fixed the puncture in the back room while I helped myself to the things I needed, adding a pair of bicycle clips that I didn't need since I was still in short trousers. I left the shop, my pockets filled with the plunder, and bicycled back to Maidenhall. I had just got to the front gates when the shop owner came up behind me on his own bike. Without saying anything (which is why I remember him being taciturn) he frisked me, found some of the things I'd stolen, then took me back to the village police station where the sergeant spoke to me and found some more things in my pocket and sent me back to Maidenhall. So I thought that was it and no more would be said about the matter. Certainly I wouldn't mention it. But let Hubert take up the shock-horror story now, in a letter to Old Joe on 6 May 1946:

My dear Joe

Many thanks for your letter; it would certainly have been a good idea, if you could have made that arrangement with St Columba's but an awful thing has happened and I am afraid the question of Joe's education will have to be considered again.

He was caught by a Bennettsbridge bicycle shop owner at our avenue gate with a number of articles which he had stolen while the man was mending his puncture. The man took him to the Guards' barracks where he was interrogated and searched by the sergeant. More things were found. He then returned to us and spent the remainder of the day without giving us an idea that anything had happened. We knew nothing until Joe had left for school, when the owner of the shop came up and told us and I went down and interviewed the sergeant. Peggy is most terribly upset by all this. I do not mean because it is an intensely humiliating experience for us but because she is so frightfully hurt by his heartless deceit. She does not feel that there is anyone else, outside you and Vera and Olive Symes who have the slightest interest or feeling of responsibility for the child. We have both of us known that there was a bad side to his character. He has clearly had far too much licence at Sandford Park, as, till he went there, he never strayed on his own into the Bennettsbridge shops and we knew exactly what he was doing. He came back from Dublin with a good deal of money on him for which he bought rather more goods than was natural. This had been worrying us and one or two other things.

Peggy and I feel that Joe's is a special case requiring special treatment and that we are not qualified to cope with him. Our method of treating him as a normal child and trusting him has failed. I can see no alternative but changing his method of upbringing, even if moving him from Sandford Park does cost you more. Sally and David will surely not grudge money spent on saving Joe from going to the bad. It's now or never.

Do you think he had better go to Ballyorney for the week-ends? I feel sure that the companionship of servants is not good for him and he makes for them if he gets the chance.

There have been four other children of his age during the whole of his visit staying here but, instead of playing with them, he has played his own games the whole time – e.g. he bought himself a box of chocolates, hid it in the kitchen and ate it by himself without any attempt to share it with others.

We can't exactly blame him, he seems impervious to influence, in fact amoral. Sandford Park has, if anything, done him harm by familiarising him with the streets. Before he went to the bicycle shop he went into a pub and bought himself a bottle of lemonade. It is unthinkable that small children of nine, staying at Maidenhall, should wander round the Bennettsbridge pubs. It has never happened before and there have been many children here.

I will not write more, it is all too close to us to suggest any course of action. I will come up to Dublin as soon as I can. Perhaps advice could be got. My opinion at present is that Joe should go to a country boarding school where he is better supervised and out of temptation. We have not said anything to Little Joe about all this as we did not know till after he'd gone what he'd done. Please do nothing and say nothing till we have seen you. I wouldn't have him for the week-end till we have conceived a wise plan of action. We feel it very important that Joe should realise that this time he has overstepped the mark. But it might do him more harm than good to scold him or threaten him with our withdrawal from his life.

Love to you both and I am truly sorry to be the bearer of such very sad and disappointing news, yet it is no good making light of it. The Sergeant said that he had a perfect right to charge Joe with Petty Larceny.

My career as a rural Oliver Twist had come to an end. Perhaps the only person who comes well out of the incident is the village sergeant for not charging me with petty larceny. Hubert's reaction seems exaggerated. There is a sense in part of his letter that he is as much concerned with Butler status in the community as with my thievery – along with the horror of a Maidenhall boy wandering round the village pubs buying bottles of pop. And then there is his phrase of my conduct as being one of 'heartless deceit', which seems a bit strong. He means of course deceit towards them in not admitting my sins when I returned from the interrogation at the village police station. But did Hubert really expect me to admit my sins? It's surely a cardinal rule among miscreant schoolboys to keep mum with the authorities over their misdeeds. Was he never a schoolboy himself? In any case my 'heartless deceit' was directed towards the surly bicycle-shop owner, not to either of the Butlers. Rather the opposite – since in part (apart from the sweets and ice creams for myself) I was trying to appease the Butlers by stealing their money, so that I could buy perfume and cigarettes for Peggy. But that equation doesn't seem to have occurred to Hubert. It's interesting, too, that, given his very liberal ethic, Hubert so takes against my consorting with servants. I can certainly remember doing this in the case of the Maidenhall and Annaghmakerrig maids, and particularly with Mary, my great-aunt Olive's cook out at Lime Hill, a roly-poly, elderly, kind-hearted woman who gave me ginger biscuits in the basement kitchen and allowed me to travel up to the dining-room in the dumb waiter. The dispossessed will naturally gravitate towards others in the same position.

As to my grandfather's reaction to Hubert's alarmed letter, he takes a different line. He writes to Hubert three weeks after my 'raid' on the bicycle shop (as Old Joe describes it in a later letter):

As regards Sandford Park I don't think there is any need for panic. I saw Allt yesterday [Peter Allt was a close literary friend of my grandfather's, a Yeats scholar who subsequently edited the Variorum edition of Yeats's poetry], who teaches at Sandford Park and was formerly at St Columba. Dr Auchmuty [the Vice-Principal at Sandford Park] had spoken to him about Little Joe and said he was difficult and too inclined on self-emphasis and self-assertion; but he was not in any great immediate anxiety about him. Allt does not recommend Sandford Park as a permanency, however, in Joe's case, and thinks highly of St Columba, and particularly of White, who has a 'house' there, and has done well with difficult boys – with one in particular, the son of a well-known man in Dublin, whom no other school was able to keep. I heard of another small boy, also a child of a well known person, who goes in for peculations, and the person who told me seemed to think that this was not uncommon in children. I will speak to Olive as you suggest, and write to you then.

On my being marked down by Hubert as an obstreperous nine-year-old, impervious to influence and amoral, the pace of the correspondence quickens between my grandfather and Hubert and others who are now brought in – a doctor-psychiatrist, headmasters and housemasters, friends and relations and my parents in Cheltenham; all of them so far a largely hidden chorus in the wings, who have the sudden evangelical opportunity to come on stage – advisors on the wicked condition of Little Joe, now strutting over the footlights, swigging stolen bottles of pop and gobbling bulls' eyes, with cigarettes and phials of exotic perfumes scattered about him: a Victorian melodrama where the fallen boy must be saved from his moral blindness. And so there follows a series of alarmed, scatter-shot letters between everybody, where the issue of 'What to do with Little Joe?' becomes a truly hot potato.

Half a dozen plans were considered – that I should see a doctor in Dublin or go to a 'childs' guidance clinic', that I should be given over to my parents in England and go to school there, that I should go to the famous (or infamous) progressive school of Summerhill, run by the dour old Scot A.S. Neill, or to Christ's Hospital school in Horsham, or that I should be farmed out once more to friends of the Butlers who took on difficult children and had a 'family' of them in the wilds of County Cork. Confusions, indeed, as evidenced by a letter from grandfather to Peggy, in mid-June, 1946:

My dear Peggy

I am afraid a hornets' nest has been stirred up by this planning for Little Joe. Nat arrived here Friday evening, unannounced. He had not answered my letter. He said he had come over to see about the child, in view of my letter; but has not actually seen the child yet although he was hanging about Dublin all yesterday. He had enquired about ordinary private schools in London, and done nothing about the other thing and says he is opposed to it. [*What other thing? Perhaps my going to a child's guidance clinic?*]

I suppose the idea was that he and Biddy could get some money into their fingers if any change was made. The only concrete suggestion he offered was that Little Joe should go to a farm in Wiltshire for the summer holidays where Biddy's sister works. A decent girl, I believe. When he came back last night, at twelve o'clock, he said he had been at the passport office for Little Joe. I am not giving him any money for Little Joe or for himself (beyond his fare back, which I must, as it is the utter sense of futility that is produced) …

Meanwhile my mother Biddy, seemingly left out in the cold over all these possible arrangements by the footling men, understandably tries to get in on the act. She writes to Peggy:

Dear Peggy

I was very distressed to hear about Little Joe. The first we heard about it was from Nat's father who wrote a few weeks ago asking us to find a school for him over here. It has been very difficult to find anything as reasonable as Sandford Park so far. A friend of ours is very friendly with one of the partners in Gabbitas Thring, the scholastic agents, and he went along to see him for me last week. Any schools I have heard from them have been in the region of £35 – £40 a term. At the moment I do not know where I am about the whole thing …

Personally, Peggy, I should love to have him at school over here because I could see more of him and see him most week ends. I can arrange to have him looked after for his holidays down in Wiltshire …

I am afraid I cannot agree to sending Joe to a clinic over here. Bickford-Smith of Gabbitas Thring thought it unnecessary. He mentioned a case of a boy he knew who went to one of these clinics and he said the little boy was infinitely worse when he came away.

Anyway, Peggy, would you write to me and let me know what is happening … I believe Hubert is in Dublin this week so something may be arranged between himself and Mr Hone about Joe. Mr Hone is so vague about everything and he emphasised in one letter to Nat that he did not want to be written about in the matter. But I would be most grateful, Peggy, if you would write to me and give me some idea of what is happening ...

Yours,
Biddy.

There is a note of desperation in this letter, which is not surprising given the vagueness of my grandfather and the vagaries of my father, which give the impression that they would both like to be shot of the whole business of Little Joe. There is no reply from Peggy to my mother in the file. But I'm sure she sent one. She was a very conscientious woman.

The next letter to Biddy in the file is from Hubert, commending a family in County Cork, where he thinks I should go for the holidays and, implicitly, where he feels I might find a permanent home.

Dear Biddy

You have no doubt heard from the Hones about Mr and Mrs Allen who have offered to take Little Joe for six weeks of his holidays. Both Peggy and I, as well as Joe's own relations in Ireland, think it would be the gravest mistake if this most generous offer was refused. I do not think it likely that it would then be repeated. Mr and Mrs Allen are connected with Newtown school and are extremely enlightened people. They know of Joe's difficulties and his rather unsettled background, which may be in part responsible for them. They have an understanding of children and I believe that under their guidance he would get through this most unfortunate phase of dishonesty and egoism.

A visit to England at this time, except to a very carefully selected school, would I believe be most harmful and unsettling to him and indeed criminally unwise. His case cannot be considered normal. I have never yet heard of a child who would be quite unmoved by a visit to the police station and start stealing from a different shop a couple of days later. Obviously his temperament requires very careful watching and handling. This I am confident that the Allens would provide and that their advice would also be worth listening to. Gabbitas Thring and his opinions are not of course worth a row of pins.

We were surprised indeed that Nat paid a visit to Ireland on the head of this matter and made no attempt to get in touch with us. You will forgive us if we are sceptical of the good effects coming of this visit to England. If you are both capable of a sustained and fruitful interest in Joe's future you would surely have given some signs of it in the past seven years.

Yours sincerely,
Hubert Butler.

This offer from the Allens was clearly turned down, since I never went to them. Instead I was taken to see a doctor in Dublin, a Dr Eustace, who practised in the posh medical quarter of Fitzwilliam Square and (as I afterwards learnt) had an interest in psychiatry having met the master, Dr Freud, in Vienna in the 1920s. I was taken to see him by my grandmother Vera and my father Nat. The two of them left the waiting-room and I was brought in to face a small middle-aged, dark-suited figure behind a large desk in a high-ceilinged room looking out over the leafy square. I can remember very little except that at one seemingly crucial point the doctor got out a board with square and round holes and a similar number of round and square pegs. He asked me to put the pegs in the right holes. I found this ridiculously easy. And that seemed to be it. I waited to be picked up by my father. He didn't turn up for quite a while, and when he did he smelt of beer. But let the doctor take up the story:

Dear Mr Butler,
Mrs Hone brought her grandchild to see me and I had a letter from Mr Hone about the position. I may not have heard the full story of the case, but I think they have told me everything, including the stealing in Kilkenny.

I do not feel that this child's psychological difficulties are such as would need a special school; he spoke to me fairly freely about the various upsets, and I do not suppose was any more untruthful than most children of his age. He is quite intelligent and I feel should do well at school.

As you know his family condition is far from satisfactory, and certainly you and your wife have been very good to the child, but it is always difficult for a child knowing he is being brought up by foster parents or grandparents. I feel that to send this boy to a special school in England is more likely to make him more difficult, as no matter how much they try to improve the conditions in these schools there is always an atmosphere of abnormality and he would have to associate with children who have much more serious difficulties.

As you probably know, this kind of pilfering by children represents an urge to compensate for some feeling of insecurity, and this is a child who must feel insecure, in that his early life has been irregular, except when he was living with you. Living in his present atmosphere, of being very much a junior child and smaller than most of the others in the boarding part of the school, he cannot but feel insecure and it makes it difficult for him to meet others on his own level.

His father talks of taking him over to England with him for his summer holidays, and I do not know whether this would be a wise move or not, but it would be a solution of how he should spend his holidays, and it may help him to know what his own parents are like.

Yours sincerely,

H J Eustace.

A very sensible letter. Though, as we shall see in a subsequent letter from Hubert to the doctor, Hubert was either puzzled or frustrated by the doctor's responses. Meanwhile I did go over to England for the holidays, for a first meeting with my parents in London. I was put on a plane at Dublin airport by Oliver Hone, the son of my grandfather's brother Pat. 'Noll', as he was known, had a senior position with Aer Lingus, and I was cosseted by the air hostess and had a bumpy flight in a Douglas Dakota, which frightened and excited me. My mother Biddy was working at that time with Tyres Scotland, a motor firm in the Kingsway, and I must have been met at the airport by my father, though I don't remember this. The first thing I remember of London was being taken by Nat to a pub on the river in Chelsea, the King's Head and Eight Bells. There were tables outside. Nat told me to take a seat. He went inside. Later he brought me a glass of cider, which tasted nice. My parents then had a flat in a big red brick mansion block on Prince of Wales Drive over the river in Battersea. I must have met my mother that evening. But I have no memory of my meeting her whatsoever. The next thing I remember – it must have been the following day– was wandering alone along Battersea High Street and being very curious about everything in this big city, the shops, the trams, the strange taxis – and a vast station I arrived at, Clapham Junction, where I stood on a bridge watching the trains beneath, amazed at the number coming in and out of the station, over the dozens of criss-crossed lines. My mother must have been very pleased to see me. My not remembering anything about her, on this first meeting, must have been an unconscious rejection of her. Or just that I had a numbed feeling about being with my real parents in London. Numbed as I had been during my first frozen year at Sandford Park. I was aware only of London sensually, visually – the taste of cider by a river, the strange taxis, the clanging trams, the incredible number of electric trains.

I do remember one day when my mother took me off to see a great friend of hers, Patsy Kilmartin, who had a flat in a big house in Carlyle Square off the King's Road in Chelsea. There were drinks and jollity with this woman and her son, who lived nearby and had come to call. A sudden feeling of ease and civilization, though I use these words only in retrospect. But I was right to feel what I did – leavening conviviality, together with good sense and intellect, a new world that had nothing to do with the petty worlds I had so far experienced, the cruelties of Sandford Park, my insecurities and thefts with the Butlers and my grandparents; all that could be put aside as nothing in this enlightened atmosphere. The world could be a kind and sensible place, among understanding, easy-going people. Patsy Kilmartin was just such a person. And so was her son, Terry Kilmartin, whom I met that summer, and who shared the awful stammer I had then. He went on to become the distinguished literary editor of *The Observer* and later the second fine translator of Marcel Proust's great novel. My mother, with her loving nature and great social gifts, got on with everyone: barmen, Irish navvies, intellectuals, literary critics and French scholars. But Hubert was not pleased with my first visit to my parents' world, their louche Bohemian world as he no doubt saw it after his experiences of having to run Nat and Biddy to ground in the Holborn bar in 1942. He writes to Old Joe in August 1946:

Dear Joe

I'm sorry that Joe has gone to England. I think it most weak of you and Vera, who, by holding the purse strings, can exercise control over Nat and Biddy, to have allowed this. I warned you that for all our good will towards Joe and you, we cannot share any responsibility for his upbringing with Nat and Biddy. We feel now that he is definitely passing into shady and unknown regions, into which we cannot, in justice to Julia and his friends here, follow him. Whether, if he is stranded again, we shall take him back here, I do not know – but very definitely one kind of chapter ends …

Yrs,

HB.

Now the melodrama moves into Greek myth, Little Joe descending into Hades, where he will face some awful Nemesis. My good great-aunt Olive will have something to say about Hubert's dire prophecies later. But meanwhile there is a reply to this letter in the file, in August 1946. Indeed, while I was away in London, my grandfather clearly bestirred himself in a flurry of letters to Peggy and Hubert:

Dear Hubert

I hope you won't think I'm keeping back that letter of yours to Biddy purposefully, for you would certainly be welcome to it, and indeed I instituted a long search for it the other day. As I said I had two editions of it, Nat having sent me his. I might have destroyed one, but would be surprised if I destroyed both, so one may turn up. Anyhow, if you ever want evidence, I will give it, that you wrote to the parents about the incident in Bennettsbridge and advised and urged that the child should go to the Allens for the holidays.

It is true that I have responded to SOS calls (from Nat and Biddy) from time to time. But I don't give him an allowance. I couldn't therefore try to prevent him taking the child this holidays in the way you suggest. We might of course have refused their request for travel facilities; but I think that course would have been morally dubious, since after all the child is theirs, and I really cannot propose to believe that they intend to ill-treat him, or teach him evil. So much for the 'weakness' with which you charge us.

Furthermore, if we had simply done nothing Biddy might have turned up here for him, which would have been a damned nuisance and expensive, as I should have had to pay to get her back to England with Joe.

I think you underestimate our difficulties. I think they are more serious than your worryings and your speculations as to some possible injustice falling on Julia in the distance, rather an absurd speculation, if you will forgive me for saying so.

Perhaps there was an original misunderstanding on your part, of which I did not clearly disabuse you. I never wanted to detach Little Joe from his parents. He was left on my doorstep, and the rest followed, including Peggy's great kindness, which makes him think of Maidenhall as his home.

I must say we found him very little trouble and saw no signs of abnormality. If I were to prophesy about his future I would think that the danger lay in excessive physical and 'psychological' normality. He might so easily, if circumstances permitted, turn into a good fellow hanging round bars, the admired of all admirers. The practical test on which he should be brought up is that circumstances won't permit that kind of leisure … Therefore I am coming to think that he might be better off with his parents – that they should have the task and responsibility of setting him to a career or employment, I helping them on his account while he is still a child. Especially since you are now doubtful whether you can do anything for him in the holidays.

Yrs,
Joe.

In another letter to Hubert my grandfather is again playing the card of handing me over to my parents, suggesting I would be living a more 'normal' life, though he must have known how abnormal my parents' life was:

Dear Hubert

I wrote to Nat and suggested that he should write to you. I get cross and stupid if involved with Biddy.

I said you were worried about certain aspects of his character which had come out lately in Joe's conduct, and that you suggested this treatment and the English school. I said in other words I was an agnostic (rather than an atheist) about 'psychology' but that I thought there were advantages in the child being near his parents as he could feel more normal, and very great disadvantages to Joe if you should feel obliged to disinterest yourself in him, as he was so fond of you and you had done so much for him, and that it was clearly unsatisfactory with us in the holidays.

Who was that woman in the Kildare Street Club? It is awful having that pistol put to one's head – 'You don't remember me' and then we both fled from her.

Yrs. Affect,
Joe.

This meeting with Hubert at the Club may have been the occasion (afterwards recounted to me by another member who was present) when Old Joe, aiming to save money, ordered just one pot of tea and one cup and saucer for Hubert, and said he would take his tea from Hubert's saucer. But here he is now in his next letter in an almost extravagant writing mood:

Dear Hubert

Unfortunately I put the wrong number of Nat's road. I have written to him again and told him of your views and how far I can go in the matter. I want him to keep further correspondence on the project between you and Peggy, and not to bring me in, until the end when you can advise me on the result. It is much better this way ...

If the other plan breaks down [*I suppose my being sent off to the Allen family in the wilds of County Cork*], I will think of sending him to the National School in Enniskerry, the Protestant one, which is very good, so good the plutocrats think of sending their children there. He could go and come home with the other children who pass the gate. Dr Eustace or some other doctor of nervous diseases could see him from time to time. There is a charming retired Irish doctor up the road here, a really nice man, who used to attend these cases, and I could ask him for the name of a good doctor of nervous diseases without saying who the case was. I don't want to publish Little Joe to all the world.

There is an article on Kleptomania in Chambers Encyclopaedia (1896). It uses words like 'inhibition' that I thought had only lately been invented. I daresay the ordinary conscientious, intelligent doctor, who has specialised in nervous cases, or if you like diseased minds, is just as good and knows just as much, as these clinics which always suggest to me an exploitation of 'Decaying Capitalist Society'.

Yrs,
Joe.

One can see why Old Joe was keen on the National School in Enniskerry, some few miles down the road from where they lived at Ballyorney House. It was free – and it was Protestant. His last paragraph, no doubt in the light of this idea of free schooling for me, is almost jokey. And of course he saw himself as very much an exploited member of a 'Decaying Capitalist Society'.

Now to return to my 'peculations' – in an earlier letter dated June 1946, from my sensible great-aunt Olive, in reply to one from Hubert:

Dear Hubert,

It really is very sad and terrible about Little Joe – and I quite agree that it is worth trying now to see what can be done to cure him.

Joe (senior) told me about it … How cruel it seems that there is no way of showing the child his errors and his ultimate misery if he goes on this way. After all he has had a very happy home with you and plenty of affection, and it is tragic that he is not influenced by Peggy's efforts.

As to other younger members of the (Hone) family taking on responsibility, I'm afraid this is not possible. The only others are Pat's family. Of these Noll is married and starting a family of his own. Moreover he will I think be saddled with some responsibility for his sister's children, as her husband is useless, and she has gone off to work in England, leaving the elder child with Pat. The younger one is with her father, John Price, and his mother, but is promised to Pat also! So you can see that Pat and Noll and the children's mother have their own troubles and cares. Pat's other girl, Leland, could not be expected to take on another cousin. She is working in England and naturally any interest she has in other people's children will be in the ones of her sister.

I would be sorry to see the child handed back to Nat and Biddy, but possibly it might make Nat shoulder responsibility and make Little Joe feel secure. I don't know that I would put much faith in this however! I have said nothing to George [*Olive's husband*] about this. He is greatly anti-Nat and no use making him prejudiced about the child.

Love to Peggy,
Olive Symes.

It can be seen from this letter how my father was not alone in the Hone family in messing up his life. My grand-uncle Pat's daughter, Paloma, was a dab hand at it, too, abandoning both her daughters in due course. Hubert now takes the stage again, in reply to Dr Eustace's earlier letter to him:

Dear Dr Eustace,

I am glad Mrs Hone took Joe to see you, but it naturally must have been very difficult for you to form an opinion on so short a meeting and so little information. I agree with most of what you say …

Is it possible for children to be born amoral, as they can be born colour blind? And, if so, is there not some way of dealing with them? I would not make this very damaging suggestion about Little Joe to anyone but a doctor, or on anything but very long experience of him. He is a very bright and attractive little boy, but ever since we have had him, aged two, he has shown no signs of being really able to distinguish, except on grounds of expediency, between truth and falsehood. We have had many other children with us, as guests or relations, and have never noticed this in them. His sense of insecurity may have something to do with it, but not everything. If his heredity is bad, something could be done about it.

We hoped that discipline at school and companionship of other boys would have helped him, but instead it has made him worse. We have no evidence that he stole before he went to school. He used to come out and see us for weekends in Dublin from Sandford Park, bringing my wife, of whom he is very fond, very handsome presents, cigarettes, scent, etc. She was worried about this, but until he admitted later to myself and one of his schoolmasters that he had been taking money from his grandfather's room and also from my wife and little girl, we did not know how he came by it.

Three days after he'd been taken to the guard's barracks in Bennettsbridge he was stealing comic papers from a shop in Sandford Road. Surely this is not normal and cannot be treated by normal school methods – beatings, etc – nor is it normal for a child to recover his spirits after such an experience in the barracks, so that until after he had left for school we had no inkling of what had happened at the barracks. He was laughing and shouting all afternoon.

I am quite out of my depth in regard to psychological treatment – but I am extremely sceptical that the normal school will handle him well. They will take a rosy view of it all – 'Boys will be boys', etc., until something disastrous happens to him. Then they'll pitch him out, lest he contaminate the other boys.

We don't want to put him out of our home, because he has no other. This is why we would sooner take a serious view of his character now than later, when he might have done some grave damage which we could not forgive.

We've never once suggested to him that this was not his home always, and trust that his relations have not done this either – because we felt this would increase his sense of insecurity. We still do not want to make this suggestion till he has recovered his sense of security and is on his way to building up his character, somehow and somewhere else, for I cannot see this happening with any of his relations or at his present school.

We have no legal status in regard to him and have no power to hold out any hopes and provision for his future. But he has been with us since he was a baby, and we cannot disinterest ourselves from him. His relations are aware of this and will, I think, in the long run accept our advice.

I feel that if some family could be found with boys and girls, which he would go to school with as a day boy, a very normal ordinary family which was interested in things like carpentry and mending bicycles, etc., and who would take a spontaneous, evangelical view about theft – this would be an alternative to psychological treatment. He is an eager and active participant in anything that interests him. It is his misfortune that none of his protectors belong to the bicycle-mending class.

Forgive this long letter. I do not see what you can do immediately. But if you bear his case in mind, it is possible that later some solution might occur to you.

Yours sincerely,
Hubert Butler.

From a classical scholar, liberal humanist and a realist in most matters, this is rather a strange letter, with what seems an almost mystical longing for truth and light about the nature of children. Had he never read *Lord of the Flies*? What is puzzling in the letter is Hubert's puzzlement. He might almost be putting my bad behaviour in a biblical context – Genesis, the Fate of Adam and the Fall of Man, instead of seeing my pilferings, my selfish and aggressive behaviour (as Dr Eustace has told him before) as commonplace – expected, indeed, from a boy with my difficult background and insecure circumstances. Does the puzzled tone of the letter suggest that Hubert wished he'd been a bad boy himself? Dr Eustace might have helped him there.

However, there is one clear fact: Hubert can't accept that my pilferings, egotism and assertiveness, my gorging on boxes of chocolates and so on, are not surprising. He saw my behaviour, I think, as a shocking failure in a world which his own Victorian parental background of high purpose and stern good works had brought him up to see as unquestionably open to enlightenment, always open to improvement through the rational, or by way of the Christian ethic. I was an insult to both these ethics, for I was not being improved. He knew full well of the darker side of humanity, but could not accept this on his own hearth. And of course, very creditably, the overriding tone of his letters about me is that I should be sensibly saved – but not at this point by warming my toes at his fire. Which was the only way I was likely to be saved.

One notices also that, in keeping with his Victorian good-and-useful-deeds ethic, he hopes that I would find a family to live with who would take an 'evangelical' view of theft. It doesn't strike him that, given my proven taste for thieving bicycle parts, such a bicycle-mending family, however evangelical, might find my presence oppressive – might soon find they were having to ride their own bikes circus style, one-wheeled with no handlebars. Finally he makes the serious comment that it's my misfortune that none of my present protectors are of the bicycle-mending class. But how could he have seriously thought that this was a misfortune? – knowing full well that none of my family, nor his, had ever been of that class. Rather he should have acknowledged how lucky I was to be in his and Peggy's very intelligent and caring hands.

Next there is revival of the possibility of my spending time, possibly permanent time, with the Allens in County Cork. My grandfather writes:

Dear Peggy,

As you know the Allens put off the visit on the 1st and suggested the 5th instead. Now I have written to Mrs Allen to say that he'd better go on the 12th. The reason is the 5th will be a hell of day to travel at the worst of the holiday.

I mentioned too that there was a question of the parents wishing to see him but did not go into details.

Did you write to the Allens? I think it would be wrong to give them the idea that there was any opposition from the parents of his going to Co Cork. It would make them feel uncomfortable.

As regards Sandford Park, he has to go back there next term, since I would be charged whether he did or not. The charges are about the same as the school you mention. The important thing about his schooling is that he should be equipped early for taking up a trade, for he will have to go out in the world early.

Yrs,
Joe.

93

There is no chance now, in Old Joe's view, of my taking up a career. A trade at best, and as soon as possible. Carpentry? Bicycle mending? This letter incurs a real blast from Hubert:

Dear Joe

It is no pleasure for either of us to take all this trouble about the child of your erring son. You have explained that you are not young enough to take much interest in him, that you are in any case probably going to live abroad, that David and Sally should not be put upon, and you admit that his parents are incapable. Aunt Olive equally says that none of his younger relatives can be expected to take an interest. Who is left? Peggy and me. You do not like to admit this but you know it quite well.

We are ready to take an interest in Joe but on our terms and safeguarding our own interests. You must see this – yet you cannot be bothered to return the copy of the letter I wrote to Biddy. Nor have I received the carbons of the letters to you giving an account of what happened to Joe here. You may not have read them, but Aunt Olive kept them for you to discuss. They are quite essential if any serious attempt is to be made to cope with Joe's difficult character. Your attempt to minimise the difficulties of Joe's character may be amour propre, but looks to me more like wishful thinking and the desire to save yourself bother.

I told you years ago, and Aunt Olive too, that we were greatly opposed to any idea of Joe being shared with Nat and Biddy.

I wonder you weren't ashamed to write that devastating sentence about the bills at Sandford Park having to be 'paid', (to begin with you would probably get a refund). I have stood out for about £50 owed me by Nat for several years, uncomplainingly. As you know I told him he must either pay properly or not interfere. He interferes and has not paid.

Of course you can easily realise that sum by selling something. Everybody else does that with infinitely less fuss. You are not the only people with 'commitments', money difficulties, children and impending old age. It is no doubt too late to take him from Sandford Park, where he first learnt to steal, but your arguments for leaving him there are futile and contemptible.

I am sorry writing like this, but the tranquil way in which you accept Peggy's unceasing efforts to see that Joe gets a good start infuriates me. You know that Peggy and I can't afford morally to abandon Joe – you are too mean. You know that we are prepared to take, if we must, a great deal of trouble on his behalf, which would be far more fittingly taken on by a member of your own family. But you are not entitled to exploit these moral scruples of ours.

Hubert.

A real stinger. How far my grandparents and the Butlers were from the carpentry and bicycle-mending class is shown by Hubert's answer to financial difficulties, implicitly for him and obviously for my grandfather, in their simply 'selling' something. Not their labour, of course, but stocks and shares. 'Everybody else does that,' he says. This surely wasn't true. Only people with a fair portfolio of stocks and shares could realize cash in this way then. As both of them could, being fully paid-up members of the (exploited) capitalist class, who were in a distinct minority in the Ireland of the times. Hubert and my grandfather were never really in the nine-to-five brigade, as most of the Irish were then, who had to earn their living with ploughs and picks and shovels – or through carpentry and bicycle mending.

I give myself no particular praise for having had many nine-to-five jobs later in my life. What used to annoy, but now only amuses, is that while every sort of nine-to-five 'job' was endlessly proposed for me, neither Hubert nor my grandfather nor most of the others concerned with my welfare then (except my mother), ever did any regular work in their lives. They didn't have to. The money was there for them already, through family inheritance, in land or property rents, in 2½ per cent War Bonds or São Paulo Tramway stock.

There is no reply in the file to this letter from Old Joe – possibly numbed and certainly hurt by its accusations, as is clear in a very sensible letter from great-aunt Olive who writes to Hubert instead, defending her brother. In fact it's clear to me now that I have great-aunt Olive largely to thank for my staying on with the Butlers at Maidenhall, and with that all the benefits I gained from them and the Guthries later. It was thanks to her that I wasn't farmed out again to a family of total strangers, with whom I might well have gone truly to the bad. It was great-aunt Olive's straightforward good sense and kindness, unalloyed with psychological enquiries into the nature of childhood or views dictated by the Scrooge-like attitudes of Old Joe, that saved the day for me:

Dear Hubert,

I am sorry not to have replied sooner to your letter, but it was a difficult letter to answer in a hurry. No one could have been more sorry than I that Little Joe went to England instead of to you. But the whole point was that you had previously said you were not having him any more, and you know we all said there was no other prospect for the boy, in that case, except to go to his parents.

Nat came over here in a great state about Biddy having left him and wanting to get her back, and you have to admit that if there is to be any prospect of a home for the children in future it would have to be with their parents, who are considerably younger than myself or Joe and Vera.

Well, when Nat came here from the boat and told me the tale of Biddy, I said, among other remarks, 'And I'm sorry to say the Butlers say they can't keep Joe any longer.' 'Well,' said Nat, rather naturally, 'He'd better come over to me, and it may influence Biddy to return to me.' I couldn't very well disagree with this, as the boy is their son, but I did say definitely that he shouldn't go over unless Biddy and Nat had some sort of home for him in the holidays … I only then heard that you had offered to take Little Joe for the holidays. This altered my feelings towards the plan, and I know both Joe and Vera would definitely have preferred to send him to you. Once Nat heard Little Joe was not to spend holidays with you any longer, it was a chance, however slight, of keeping Biddy and inducing both her and Nat to start some sort of decent home for their family.

You say Joe is an egoist; I can't agree. He does his best for Joe junior and for his family, under very difficult circumstances, and if you talk of worries, very few fathers, luckily, have had such a perpetual worry and expense as Nat has been to him.

I think you are unfair and unkind to say 'we' were all ready to exploit Peggy's affection and care for Little Joe as long as it suited us. Don't bring me into it all. I have always been wholeheartedly in favour of his being with you, and have never exploited you in any way. I have enough to think of and arrange with the other two, Geraldine and Antony [*my siblings, whom aunt Olive was taking financial responsibility for while they lived with my mother's parents in south Kilkenny*].

Joe tells me the child is with his father, and none the worse for the time over there. I rather think Biddy never came back, but no one has definitely heard. At least I haven't.

Now as to any idea of Joe going to school in England. I'm afraid it's hopeless. He is too old to pass an exam to any of the state aided schools, and they are so crowded they don't want boys even if they are paid for. The County Council schools only keep boys till 15 or 16 and in London you get a type of boy who would do Joe no good; the type who failed in the exams, and the underdeveloped and the wild type – so I'm told anyhow. This only leaves the public schools, beyond the reach of Joe's purse.

Now do let me make an appeal to you not to cast the child out of your life because he went over to his father. I quite see you are not going to have him regularly, but I was so pleased that you had considered having him last holidays, and do forget this unfortunate affair and ask him again; it is his best hope and you are doing the child real harm if you leave him nowhere to go in any holidays, except Enniskerry, where he has nothing to do, or London, and this is most improbable I think.

Joe was greatly hurt at your telegram; he is a sensitive man and an affectionate one too and he felt very much that you would not come and let him explain his difficulty over the matter.

I wish you would ring me if you are in Dublin; I would like to talk to you. Let us try to forget any recrimination and give the boy a chance. I'm sorry to have written you such an epistle. I do so hope you'll see our point of view over this episode and let it sink into the past.

Yours sincerely,
Olive Symes.

'Telegrams and anger' – one thinks of E.M. Forster, an author Hubert much admired, where Hubert's beliefs closely paralleled Forster's liberal-humanist ethic. But here again, Hubert has been unable to maintain this ethic. I have sympathy with both sides – for Hubert, other than with my great-aunt Olive, has clearly had great trouble in getting anything straight with the Hones. 'Only connect' – that was another Forsterian challenge for Hubert with my family.

It is also interesting that great-aunt Olive writes of Old Joe as an affectionate man. I didn't figure greatly in his affections. But I can understand this. For some it can be impossible to show affection towards the innocent cause of all one's troubles and pain. My grandfather's life, so far as I knew it, was dominated by Nat's increasing 'prodigal son' behaviour – and by the decreasing value of his São Paulo Tramway stock. And that's a pity, since of course showing affection beats any amount of tramway stock, and had Old Joe been able to give this to my father as a child, he might have prevented Nat from becoming a prodigal son. Affection in my grandfather had been choked by his family circumstances. The possibility of an openly loving nature may have been strangled in him at his own severe Victorian prep school, to the like of which, and worse, he had consigned me. My father was in part a casualty of my grandfather's early schooldays. I very nearly was.

And here, too, in this letter, is another mention of Biddy leaving Nat. I don't know any details of this, and there is nothing in the file from her about her leaving. But I imagine that, like Old Joe, she became unable to support Nat's moods any more, his illness, depression, his futility, his sponging off her. She didn't have Old Joe's money, though. So there is a letter from her to Hubert from a boys' prep school in Scotland, where she has got a job as junior matron or some such, with board and lodging and three pounds a week. And it must have been at this point, in Scotland, that she met Ian McCorkadale, the rich Scots business man, who became her lover, and who I met on subsequent holidays in England: the three of us touring the 'shires in his smart Sunbeam Talbot, and later doing the same in Ireland when Ian came over and met me with my mother in Clonmel, not far from her parents, and we all had 'refreshments' in the Commercial Hotel there.

Ian was a big kind jokey man, with sandy hair and a moustache; a gin-and-tonic Scots hearty, with the typical drinky, hail-fellow-well-met slang of the time – 'Top of the morning!', 'Bottoms up!', 'One for the road!', 'Wizard prang!' and so on. He might have been in the RAF during the war. I certainly enjoyed my trips with him and my mother – mostly, I see now, because he had a speedy car and spent money freely and happily, which was something of a change, to put it mildly, from my grandfather's and the Butlers' way with cash.

Yet thinking of this now, of Biddy's understandable departure from Nat and taking up with Ian, I can put myself in my father's position and have sympathy there too, for this once gilded youth, now left alone and penniless in Peter's Bar playing shove ha'penny, saddled with his grim demons and decaying lungs – coughing, spitting and drinking his life away.

At any rate, despite this flurry of confused and angry correspondence about what to do with me, a line of least resistance was apparently taken and I was returned that autumn term in 1946 to the sadist Dudgeon and the untender mercies of Sandford Park School.

SIX

Aside from its prison-like aspect (for us boarders at least), Sandford Park School in retrospect has an air of music hall and high farce for me. Of course, remembering those old British POW Colditz movies and the prisoners' desperately jolly stage shows, this is appropriate. The teachers at Sandford Park, as much as the boys, sometimes took major roles in these theatricals. Some of them, no doubt, like us, were in fear of Dudgeon. And I imagine that, apart from the several genuine eccentrics, these teachers sometimes clowned around or behaved oddly whenever Dudgeon wasn't about as a release from his all-seeing beady eye, his endless diktats and prohibitions. Fear finds a ready release in farce.

So when in a benevolent mood I look back on the place, the bizarre personalities and antics of some of the staff come first to mind, overlaying the pain. Like an old music hall playbill I see the various star turns: Froggy Bertin, the small, portly caricature of a French teacher, a Belgian refugee from the Great War who had stayed on in Dublin, a near replica of Monsieur Poirot indeed; Furness, the lanky Northerner, who did Maths; Cookman, one of the idealistic young housemasters from Wexford; Len Horan, the very decent, tall, muscular and fiercely moustachioed Irish teacher and rugby coach who had once played prop forward for Ireland; and Peter Allt,

Yeats scholar and my grandfather's literary friend who had unaccountably come to teach junior English. Unaccountably, since he was a brilliant academic, had taken a First at Trinity College, had a Lectureship there in French and English and among many more original and imaginative academic gifts could apparently quote from memory every poem that Yeats had ever published – and the ones he hadn't.

Allt came into the category of genuine eccentric. My first experience of him was in the fourth form, in the big assembly hall, the old ballroom with its minstrels' gallery to one side where discarded school books were stored. Allt was taking us for poetry, and we'd had to memorize Tennyson's 'Ulysses'. He went up the stairs to the gallery, lay flat out on his back among the old books, and one by one, down below, we had to quote the poem from memory a verse each. And each time that any of us forgot a word or a line a book would fly down, tossed willy-nilly by Allt from his recumbent position, hitting this boy or that or flying off the far wall, a saturation bombing raid that went on for most of class till the floor below was littered with copies of Kennedy's *Latin Grammar* and Durrell & Fawdry's *Mathematics*. I can remember Tennyson's poem almost in its entirety to this day.

But this aerial sport was only an entr'acte to Allt's subsequent floor shows. Later on that winter term we had a grammar class. I've mentioned the tall, red-hot, cast-iron stove at one end of the hall. Allt on this occasion put it to educational use. There was a boy called O'Grady in our class, an owlish innocent swot, with pimples and spring-wired specs that clipped on behind his ears, a boarder from County Cork with a shock of black hair that would never lie down so that he greased it heavily with Brylcreem every morning – a natural victim in short, who fell foul of Allt that day in the matter of some grammatical construction. Allt wore a grubby tattered black gown, one arm of which he had tied into a hard knot.

'That is not the answer, O'Grady,' he said ominously. He then proceeded to whack the desk in front of the boy with the knotted sleeve. Whack! Whack! 'The answer, O'Grady is …?' No reply. O'Grady was stunned. 'Come, O'Grady, perhaps we may tease the answer out of you in some other manner. Come.' Bringing a chair with him, he beckoned O'Grady up to the stove. 'Stand on that chair, O'Grady, and take your spectacles off.' O'Grady did as he was told. Allt opened the top of the roaring stove, and taking O'Grady's head started to push it down towards the fiery opening. 'The mood we were curious about, O'Grady, was the ...?' 'Please Sir!' O'Grady was petrified now. And then there was the smell, a burning perfumed smell – it was the Brylcreem on O'Grady's mop of hair, beginning to warm and singe. 'The mood, O'Grady?' 'Please Sir! It was the pluperfect.' 'It was not the pluperfect.' The head was pushed a little closer. O'Grady started to yelp out answers any old how. 'It was the past tense!' 'No.' 'It was the future indicative!' 'No.' 'It was the past perfect!' 'No.' The head getting closer to the fiery furnace. 'It was the subjunctive, Sir!'

Allt pulled back O'Grady's head. 'It was indeed, O'Grady. Sit down.' O'Grady descended, mopped his brow and sat down. Allt glared at the rest of us. 'The subjunctive. I suggest you don't forget it.'

These days, of course, Allt would have been arrested. But then these days most pupils don't know any grammar. What Allt, with his academic brilliance, was doing at a less than third-rate school, where he stayed for a year, I've no idea. Perhaps he needed the money. Many people did in Ireland in those days, and teaching jobs in the few Protestant schools were scarce. In any case he went on to Cambridge, where earlier my grandfather had introduced him to the Yeats scholar T. R. Henn, who appointed him Senior Research Student at St Catherine's College. Here Allt worked for several years on the great Variorum Edition of Yeats's poetry, and, in 1954, absent-mindedly, he stepped off the wrong side of a London suburban electric train, onto the live rail where, more than the hapless O'Grady, he frizzled.

It was a tragic end for Allt. Yet I have to see him as part of the jollier times at Sandford Park, these lighter incidents (though O'Grady would not have seen it that way), so as not to harp on the background terrors. I see a disconnected medley of such bizarre moments, like clips from a farce-horror movie that was never released.

Froggy Bertin, moving gently up and down, warming his tummy and privates on the central radiator in one of the garden classrooms, while reciting verbs: '*j'ai, tu es, il a* ...' 'Ha! Ha!' from a tease in the back of the class. 'Zat boy will take fifty lines: "I must not make zee monkey out of zee French teacher."'

Mr Furness, the tall, somehow mysterious, crinkly-haired Maths teacher from Belfast (there was a rumour that he'd had some unfortunate experience with a woman – or women!), getting in a terrible bate and clipping me over the ear one evening when I was playing 'Oh Rose I love you!' on the assembly hall piano. 'Why, Sir? There's nothing wrong with the song.' 'It's a dirty song, Hone. That's why.' (I didn't learn why until later when Wilshire, an older, knowing day boy, told a group of us round the stove the dirty version of it: 'Oh, Rose, I love you, won't you let me come and have a screw?') Lots of prurient sniggering, before Wilshire turns to me. 'Go away, Hone, you're too young for this sort of talk. Move off.'

Mr Cookman, the genial young housemaster from Enniscorthy, testing the new pulley-and-sling fire escape from the top dorm window; the other part-time housemaster, Mr Elliot from Sussex, forever studying medicine in Trinity, and all us boarders, looking up expectantly. Cookman puts the canvas sling under his arms, gingerly pushes himself out the window, lets go, and falls like a stone. He hits the ground hard, lying prostrate. It looks like he's broken his leg, or at least twisted his ankle. We hope. In some pain certainly. We are all agog, doing nothing. Mr Elliot moves forward, giving medical succour to Cookman, gently feeling his ankle. 'Get Matron', he says. 'Matron's out, Sir. She's gone to the pictures.' 'Can we go to the pictures, Sir? Tonight at the Sandford cinema? They're showing a very educational film, *The Blue Lagoon*, about fishes and things in the south seas.' Mr Elliot looks up. 'I'm not quite the fool you think me, Mather. Fishes and things … here, help me with Mr Cookman.' Half a dozen of us rush forward now, helping Mr Cookman up, carrying him indoors. And Mr Elliot breaks into song, while we struggle along, Cookman squeezed uncomfortably amongst us like a side of beef. 'For he's a jolly good fellow! For he's a jolly good fellow … and so say all of us! And so say all of us!' We all join in, a loud chorus, all of us happy now, with the exception of Mr Cookman, no doubt.

Lugging Cookman up the stairs to where he had his room next to our dorm on the top floor, another dream-like clip comes to mind. The dorm was a long room with six iron beds running along either side, and another curtained-off bed for the dorm captain at the end, and a big cupboard against the far wall where we kept our clothes. And in it, since we now went to Cubs at Sandford Church Hall along the road, were our Cubs outfits: the cap, scarf, toggle, green pullover with its badges of merit, short trousers, long woolly socks with the penanted garters and so on. There was a boy called Thompson in the bed opposite me, at the other end of the room by the window, a small boy, new to the school, who spoke hardly at all. That his parents were out east, his father a rubber planter in Malaya, was among the few facts we'd managed to get out of him. I woke one night and, with the moonlight from the badly-curtained window, I saw the small figure of Thompson making a slow and stately progress down the centre of the dorm between the beds. I supposed he was going to the lavatories, or that he was sleepwalking. But then I saw that he was completely dressed in his Cubs outfit. I got up and whispered to him, 'It's not Cubs night, Thompson. Where are you going?' 'Back to Malaya,' he said in a sensible voice. 'I got my pathfinder's badge last week, you see.' 'Don't be stupid, Thompson, Malaya is thousands of miles away. Get back into bed before someone hears us.'

Someone did hear us, the dorm captain, out of bed and on his feet now. 'What are you two doing? Get back into bed at once.' And then Thompson shrieked out, 'No, I can't! You see I'm going home to Malaya. I am! I am!' he yelled. And then the whole dorm was awake, with Mr Elliot in the room and the lights on. Sensation! Subdued chatter. 'Thompson's going back home to Malaya!' 'He's mad!' 'How's he going to get there?' 'He'll fly BOAC, from Heathrow, in one of their new Stratocruisers.' 'No, he's going to walk, it'll take him months, and he'll have to learn to walk on water.'

'Shut up all of you.' Mr Elliot led Thompson out of the dorm. He brought him downstairs to Matron, we heard later, where the boy spent the rest of the night in her room. Next day Thompson wasn't there. He'd left the school. Walking on water all the way back to Malaya! What a laugh, we thought. Thompson was a great joke for all of us over the next week. I didn't see then, as I see now, that Thompson's shrieks for home were mine as well. But I kept my mouth shut, hated the Cubs evenings, and never got a pathfinder badge to find my way home with.

And another vivid clip – Len Horan, the kind-hearted, hugely muscular Irish teacher with the glary eyes, bristling dark eyebrows and fierce moustache, at the high desk during second prep in the heavy sighing silence one evening. He's seen something and is stalking a boy at a back desk, light and soundless on his feet. The fat boy Louis Watson, with his head down, is fiddling with something in his lap. Horan pounces on him. We all turn. It's nothing more than a handkerchief in Watson's lap, which he's been screwing round in his hands. I wasn't far away from him. I see his face, all stained with tears when he looks up.

There were always tears before bedtime at Sandford Park.

Few things saved me from the awfulness of the school. One was sports, which I became good at – cricket, rugby, tennis, table tennis, and particularly athletics, under the enthusiastic tutelage of Len Horan: the sprints, high and long jump and especially the seven-pound shot. Horan had been an Irish champion at the senior, sixteen-pound level in the shot and he showed me how to do it in a far corner of the park – how, crouching right down, with one's back almost to the field in front, one had to skip across the circle at great speed, then let fly by straightening up, torso, arm and wrist moving one after the other at an ever greater speed, in one flowing movement, which ended in my hopping about on one foot, at the front edge of the circle, watching the little cannonball disappear over the horizon. Well, not quite. But I became pretty good at the shot and athletics generally, winning more or less everything at the annual school sports, and the same with cricket.

This success gave me some immunity from the bullying and dismissive attitude of the other boys. The all-knowing, derisive, wiseacre Wilshire, for example, who did no sports at all, always carried a letter from his mother saying he had asthma or flat feet or something. But my athletic gifts put me out of his reach and on a level with older boys in the senior sports teams.

To be good at sports was, and still is, a way out of the pain and boredom of school, and any failure at school learning. And a way of being admired, by the other boys and some of the teachers. I was grudgingly admired – grudgingly because I always felt at Sandford Park, and later when I went to St Columba's College, the public school up in the Dublin mountains, that this admiration for my sporting prowess was mixed as much with cynical surprise – for it became well known in both schools, by boys and masters, that I was a wicked and lazy lot in most other ways. Smoking behind the bicycle shed or the cricket pavilion, being caught out of bounds intent on a bit of shoplifting down Ranelagh Road, skiving off this and that and doing little or no work, and being beaten regularly for all these things.

So there was ironic comment that in the field of sports I was tops. This didn't add up for the authorities. I think it seemed unfair to them that, being clearly a bad lot, I should win those most admired things in schools of the time: all the glittering sports prizes. If you were bad, then you should be bad at everything. And if you were well behaved, then you should be good at everything. That was the natural order of school expectations in those days. I was an insult to that order. This annoyed the authorities. And pleased me.

I was bad at schoolwork, except in writing English and History essays and doing elaborately coloured geography maps. Indeed in English I once won the form prize in a short story competition set by a new English master, the delicate, wispy-voiced, literary-minded Mr Sheehan. But this was largely achieved through prior advice from some of the other more knowing boys, who must have recognized my gifts as a fantasist long before I did, and encouraged me to write reams of fiction, much more than was asked for, about a mad schoolboy who does all sorts of mad things, including eating a mound of marshmallows and then nearly drowning in a lake of liquid chocolate. I wrote at such length simply because Mr Sheehan had told us that whoever won the prize would read his story out in the next class. And of course, as we saw, the longer the story lasted the less difficult grammar work would have to be done that day. And we all remembered the near immolation of O'Grady in his failure to identify the subjunctive, so that my story, when I came to read it out, lasted the whole fifty minutes of class. The boys cheered me at the end – for being let off parsing and analysis, not for the story, I'm sure.

Dudgeon, in due and painful course, disappeared from Sandford Park, before my five years of incarceration there ended. Did he resign, or was he removed by the Governors? Years later someone told me that he'd become headmaster at a public school in England. Perhaps in those days there were still some public schools where Dudgeon's subtle tortures and open brutality would have been welcomed.

In any case Sandford Park, by 1949, was in a poor way. And it was at that moment, aged twelve, that I should have been removed from it, and sent somewhere else. I wasn't. Meanwhile the Governors, deciding to cut their losses, put the lease on Sandford Park up for sale. It was bought by a Major Wormell, middle aged and recently retired from the British-Indian army. The Major was in retreat from the Labour government to Ireland perhaps, as many British were at that time; he probably bought the lease for a song, given its few pupils and very doubtful reputation. And now another complete transformation occurred, the school changing character from Dudgeon's sadist bunker to British military circus.

Major Wormell – the Mad Major as we soon dubbed him – was tall and of great girth, with crinkly brown hair parted severely in the middle. Yet his face was relatively small and he had curious, slanty eyes – a monkey face that jerked alarmingly every few minutes, a nervous tic (the result of an old war wound) accompanied by a grimace, giving him the air of a huge puppet on strings being badly handled. An impression emphasized by the quick tiny steps he took, arms swinging, as if heading a parade of sepoys in Chandrigar. He walked like this with particular speed, we soon noticed, after the day boys had gone home at three o'clock, down the laurel drive, to McCaulay's public house near the school gates.

He had a younger, leggy, wasp-waisted, blonde and bosomy wife, a woman the like of whom we had not seen before – a Betty Grable gorgeously swum into our ken. We eyed her with the confusions of half-awakened sexual greed whenever she was on parade, which was rarely since she kept to herself in the new head's quarters, a bedroom made over from Matron's old room, and in the ornately gilded drawing-room next door. The previous matron had been dispensed with, since there were now only about six boarders, and Mrs Wormell was to take over her matronly duties. We all hoped to be ill, so as to test what we thought would surely be her stimulating ministrations. Unfortunately I was never ill.

The Major, with the end of Empire in India, was clearly keen to continue things in the imperial manner at Sandford Park. Indeed he must have thought the Republic still part of the Empire. He found a Union Jack in the attic and brandished it about of a summer evening, well oiled from sessions at McCaulay's, when he would take we few boarders for military drill in the old ballroom together with a new teacher, a nice but rather ineffectual ex-army friend of his, a Captain Villiers. The two of them, among other military drills, put us through the slow march of one of the Guards regiments the last few inches of each step being slid forward, airborne, just before touching the ground. By now there were only four boarders, myself and the two small Brownlee brothers and another bigger boy called Bowden. Up and down we went, the length of the ballroom, between the desks, a ragged, out-of-step troop. I see the Mad Major now, annoyed with our progress, showing us how to do the Slow March – a huge figure, light but unsteady on his feet, swaying slightly on one leg before the touch down with the other, Captain Villiers with the Union Jack rampant behind him.

The following year, with the boarders now reduced to three and the day boys to about thirty, the Major must clearly have seen that he would have to take dramatic steps to increase the school rolls or go bust. And what better way to this end than by improving the recreational facilities? So with the help of potent sundowners in McCaulay's and the large supply of bottled lager that he kept in the little pantry next to his study, he hit upon a splendid scheme: since there was no swimming pool, he would drain the pleasantly exotic garden pond and turn it into a pool. But discovering that this would be both expensive and impractical, he reduced his ambitions: he would convert one end of the pond, by the little covered boat house. Or rather the boys would, boarders first thing before breakfast (with the promise of an extra fried egg) and day boys in their lunch hour.

The pond was drained and then in a ham-fisted and literally sloppy way, over months of the spring term, with shovels and wheelbarrows, the mud was lifted from the boathouse end; with little effect, for overnight the squelchy liquid from the rest of the pond would seep across into the cleared area and we had to begin all over again, emerging each morning for our extra fried egg covered in green slime. The day boys made themselves scarce over lunchtime, pleading dentists' or doctors' appointments. Progress was slow. Eventually, however, with a sort of wooden coffer dam to keep the squelch away, one end was cleared, cement and a concrete mixer were obtained, and, with the Major himself now in daily charge, we started to concrete the bottom and replace the coffer dam with a brick wall halfway along the pond.

The Major got a plumb line and large wooden set squares from the carpentry shop and gave us an inspiring talk about how he'd been in charge of Army Engineers out in India, constructing rope and pontoon bridges over roaring torrents and great rivers; and how, by comparison, this building work would be easy. It wasn't. With water seepage from beneath, the concrete on the bottom failed to set, the unsteady, half-built brick wall tended to collapse overnight, and the Major got into mighty tizzies, his neck twitch going into overdrive as he shouted commands like an overblown pyramid slave master. 'Brownlee! Have you no idea how to set a brick on a brick wall straight?' – Brownlee up to his ankles in damp, unset concrete at that moment.

I will give the Major one thing – he was persistent. The pool was completed and very slowly filled with water from a number of leaking, thrashing garden hoses, with which we had good fun, deluging each other when the Major was taking 'refreshments' in his pantry. We swam in the pool only half a dozen times, for there was a distinct problem in attempting any full immersion. Owing to various miscalculations the pool was only about two feet deep or three at the most, so that any proper swimming was impossible. And it soon emerged that the pool had several other basic faults: there was no water inlet, no outlet back into the main pond and no chlorine cleaning, so that soon the water became stagnant and slimy, pee-smelly and very uninviting.

The pool and swimming lessons were tactfully forgotten and the Major set his mind to another means of increasing the school rolls – by improving our academic work, in face of the Irish Ministry of Education's Intermediate exams which were to take place the following summer. The Major knew that in one particular subject we (apart from Wilshire) were real dunderheads: Latin, in which we were required to get at least a pass mark of over forty per cent or fail the exam, and find our future careers severely blighted. Most of us were likely, and me especially, to get about ten per cent in Latin, if that.

Faced with this problem the Major pulled off what proved to be an academic masterstroke: he employed as Latin teacher a Mr Carpenter, a small, mild-mannered, apologetic, clerkish gent who always wore a long black overcoat, even in class, and always carried a briefcase. A caricature of a civil servant. In fact this was just what he had been, having spent a previous career with the Ministry of Education in Dublin. The Major's unintended masterstroke (or was it intended?) was based on the fact, as I learnt later, that Mr Carpenter had filled his days at the Ministry in the department that dealt with the setting of public exam papers – in his case, as it conveniently happened, with the setting of the Latin papers. We half-dozen boys in the Intermediate year knew nothing of this at the time, of course. And Mr Carpenter, of course, made no mention of his previous career at the Ministry.

We continued to struggle thought the Latin syllabus – '*Amo, amas, amat*', endless sentences from Latin into English and vice-versa, together with Virgil's *Aeneid* and Caesar's *Gallic Wars*. Even with the forbidden cribs we had for the *Aeneid* and the *Gallic Wars* all this was pretty well Greek to most of us.

The June week of the Intermediate exam approached, to be taken at another school in the suburbs. Latin was the first exam. Someone, Wilshire very probably, had told me that if I only managed to put my name, school and date at the top of my exam paper I would at least get two marks out of a hundred, since the authorities were keen never to give a zero mark. I expected to get two marks.

There was a tradition at Sandford Park that the subject master gave us a final revision class on the night before the exam, in one of the garden classrooms. Mr Carpenter brought us all together on that bright summer evening. I remember the fluttery golden light on the old apple and pear trees, for this part of the grounds had been an orchard. What did failure in the Latin exam matter? I'd failed at most subjects in Sandford Park. I gazed at the trees from the window, the wind stirring the leaves, dreaming. Mr Carpenter politely interrupted my reverie.

'Hone, you might care to pay attention – all of you. I'm going to give you, on the board, a mock outline of the sort of Latin exam you may expect tomorrow. Six sentences English into Latin, six Latin into English.' This he proceeded to do on the blackboard – translating each sentence into the appropriate language. We started to take notes of his translations. 'No,' he said. 'No writing down. Just memorize these translations.'

Now though some of us realized that something important was happening, we weren't sure what. 'Memorize these sentence translations carefully.' Mr Carpenter went on in his mild, self-deprecating way. 'Take a good look at them,' he said, 'while I'm outside for a moment.' He left the classroom for a cigarette. And now we realized what was happening. Mr Carpenter had been giving us part of the Latin paper for tomorrow morning. We said nothing, of course, when he came back and rubbed all the sentences off the blackboard. At the end the class he said, 'Oh, and by the way, boys, take a good look at the first paragraph of Chapter Seven in the *Aeneid* and the same with the third paragraph of Chapter Two of the *Gallic Wars*. We knew, of course, that we could get the English translations of these paragraphs from our cribs. 'Good luck tomorrow, boys!' Mr Carpenter said in as bright a manner as he could ever muster, and left the classroom with his briefcase.

The day boys rushed home to consult their cribs for a session of intense memory work. And I did the same, back in the boys' common room, being the only boarder doing the exam, for now there were only three boarders, me and the two small Brownlee brothers. But there was a problem. One of our class, a day boy, a genial friend of mine, Charlie Culley, had been absent from the revision class. I would have to telephone him and at least give him the chapter numbers and paragraphs of the two set books for the exam. Here was another problem. The only telephone in the school was in the Major's study. Since it was now around nine o'clock I was pretty certain he'd be engaged with his bosomy wife, on the other side of the hall in her gilded boudoir, downing whiskey sodas prior to other stimulations.

I was right. There was no light or sound from the study. The study had two doors, one leading in from the hall and a side door leading out to the Major's private drinks pantry and the back stairs. I crept into his study by the side door and phoned Charlie, giving him the chapter and paragraph details. At the end of transferring my vital information, I heard the Major's footsteps coming across the hall, so I bolted out the side door of the study, making for the back stairs. But the Major was coming towards me, along the back corridor. I was standing in the doorway of his forbidden private pantry. All hell broke loose. He was well on, eight parts cut and sweating, his nervous neck tic in sudden ominous movement. 'So, Hone, caught in the act getting at my drinks! You blackguard!' He dragged me into his study, got the cane out in an instant, and whacked me half a dozen times. Whack! Whack! Whack! Then he marched me up to the top dorm where the two junior Brownlee brothers were getting ready for bed. 'You two,' he shouted. 'I want you to keep Hone under house arrest until he goes to the exams tomorrow morning. Close arrest', he added. 'Yes, Sir!' 'Yes, Sir!' they said, terrified. Since the Brownlee brothers were small and I was quite the hulking athletic brute, this idea of their managing to keep me under house arrest seemed unlikely if I decided to make a break for it. I didn't. I wrote down and memorized as much as I could of the Latin/English sentences and the two set book passages, and went to the Latin exam next morning.

Sure enough the Latin paper was exactly as Mr Carpenter had outlined it, and sitting on my sore backside I answered all the questions with relative ease. When the results came out I had failed in most subjects – but in Latin I passed with honours, with something just over 60 per cent. Wilshire got 96 per cent, having had to make mistakes, he told us later, not to get 100 per cent, which would have been suspicious. I thought then how lucky it was that I'd been caught by the Major next to his drinks pantry, his thinking I was thieving his lager. Had he caught me in his study on the telephone he would have wanted to know who I was phoning – and why. And the truth of Mr Carpenter's tactful help might have emerged.

In any case I see that Mr Carpenter probably gave us the Latin paper in advance in order to make sure that we would all pass the exam, so that the school rolls and reputation might be increased and he would keep his job at Sandford Park. Full-time Latin school-teaching in Dublin, in a Protestant school, was likely hard come by then. Like Peter Allt, Mr Carpenter was simply keeping the wolf from the door. 'All Gaul is quartered equally in three parts' – what I remember is the old chestnut about how the first sentence of the *Gallic Wars* went, though as far as the Irish Examination Board was concerned I ended up being reasonably good at Latin.

But thinking of that Latin exam now, of Mr Carpenter and the Major, I see another side to things – some understanding of all their mad and dishonest efforts: the Major valiantly trying to keep the school going, pouring himself another chota peg in the gilded boudoir, dreaming of creating a great British prep school in republican Dublin; Mr Carpenter, in some small, lace-curtained suburban villa, equally brave in his very risky academic deception, simply trying to make up on his overdue mortgage payments.

Finally, I imagine the Major dying penny-pinched in a faded south coast hotel, with a last dream of Empire, and loyal sepoys marching to Kabul, his head resting happily on what I hope were those still-bouncy bosoms of his wife. And Mr Carpenter in his suburban villa likewise, expiring carefully, arms crossed on his chest in his single bed, one of his old students reading Tacitus to him – 'Fortune favoured him, in the opportune moment of his death' – as indeed it had, his having just the week before paid off his mortgage. These things matter, a good or bad death – not crazy swimming pools and not deceptions over exams. Not even my great and unexpected success in that Latin exam. (I wonder if I might have got into Balliol?)

Neither the Major nor Mr Carpenter did us boys any real harm at Sandford Park. Nor did the other teachers with their sometimes bizarre behaviour, which probably came as a result of their having to take on theatrical roles, in order to endure the dull process, year in and out, of teaching dim and unwilling boys. The teachers, like the boys, had to put on the motley now and then to survive.

So there was benefit in these comedies for us boys, a touch of extra-curricular drama from the teachers, giving us, or me at least, an early experience of the marvellous quirks of human nature, more valuable and lasting than the messages in Caesar's *Gallic Wars*: a first sense of the world's strange foolishness and excitements – from Froggy Bertin and 'Dirty Songs' Furness, from the fiercely kind Len Horan, wispy Mr Sheehan keen on Katherine Mansfield and Peter Allt of the lofty Yeatsian surmise, from jovial young Mr Cookman and the chronic medic Mr Elliot. And I think of Bull Cordner, too, when I first came to Sandford Park, looking out on the playing field at the house cricket match – 'Ah, the boys in their whites. Their summer whites …'

The Bull is a spectator now, I hope, in a deck chair, at the edge of some Elysian cricket field, watching an endless game, with the poet Francis Thompson, the two of them reunited with the great cricketing heroes of their youth:

For the field is full of shadows as I near the
          Shadowy coast.
And a ghostly batsman plays to the bowling of
          A ghost.
And I look through my tears on a soundless-
          clapping host,
As the run-stealers flicker to and fro,
          To and fro –
O my Hornby and my Barlow long ago!

Now those great players are no longer ghosts for the Bull. He's with Hornby and Barlow, watching them hit sixes for eternity. *Goodbye, Mr Chips* to them all. It was only Dudgeon who caused us real harm at Sandford Park. I hope he's in some fiery scholastic underworld now, writhing in pain, with all the other sadistic headmasters and teachers.

As to Sandford Park and the Major, unfortunately our academic success in Latin didn't help him. He was gone by the next term, and I was gone at last from the painful and bizarre school as well. Fresh woods and pastures new. There were other pastures grazed, though, upon during those Sandford Park years, at home in Maidenhall and in Dublin.

SEVEN

'The past is another country – they do things differently there' L.P. Hartley famously wrote in *The Go-Between*. Was he entirely right? If some incident in the past was important enough we can find they do things just the same there. We can regain the past almost exactly as it was in a vivid mental photograph, because the intense feelings we had at those moments lead us back to the actual vision. These strong emotions remain imprinted within us, preserving the past – the feelings waiting their resurrection, when we can experience those vital moments again.

I must have been about nine or ten, at my grandparents' Grange House in Rathfarnham. Our next-door neighbours the Phipps family, who lived in a larger, tree-surrounded house, had two daughters, a little older than me. Playing together one hot afternoon, we went into the porch and shared some lemonade from a pewter tankard with a glass bottom. Fooling round with the tankard when my turn came, I lifted it right up and suddenly saw the face of the older girl through the glass distorted with the swirls of liquid, so that her smile danced. She was laughing, happy. She liked me. And the excited feeling I had from her then gives me the image of her face now, a round face, short fair hair, bubbly lips. Laughing. And I can feel and see the afternoon now as well, the heat and the big chestnut trees around the house, the heavy summer shadows. And that I was aware of an emotion, for the first time, quite clearly, as I am now, sixty-odd years later. I liked her. It was more than that, though I didn't recognize it as such then – it was a first hint of sensuous attraction. So the future of love came to me first through a glass lightly.

It was the start of a long river of girls, and of women, who floated past me later on the water with beautiful indifference, or with whom I jumped in for a flirting mile or two downstream, or house-boated with for longer stretches, or whom I escaped from, swimming thankfully for the bank; or women who nearly drowned me in the flow.

The file has a letter from my grandfather, in 1950 to Peggy, discussing my summer holiday arrangements – a time during which, unbeknown to my grandfather or to the Butlers, I experienced the first obsessive longing in my life for another:

My dear Peggy

Olive speaking to me on the 'phone today reminded me that it was only on cer-tain conditions that we agreed to let the child go over to his parents in England. She knows what they are like. [*My memory of Nat's visit here has the incoherence of a dream, so I leave it to Olive and Vera to decide whether the conditions are fulfilled.*] So he may very well be in Ireland after all, and go to you for two weeks if you can still have him, and then to Col. McLeod – who we all think sounds excel-lent for him, especially for the boat building on hand. It would be a great thing if Joe could get some experience in tar painting (or carpentry).

Yrs. affect. Joe.

My grandfather now clearly seems taken, as he had been in his hopes of my joining the merchant navy by sending me to the Napoleonic wars hulk in Colwyn Bay, by the chance of my making a nautical career, though not officer class, of course – still before the mast, as a tar boy or ship's carpenter. The letter reflects nothing of my real interest in the McLeod family whom I'd known for a year, and I certainly wasn't interested in the boat building and the tar painting offered. I was interested in Angela, the eldest daughter, and so more than anything I wanted to stay with the family that summer.

Angela was beautiful, one of the few women I've met that I can hon-estly describe as ravishingly beautiful. Tall, a perfect figure, easy movements, grace. Pale faced, with dark, silk-shiny hair, high cheekbones, narrowing down to a sharp chin – literally chiselled features.

I was about twelve when I first met her and her younger sister Lucy. Angela was a year or so older than me, the eldest daughter of a Scots family who had come to live near us at Maidenhall in the Mill House in Thomastown, a small town lower down on the river Nore. Her father, a retired Colonel (another Tory escaping from the new Labour government's strictures and privations in England perhaps), was a remote figure: always busy, not unfriendly but otherworldly, with eyes that flickered unfocused, or roved about intensely, fiercely, looking for something.

These searching looks might have been explained when I afterwards learnt from Hubert that the Colonel was a member of the British Israelites, a bizarre sect who thought the British were one of the lost tribes of Israel – and further that they were the Master Race, something he was perhaps intent on proving in Ireland, where, Hubert suggested, the Colonel imagined that the lost tribe might finally have settled with the Ark of the Covenant, beneath the Hill of Tara in County Meath, where the old Irish kings had been crowned. The Colonel was a maverick. So, in their way, were his two daughters, which was one reason, I think now, why I came to see Angela as the be-all and end-all of love. I knew I was an outsider, too. We were the same sort, so it was first love, as if there could never be another.

I can't remember the mother or my first meeting with the two girls, though I think it must have been on some shared Maidenhall pony business, for the two girls were passionate horsewomen. I had no interest in horses whatsoever, but I sometimes tagged along on my bike, with Julia (Hubert and Peggy's daughter) on her pony Pat, to meets of the local hunt. And it must have been at a meet that I first saw Angela – mounted, proud, tightly encased, top to bottom, in a hard bowler, tie-pinned white stock, a dark jacket, breeches, high black boots, pink-cheeked in an icy wind. I was smitten. Though I wasn't able to see that the smile was somehow icy, too.

In any case I was soon sweating furiously on my bike, cycling the six miles from Maidenhall over to the Mill House, as often as I could the next summer. I can't remember much of what we did. The girls were being educated at home, as I remember. They were fiercely and, to me, startlingly independent, quite unlike any of the local girls I'd met. They did what they wanted. Daring. Tomboyish. They seemed to have no other friends. There was no boat building or tar painting, but everything else we did was open aired. Walks with the basenjis, who weren't my sort of dogs, with their curled-up tails and back hairs going to wrong way; swimming in the rushing mill stream, where once, arriving early and from a distance, I saw the two girls getting out of the deep water naked – a vision which I though to be improper and so the more exciting. For the rest I hung about the stables, watching the girls tend their ponies, mucking out, feigning interest.

And that was one problem. I had nothing in common with the two girls, or their horsy lifestyle. I just needed to be in Angela's orbit, and would go to any lengths to achieve this, following her with the hunt the next winter on my bike, not just to the meet but lugging the bike afterwards along muddy tracks, over the hills and mountainy gorse bushes above the river. And that same winter, hoping to see Angela at one of the teenage dances Julia and I went to then at the houses of the local gentry – longing to dance with her, steeling myself to do so as she stood against the wall with her sister, for few of the boys danced with her, put off perhaps by her cold, knock-you-down beauty. Neither of us was much of a dancer. I remember the chill of her hand as I held it in the dance, and the smooth hard feel of her white satin ball dress as I nervously touched the back of it with my other hand, stepping on each other's toes to the blaring of the little local dance band.

I longed to be with her more often. So when the Butlers suggested that I might stay with the family that summer I was all cock-a-hoop. I might now have the opportunity properly to press my suit, and she might thaw.

In the event my summer stay at the McLeods, with my visions of further glimpses of the girls' nakedness in the chilly mill stream, was cancelled, and I was sent off to my parents' cold-water flat in Cheltenham instead. The torrents of young summer love never occurred, and I thought myself very unlucky in this at the time. On the other hand, had my suit been even vaguely returned, I might long since have forgotten Angela. One tends to forget early success with girls in the youthful merry-go-round of flirtation and mild sensual experiment. As it is Angela remains a vivid emblem of the obsessively loved ideal by being unobtainable, unpossessed; whereas other warmer-hearted women, with whom I was later to some degree successful, have largely disappeared from memory.

I didn't stay with the McLeods that summer because my mother wanted to see me over in Cheltenham. She writes to my grandfather from their first flat in Cheltenham at 4 Selkirk Street in June 1951:

Dear Mr Hone

I was very disappointed to hear your news this week about Joe. But of course I can understand your point of view. [*His point of view must have been that it would be a very good thing for me to do a bit of boat building, tar painting and carpentry with the McLeods for the summer holiday.*] However, Joe has been looking forward for months to coming over here [*This seems strange, since I was much keener to go to the McLeods*] and I cannot disappoint the child. I will send you the ticket next week – a friend of mine has offered to pay for it [*This may have been her part-time lover, Ian McCorkadale*]. I don't mind him staying with the Butlers for the first two weeks if you have already arranged that, but I would like him over here then.

Months ago I mentioned his holidays to you and said not to arrange anything. There is room for the child here. I have not seen the child since Easter twelve months ago. I could not see him when I was in Ireland last year. Things are never very pleasant for me when I do go to Enniskerry. If you will let me know which route Joe will be coming on I will send you or the Butlers his ticket.

I am sorry if this is going to cause a lot of trouble for you but he is quite big enough to more or less arrange things for himself.

Yours sincerely,
Biddy.

So over I went to Cheltenham. I suppose I shouldn't have minded. I was never going to have any relationship with Angela. But I was never to have any real relationship with my mother either. She remained as a distant aunt to me – someone never known in my early years, awkwardly introduced to when I was ten and rarely seen afterwards. I later came to understand her very difficult circumstances, which my father had largely imposed on her, but for me there were only the formalities, never the feelings, of a mother-son relationship with her.

My grandfather at least understood her predicaments, as he writes to Hubert Butler, on receiving my mother's letter:

My dear Hubert

I enclose a letter from Biddy. I suppose if Biddy sends the ticket we will have to dispatch Joe over to her, though I feel that the ticket may not materialise. After all, she doesn't get much joy out of life, and I/we can hardly refuse. I have written to say he will be with us when you and Peggy come up on the 14th.

I saw an interesting letter of yours in 'The New Statesman' and had to quiet down my demon of argument!

Joe

No, indeed, Biddy didn't get much joy out of life. I wonder now how – apart from her leaving my father several times and furthering her affair with Ian (which was no real improvement since there was to be nothing permanent there) – she could ever have improved her situation? Other than the brief happiness she must have had by my mere presence, I, to my discredit, did nothing positive to help her. My presence with her in Cheltenham, since it was wished on me, was a duty. One of the few distractions I found there was that I could go with impunity to the various pubs in Cheltenham that my parents frequented. I was free of such prohibitions and the other formalities of life at Maidenhall, Annaghmakerrig and with my grandparents – where such pub life, for example, was out of the question. I wish I could say that I picked up something interesting by exposure to this very different style of life – the revealing argot, the raffish manners and mores, perhaps the shabby secrets of the Cheltenham lunchtime regulars in Peter's Bar. I didn't. They were mostly reticent retired servicemen, nursing small pensions over smaller beers, or faded remittance men like my father, who said very little, bent, like him, over their *Telegraph* crossword puzzles. There was a putting green opposite Peter's Bar in Montpellier Gardens. I spent a good deal of time there, at sixpence a throw, putting against myself.

But it would be wrong to give the impression that my holidays with my parents in the late forties and early fifties in Cheltenham were altogether unrewarding. If my father was antisocial, my mother certainly wasn't. She had made many interesting, talented and congenial friends about the town

– in Peter's Bar, the Cotswold Lounge (a select bar attached to the Queen's Hotel) and the Restoration Inn down on the High Street. This last was a haunt for some of the town's literary and artistic set. Here she had met, as I did later, Ben Howard, editor of the local literary *Private Eye*-style magazine, *Promenade*; Alan Hancox who ran a fine second-hand bookshop; the celebrated Scots poet Sydney Graham together with his wild painter friends Colohoun and McBride; Noel Woodin another young poet from London; and the *Ascent of Man* Dr Bronowski who, before ascending those heights, worked prosaically for the Coal Board in offices opposite the Ellenborough Hotel, another more select watering hole for topers in the professions, where the formidable owner, Mrs Davis, would let favoured customers stay for drinks after hours.

So, among the intelligentsia and the arty set, there were several of these little drinking schools about the town where my mother was a welcome scholar, not because she was literary – she, like my father, read nothing but the odd 'tec novel – but because, in her attractive, easygoing manner and intuitive sympathies, she was an addition to any company. Furthermore, beneath the accommodating surface she was no fool and always stood her round. Everyone liked her and several friends, knowing of her financial and other difficulties with my father, became particular confidants and helped her with cash advances. My father, in the often fizzy, talky, Guinness-charged company down at the Restoration Inn, made rare appearances. He preferred the depressing lunchtime silences over the crossword at the end of Peter's Bar. I, on the other hand, was attracted by the company of these writers, poets, and their hangers-on – not because I had any real interest in poetry or other literary matters then: I was taken by the general vivid devil-may-care chatter, and by some of the Bohemian girls in the company.

But here I should make a correction: I had become interested in literary matters, but only in modern French literature – the works of Gide, Camus, Cocteau, Mauriac, Alain Fournier, Raymond Radiguet and the Paris novels of Henry Miller, the two *Tropics*. This unexpected literary interest – unexpected in someone who was very bad at French, had few intellectual tastes and was successful only as an athlete at school – had come to me in my early 'teens through Kingsley Scott, a Dublin schoolteacher friend of the Butlers who had come to stay at Maidenhall in the late 1940s when he had taken a first post at Kilkenny College teaching French. Though I don't remember it, I had met Kingsley some years before at Annaghmakerrig, where he had come up to give French lessons to the Fitzsimon boys who lived then at the back end of the big house. Kingsley told me years later how he had first seen me walking down the main staircase in a glow of lamplight, and had immediately been taken by 'the vision of this unknown boy'. Auden writes, in a memoir of his own and other authors' schoolday reminiscences, of how

> the authors remember at least one master with pleasure and gratitude, either because he stimulated their minds or because he treated them like human beings … Many boys, too, can remember some adult, neither a schoolmaster nor a relative, who took an interest in them and taught them something not in the school curriculum. Behind this interest there is usually an element of homosexual feeling, sublimated or overt … The corresponding figure in my life … was a practising homosexual … He made advances, which I rejected … Instead of dropping me, however, he continued to give me books and write me long letters full of encouraging criticism of my juvenile verses. I owe him a great deal.

Other than that I wrote nothing literary for him to criticize then, this almost exactly describes my subsequent relationship with Kingsley. And I owe him a great deal. Without his friendship and his literary interests, I might not have taken up any literary interests or come to write books myself. I might have become a hulky shot-putt champion, or a professional cricketer, or just dawdled round the Dublin bars after I'd left school – becoming the sort of person my father was, a possibility that the Butlers, given my earlier haunts round the Bennettsbridge pubs, obviously feared.

Yet Kingsley's influence formed only a further and more serious part of my literary education, since I'd already been spellbound as a child by Peggy's dramatic readings and found a passion for boys' adventure stories once I could read myself. I'd sensed, too, the huge importance of books, unread, in Hubert's large library, and, if not literature, I had absorbed from Tony Guthrie in Annaghmakerrig what Henry James considered the essential in fiction – 'Dramatize, dramatize, dramatize!'

But Kingsley gave me something else – access to classic modern French books and the forbidden Henry Miller novels, and so an early entry into adult life. But initially the great thing for me about Kingsley, when he came up to teach in Dublin at St Andrew's College, another and better Protestant boys' school, and I was still marooned in the horrors of Sandford Park, was that, vouched for by the Butlers, he started taking me out on Sundays for meals downtown at the Dolphin or the Hibernian hotels, or to the Old Red Bank or Bentley's fish restaurant in Molesworth Street. My early doings with Kingsley had nothing to do with literature, but in typical greedy schoolboy fashion had everything to do with good food that I had never known in the repulsive Sandford Park meals. With Kingsley I came to taste the best of Dublin food and wine, thick pea soup and sizzling steaks cooked over the charcoal grill at the Dolphin; spring-minted lamb and carafes of claret at the Hibernian. Kingsley was relatively wealthy. His father had been a Dublin wine merchant who had died early, as had his mother, when Kingsley was in his early twenties at Trinity College a few years before. He was an only child.

I was about thirteen when, precocious and very ready for fine foods and adult company, I made this sudden entrée to sophisticated, expensive big-city life, arriving in the grand hotels, porters and waiters hovering attentively round us; for Kingsley, on his own, was a regular patron of these hotels and restaurants. Kingsley was moody. In his schoolmaster mode he tended to be fidgety, abrupt, contrary, either a bit of a pedantic stickler or a fumbler in the mind. Gangly, absent-minded, pipe-in-air – here he was Monsieur Hulot. But out and about in the city he was more Gregory Peck – tall and handsome in a craggy-featured way, with a wry smile and good tweed sports jackets from Kevin and Howlin. He did in fact look a bit like the Hollywood star and was sometimes taken for him by other diners, who gazed over at him admiringly as we savoured the sole *bonne femme* and sipped the Vouvray.

If I liked the food I thrived just as much in Kingsley's red MG sports car, on speedy wind-blown trips up the Wicklow mountains and visits to the first-run picture houses in the city after the Sunday lunches – stall seats at the Adelphi or the Theatre Royal, where in those days there was a dazzling variety show on Sunday afternoons, with Scots comics, short-skirted, sequinned-bodiced dancing girls, conjurers, crooners, Joe Loss and his big band, as well as the movie: three hours of solid entertainment, with ice creams at half time – a bonanza of glamorous afternoons.

There was only one problem in all this happy Sunday high life: Kingsley was in love with me, and I didn't return the suit. I just took the food and drink and the flashy motor trips up the mountains. This sounds discreditable. Yet I wasn't trifling with his affections, since I didn't know the nature of them at first. I saw him simply as a generous uncle, just as I had earlier seen my mother's lover Ian McCorkadale. I was unaware of homosexuality since, though there had been every other sort of untoward behaviour at Sandford Park, there was, surprisingly, never any of that at the school; and Kingsley never made more than the vaguest physical advances towards me. It was only a year or so later that I realized the nature of his feelings for me, and when I did I continued to take the food and drink and the picture shows – because they were freely offered and because I longed for these happy Sunday releases from the horrors of Sandford Park. It might be said that I should not have taken the sole *bonne femme*, the Vouvray and the ice creams. I should have withdrawn. I leave that argument open. But it's an argument that takes little account of schoolboy deprivation – and simple greed. And there is the other point that, finding my responses unsatisfactory in that department, Kingsley could have dropped me, which he didn't – which is why I owe him a great deal.

No doubt for Kingsley it was a frustrating relationship. Yet this perhaps was a dilemma based in his own idealism, in that what he really wanted was a romantic relationship with an adolescent boy, but with one who would never grow up – the Peter Pan attraction. He wanted a happy balance between the carnal and the virginal, but was faced with the likely problem that with the vision, the beauty, the ideal, there may well come an irresistible longing for the sex; just as with nothing but sex in a relationship one may well come to wish for the ideal. This perhaps creates a frisson of excitement for some homosexuals in riding Browning's 'giddy line midway, the dangerous edge of things'. But it was not for me.

What was for me later were some of the books he had in his little top-floor bedroom at St Andrew's, in Clyde Road, where I usually went back with him after the Sunday outings. The many translated French novels – Gide, Camus and so on, along with Henry Miller's *Tropic of Cancer* and *Tropic of Capricorn* and some volumes of Havelock Ellis's *Studies in the Psychology of Sex*. Kingsley didn't push these books on me; I just found them out on the shelves, browsed in them when he was downstairs on some school duty, and borrowed some of them.

My initial interest in these seriously literary French books was not very worthy. I was tempted by what I saw as exotic and hoped would be sexy in them, which didn't turn out to be the case, not even with the two *Tropics* which I had to skim through repeatedly to find anything exciting. On the other hand Gide's books roused, or just confirmed, rebellious feelings in me, particularly his paean to sensuous freedom in his *Fruits of the Earth*. His fierce advocacy, addressed to a young man, of complete freedom from all bourgeois confines showed me how restrictive the conventions of my own background were, and how the prohibitions and cruelties of Sandford Park were even more imprisoning.

Gide, in *Fruits of the Earth*, passionately urges every young man to escape all such conventions and diktats. I'd been doing quite a bit of this already, and Gide encouraged me in this path – all the more since it was a direction underwritten by the highest literary authority: as was proclaimed on the covers of his books, Gide had recently won the Nobel Prize for Literature.

Along with these literary introductions Kingsley, as a passionate Francophile, gave me something else just as important: a first taste of France – in his Gitanes, through his big record player, with the voices of Piaf, Trenet and Molouji drifting over the shouts of the rough boys playing in the school backyard.

Years later, when I first saw Jean Vigo's bitter indictment of prep school life in his movie *Zero de Conduite*, I was straight back in the horrors of Sandford Park, even down to the famous dormitory sleepwalking scene in the picture, which more or less paralleled what I had witnessed at Sandford Park with Thompson, the lonely boy walking down the dormitory in his cubs outfit. But *Zero de Conduite* also brought me straight back to Kingsley, whom I immediately recognized in the figure of the waggish, humane young teacher who mimics Chaplin's waddling walk and leads the Sunday crocodile of boys off at a sudden tangent – pursuing an attractive woman in a fur with nice ankles.

Nought for conduct. And lessons. That was me. But again, as I had already seen with Tony Guthrie's unconventional theatricals at Annaghmakerrig, I saw, through Kingsley, that getting nought for conduct and being beaten regularly by the sadist Dudgeon was not the final measure of all schooldays' life, and need not be a measure of anything in real life; that there was another world out there – seen through Kingsley, his risqué books, his pungent smokes and the throbbing bal-musette music – a world where the exotic and forbidden were not forbidden, where there were no exams or beatings, a world which one could embrace *à la* Gide, tasting fruits which would not have been recommended by any of my minders or teachers. At the very least it was a turning, which might lead me to girls with nice ankles.

Years afterwards when I was over in Dublin, long after Kingsley had left St Andrew's and the school itself had moved, I would walk round to Clyde Road and look up at the high window where I had smoked Gitanes and listened to Piaf and thumbed through the *Tropics* looking for the juicy bits. But now there was more to that little rooftop room – it held an aura almost of sanctity for me, the gilded tomb of youth.

However, to return to the continuing discussions of 'What to do with Little Joe'. There now comes a bombshell of a letter from Hubert to my grandfather, early in January 1950:

Dear Joe

We had a discussion about Little Joe at Xmas at Annaghmakerrig, and we were all of us agreed, Mrs Guthrie, Tony and myself that under present conditions it is not wise to prolong the relationship with Little Joe, and that it should be dissolved by degrees in a way that will not be hurtful or harmful to him. We are truly upset about this, Peggy in particular, but we see no way out and think that in the end it will be best for Joe. It is not his fault, we want to be quite clear about that, and that, as friends of his, we shall always feel affection and interest in him. But Nat and Biddy have in the past few years made the situation impossible for us, or perhaps it would be fairer to say they have complicated rather than eased a relationship that in any case would have been difficult.

I did several years ago explain to you all, with what I thought at the time brutal candour, that we could never share responsibility for Joe with his parents – and I had years before explained the same thing to Nat and Biddy. Either I was to have guardianship of Joe or else Joe must be with us not as a member of the family but as a child-guest we sometimes have. We couldn't take responsibility without having authority. They refused us the authority and of course have never attempted to keep the terms of the written agreement – or even tried to explain their reasons for failing to do so.

However, when they did start intervening on a large scale we still hadn't the heart to part with Little Joe – and, even now, though not financially easy for us to keep him, we would try to do so, if we thought it in his interests, but we do not think it is. We feel that poor Little Joe, bandied about from home to home and knowing that his parents have not written to us more than four times in ten years, is in a bad mess psychologically, which will become increasingly worse … and that we are quite helpless to cure it. Any suggestions we make will be disregarded. Also Joe is very isolated here, there are no other small boys, only girls, and he is thrown very much on his own. He is becoming a complete lone wolf, very unco-operative, self-centred, predatory. And though he is very warm-hearted, spontaneous and gifted – he does not seem able to adapt himself to our family life. He is always obstructive and critical. WE DON'T BLAME HIM FOR THIS. He feels divided loyalties and cannot find his equilibrium. He was stammering badly when he returned from school, and that is always, I think, a sign of bad adjustment. His stammer is never permanent. He is learning from his parents quite different standards to those we use here – particularly about money and self-indulgence. In some ways he is frighteningly precocious.

We were all agreed at Annaghmakerrig that it is no good for Little Joe to stay on here and that it is bad for Peggy who has lavished on Little Joe for many years treasures of affection and solicitude which Nat and Biddy have not shown the faintest sign of recognising. Now it has definitely become too much for Peggy. She has many responsibilities and worries of her own – if Joe turns out badly it would break her heart. We have no control over his future, so we must refuse any share in responsibility.

Please, on no account, let Joe feel that we are wishing to part with him because of anything he has done. We don't want to blame him at all. He has done his best and we are fond of him. In fact it would be much better not to mention the matter to him at all. But as these holidays have driven us to certain conclusions, regretfully and with painful deliberation we thought it fairer to let you know immediately and in writing our decision. We hope to be in Dublin for a few weeks very soon, let us meet then and discuss this more fully.

With love to Vera,

Yours, Hubert.

There is no follow-up correspondence in the file from Old Joe, aunt Olive or anyone else about this letter. In any event the parting took the shape initially of my being sent to stay for the next Easter holidays with a cousin of mine, the kindly Leland Bardwell (my grand-uncle Pat's daughter) and her husband Michael, who had come to live in a small cottage near Maidenhall, while Hubert, Peggy and Julia went off on a holiday to Normandy. The next summer holiday I stayed with the Bardwells again in London, where they had moved to a flat on the Holloway Road, while the three Butlers went on holiday to Switzerland. This was the Butlers' tactful way out of me, and, though the Bardwells were very kind to me, I certainly wasn't happy with the new situation. I missed the two big houses and wondered, since by now I saw myself very much as a member of the Butler family, why I'd not been taken with them on this and the other holidays they took without me.

For some reason the Butlers must have had a change of heart since things returned to normal and I spent the next Christmas holidays, as usual, at Maidenhall and Annaghmakerrig. What made them change their minds? I don't know. It's certain I'd had a lucky escape, in not being abandoned again to spend the rest of my adolescence with my sad, impoverished parents, or my pernickety grandfather, or marooned with some unknown guardians or foster parents in County Cork or in England.

Sarah Cooper (1857–87), of Cooper Hill, Co. Limerick. JH's paternal great-grandmother, one of seven beautiful Cooper sisters, who died of tuberculosis.

Julia Marlowe (1880–1947), my grandmother Vera's aunt, the foremost classical actress of her generation in the USA.

Vera Hone, 'The Roscommon Dragoon' painted by William Orpen c. 1913.

My grandfather Joe's family at Palermo, Killiney, Co. Dublin, c. 1920.
Left to right, above: *Vera Hone (1890–1979)*, née *Brewster, grand-uncle Pat Hone,*
Joseph 'Old Joe' Hone (1879–1959), Maria, the German housekeeper; left to
right, centre: *William Hone (1860–1920), my great-grandfather, Olive Symes*
(1890–1953), née *Hone, my grand-aunt Mary Hone (c. 1890–1945),* née *Collis,*
Pat's wife; left to right, below: *Sally Hone (1920–2003), my aunt, Nathaniel 'Nat'*
Hone, (1911–59), my father, Oliver 'Nol' Hone (1925–2005), son of Pat.

My father Nat Hone, c. 1930, at New College Oxford.

Nat Hone, c. 1933–34, in the uniform of the Royal Air Force Volunteer Reserve.

'Old Joe' Hone, April 1933, photographed in D'Annunzio's house, above Lake Garda.

Augustus John and 'Old Joe' Hone, c. 1948–49, Sussex.

*JH's christening, August 1937, at Virginia Water, Surrey. On the right is
Desmond FitzGerald, JH's godfather.*

Little Joe, three years old, Annaghmakerrig, Co. Monaghan, 1940.

*Early days at Annaghmakerrig: JH on Sugar Spice, Susan Butler leading,
Jennifer Cullen following.*

Julia Butler and JH, aged seven, 1944.

Dublin studio photo of JH aged nine, 1946.

*JH aged eleven, 1948, at Piltown,
Co. Kilkenny, near maternal
grandmother's cottage.*

Paying guests, the Maidenhall brood, 1949: back row, *Eleanor Arkell, Julia, Hubert, Little Joe, Phillipe Fouchas, Clodagh Harrison, Peggy;* front row, *Thomas Arkell, Roisin Harrison, Bridget Harrison.*

Hubert Butler (1900–91), my foster-father, at St John's College, Oxford, 1919.

Hubert, Julia and Peggy Butler, Maidenhall, Co. Kilkenny, 1950.

Maidenhall, 'The house on the hill', Co. Kilkenny, 1950.

Maidenhall, c. 1952: Under the maple tree, from left, *Hubert Butler, James Delahanty, Julia Butler, Peggy Butler, Benedict Kiely.*

Sandford Park School Cricket XI, 1951. JH bottom left, below 'Mad Major' Wormell;
centre back, *Charlie Cully.*

The athlete JH at St Columba's College, Summer 1953:
shot-putt record, 58'6" – still unequalled.

St Columba's College athletic team, July 1953, JH on right.

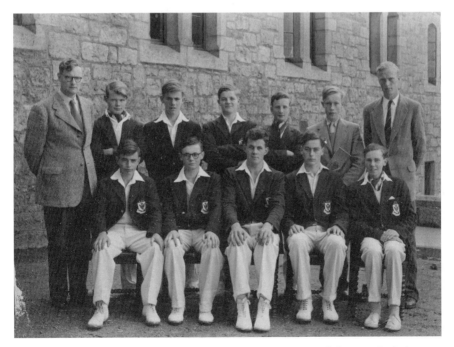

St Columba's College first Cricket XI, summer 1953, JH second from right below.

The 'Ivor Novello' bodyshot: JH 1956, auditioning for young Alexander the Great in Robert Rossen's film of the name.

Geraldine Hone (1938–), JH's sister, at Mount Anville School, Dundrum, Dublin, aged seventeen or eighteen, c. 1956.

Annaghmakerrig, 1961 (the start of my drama days): from left, *Judy Guthrie, née Bretherton, of Tunbridge Wells, JH, Bunty Worby (nurse-companion to Nora Guthrie, Tony's mother 'Mrs G'), Tony Guthrie, Evershed Martin.*

Hubert and Peggy Butler, with cats Jones and Ethel, Maidenhall, Christmas 1983.

Kingsley Scott (1923–2007), teacher, with Jacky Hone, née Yeend,
outside Manor Cottage, Oxfordshire, c. 1985.

EIGHT

For what it's worth – after all, this isn't a life-or-death story – can one make any judgment yet as to whether my minders behaved particularly insensitively? Or was I often understandably charged with being a wilful difficult thieving selfish greedy arrogant boastful boy?

Probably both – they were sometimes foolish, I was often difficult. There is no emotional science in the past. Years later there can be little certainty as to precisely what and why and how things happened: the details have dissolved with the death of the minders, and into the cloudy drifts of memory with the elderly subject of the minding. And if one hopes to get closer to the truth by writing it down, there are other pitfalls. There is the possibility that my account here may be subtly or blatantly biased, knowingly or unknowingly slanted. It's the flaw in all memoirs. In writing of any of the people with whom one was closely involved, there can of course be crucial omissions, downright lies or tactful readjustments in the tale, which those concerned are no longer there to point out. And, if they were there, and did so, they might still be wrong, slanting or forgetting crucial things themselves.

The real point is whether or not I would have been better or worse off, a happier or unhappier person, if I'd been brought up by my own parents instead of the Butlers. Given the impoverished, drinky, irresponsible situation with

Nat and Biddy, I think there can be no contest there – I was infinitely better off being brought up by the Butlers. So the next question might be, what was the quality and amount of their love for me? For it's that which really shapes the way we see ourselves as children – then, now and afterwards, whether or not we see ourselves in later life as happy rather than unhappy people. Had I been brought up by my real parents it's certain I would have ended up truly unhappy. That I didn't was entirely due to the Butlers' care and love.

So what was the quality and amount of that love? Peggy's for me was generous in quantity, for she was a highly emotional woman, but often critical in quality. Her love was not unconditional. She could be openly critical about people and their relationships. Just as she was wonderfully helpful, kind and understanding with those ill-favoured by nature or down on their luck, she rarely minced words about failings in people who should have known better. In this, as in everything else, she was high-principled and so could be brusquely condemnatory, as befitted her Scots-Victorian Tunbridge Wells background. I have taken from Peggy much of her plain speaking – to my advantage in my need for truth telling (reacting against my minders' lies and evasions when I was a child), but just as often to my cost in relationships with others.

I have sometimes been openly critical of those I have loved, as Peggy was critical with me. 'Faithful are the wounds of a friend' she used to say, criticizing me after I'd done or said something untoward. Yet perhaps even more important than her love was her honesty to me. Peggy gave me the clear sense of what was good behaviour, and what in the longer term lay in wait for you if you continued to behave selfishly, stupidly or badly – not juvenile punishments but adult unhappiness, loss, despair.

Hubert's love for me was always difficult to tell. He lived mostly on cloud nine, with his intellectual concerns. I think he found it difficult to love but I don't think I suffered from it. Had Hubert been more of an emotional father to me, with interests in my line of things as a boy – model trains, sports, cricket – would I have been less difficult as a child? Yes, quite possibly. On the other hand I might have found an emotional Hubert difficult to handle, embarrassing, as I sometimes found Peggy's intense show of feelings towards me.

In any case, one must deal with things as they were and Hubert as a distant surrogate father was far better for me than poor Nat's sad, shove-ha'penny paternity would have been. I can't see Hubert as a fly in my childhood ointment. For a start he was part of my coming to books in his big library, and even if I read very few of them when I was young, he showed me indirectly the huge importance of books, their stories and myriad ideas. Besides, Hubert's lack of emotional or critical involvement with me was a restful thing. I could sit by the fire with him, when Peggy was away, in happy silent lamplight, he with his Serbo-Croatian texts, me with my cricket book, an account of the MCC in Australia, 1932-33. But as we have seen when Hubert put pen to paper about Little Joe, he could be very active and critical about me. He, like Peggy, lived the moral life, though he did this mostly on the typewriter – his approach was intellectual, hers intuitive. The chalk-and-cheese marriage, which came to work so well 'Les extrèmes se touchent'.

To return to the fray of wider judgment about my early life, I wonder if there can ever be a fair balance sheet here for the reader to judge? Kingsley, for example, would very likely have a different slant on it – that in denying him the physical things he wanted of me I teased him, for the sake of foody treats in the Hibernian Hotel and racy trips up the Wicklow mountains. And I may have got it wrong about other people. Angela McLeod may not have been an ice maiden but simply found me a crashing bore, a moony suitor who barely knew one end of a horse from another – and didn't like her dogs. There are other scenes I may have slanted in my favour. Major Wormell, for example, was right to call me a blackguard and beat the hell out of me, not because I was thieving his drinks, which I wasn't, but because I was party to a dishonest scheme in phoning Charlie Culley in his study with answers to the Latin exam paper. I could be an unreliable narrator. For that's the flaw in most factual accounts – there is more possibility of truth in fiction than in fact, for in fiction one can get to the heart of the matter, display hidden thoughts and feelings – the shabby secrets, the frustrated love or whatever – of the protagonists, in the moment, as these emotions actually occur. Let me return, however, to the file of letters.

When I was nearly fourteen, it at last dawned on my grandfather what Hubert had seen long before: Sandford Park was no longer suitable for me.

So he set himself to various schemes and ideas for my further education, and singled out St Columba's College for me, a public school (the only one in the Republic) up in the Dublin mountains. He writes to Hubert sometime in 1951:

Dear Hubert

Sowby, the Warden of St Columba's, is very keen about getting me to write a history of the school. I feel tired enough, but I have considered the suggestion and yesterday I went to see the proposed publisher who does not think it a very promising business proposition; it might be possible if I did it gratis. Well, that is out of the question, but it has occurred to me that St Columba's might pay me for the work in the shape of educating Little Joe on a scholarship basis or a really large reduction in the fees.

They certainly would not pay me cash, but an extra boy doesn't make much difference – I mean I would gain more than they would lose, so the Warden might consider it.

The question is: shall I put this proposition? Is St Columba's the right school for Joe? On this I seek your advice and Peggy's, asking you to bear in mind that when he is seventeen or eighteen he will have to go out in the world. Should he not go to a school where the other boys' parents are in the same position as he will be, where the education is entirely practical? My means will not allow me to support him beyond seventeen or eighteen, even with home and clothes, unless manna falls from heaven.

There is no good pretending it is otherwise. If I were to die tomorrow, Vera I hope would be able to carry on Joe's education on a modest basis for a few years, but after that there would be nothing – what there is must go to my own children. Sally [*my aunt*] especially has to be considered, as she could never earn a living which would give her anything like the life she has been accustomed to, and to which she has a right of assurance, so far as I can assure it.

St Columba is not of course a school for the rich and idle classes, but most of the boys have well-off parents, and go on to Trinity, which Joe could not do unless he got a scholarship and this I don't think one should count on.

Yrs,

Joe Hone.

Old Joe, as usual, is first of all pondering money and barter deals here, before any considerations as to the suitability of the school for me. Interesting, too, are his remarks about Sally, that he must try to assure 'the life she has been accustomed to', by implication a moneyed life he has so far provided. For the first time in his letters he lets the cat out of the bag, suggesting that his family life was relatively well heeled. And this of course was not a fact he ever wanted to reveal. All sorts, besides my father, might have been at his door at once.

In fact Sally had not had any pampered, moneyed life. She had been working for her keep in England right through the war, as a secretary with Bomber Harris in his High Wycombe bunker and afterwards as a cipher clerk at Station X, the top-secret Enigma decoding operation at Bletchley Park. This my grandfather would not have known, believing she was just a secretary in some run of the mill war-effort institution. None the less Sally would have to be financed, dowried in the traditional manner, for entry into the marriage arena. On the other hand, to finance my future education he is considering writing what would have been a long history (the school was founded in 1842) of St Columba's College – or else getting me into the bicycle-mending business. Poor Old Joe, beset with problems, some of his own making, since, even at this point in the early 1950s, he was not that poor and could well have afforded (as he subsequently did, if only for one year) to pay the very reasonable fees at St Columba's.

Before a final decision about my future schooling was made there was still a good deal of footling letters between Hubert and my grandfather about a choice of school. There are letters from Christ's Hospital school in Horsham, Sussex; from Portora in Northern Ireland, and one from A.S. Neill, the head of the famous (or infamous) progressive Summerhill School in Suffolk. But it seems Neill didn't think me difficult or progressive enough for Summerhill – he writes to Hubert that he has no place for me. So there are frustrated, even angry responses from my grandfather over it all, as is clear in a letter to Hubert sometime towards the end of 1950:

Dear Hubert,

I was at St Columba's the other day where I saw the new Warden, a young Englishman. He seemed to think it would be almost impossible for a boy arriving in England from Ireland at Joe's age to get into any school whatever, from County Council (owing to his age being beyond eleven) to Eton!

Austin Clarke [*the well-known Irish poet*] who had his boys at Sandford Park, says they learnt nothing there, and there is no order or discipline, so he took his boys away. I dare say Sandford Park has done more harm to Little Joe than a few weeks with his parents in England ... By all accounts the Harcourt Street school [*the High School*] is good for getting boys to work ... My 'psychological guess' about his 'psychological mess' is that he has an innate tendency to idleness, as Nat has among the male Hones.

This was written before I saw you today. I am sorry I vented my spleen on you, but the incoherence of life – and of my own life – has pressed on me of late. Peggy being ill, there can be no question of your decision now, but I was irritated by your talk of psychological problems and solutions, when the commonsense issue was so plain and so insoluble.

I can see how Hubert, with his liberal ethic, would still be pondering psychological solutions for me, while Old Joe, with his right-wing views, would have been annoyed by such solutions, favouring the severely practical: 'Bring on the broken bicycles for Little Joe!' he might have said to Hubert, venting more spleen. 'Or the carpenter's shop. Or even the Hong Kong police!'

The first view of St Columba's College, as one came up the winding drive through the parkland, was (and still is) attractive: a pleasing, white-stuccoed Georgian house, set well up in the hills with a splendid view down over the city and Dublin Bay. But behind the house, more or less unseen, lurked something very different – a number of dark, heavy granite neo-gothic Victorian buildings; a Puginesque chapel, cloisters, a long dining hall and dormitory above, a longer hall across the lawn. Another world, not Ireland.

St Columba's in the early 1950s was in some ways even more of an anomaly in the Republic than Major Wormell's Union-Jack-waving Sandford Park. Though this wasn't immediately obvious. St Columba's didn't need to emphasize its Protestant Empire ethos, its muscular Christianity, its ideals of service to the King over the water. This was implicit. It lay all over the place, in the huge Victorian scholastic shadow that Dr Arnold had cast, even across the Irish sea, in the mid-nineteenth century: an ethos confidently enshrined at St Columba's a hundred years later – in hymns ancient and modern, on brass plaques in the chapel naming old boys killed in the Great War, and on the much longer list of names in the cricket pavilion declaring the players of the First XI, the lists going back eighty years or more. 'Play up, play the game!' The Great Game of defending the North-West Frontier from the Ruskies and stamping out any restlessness among the Irish natives.

To be fair, St Columba's had been founded originally in 1842 not to put down the native Irish but to save them from the perils of their Catholic faith – and to feed them from soup kitchens when the Irish Famine came in the late 1840s. It was a proselytizing foundation, started by two fervent British evangelicals, the Reverend Dr Sewell and the Reverend Maunsell, who only a few years into their Irish evangelizing mission fell out, so that the Reverend Sewell left in a huff, went back to England and founded the sister school to St Columba's, Radley College near Oxford, in order to be entirely free to implement his low-church Protestant gospels. The hard shadow of all these punishing Victorian beliefs lay behind the pleasant Georgian house.

I arrived at St Columba's in the autumn term of 1952, all kitted out with the usual public-school prisoner's clothes and baggage, packed in an exotically labelled trunk (hotels in Lake Garda, Mentone, Portofino) of my grandfather's. There was the regulation kit I had to have: a horrid rough-scratchy herringbone best suit, flannel suit for ordinary, a short black gown, a white surplice, dried muddy rugby boots ex-Sandford Park, two ties, three this, four that and six of the other – and an old tuck box, belonging to my uncle Pat for which my grandfather had given him half a crown. I was ready, but not very willing.

Mine was an awkward arrival, one that exposed me embarrassingly. I was coming to the school very late, at fourteen instead of eleven or twelve. I was neither a senior nor a junior, an in-between boy. I was put in a new House, Gwynn, run by the ex-Balliol classics master, G.K. White, long a fixture at the school – put in his house no doubt because White was a friend of my grandfather's and had been in charge of my uncle David, in another House, ten years before when David had been at the College; the assumption being, I suppose, that G.K., as he was known, liked and knew how to deal with the Hone family, many of whom had been at Columba's in earlier years. Certainly, as I learnt afterwards, he liked David, not only for his good behaviour but also for his artistic talent. It was not to be the same with me.

Two incidents occurred on my first day that set the tone of my experiences at the school, reflecting the position in the College of the two Irish classes, two religions, the two utterly different sets of values that the College lived by: on one side the many maids ('skivvies'), other servants, gardeners, groundsmen, and odd-job men – the Catholic Irish, impoverished, decent but largely ill-educated; on the other side their masters: the mon-eyed, well-educated Anglo-Irish Protestant boys and teachers. While one side imposed their sanctions through the confessional, the other took to floggings with the birch, and rarely did the twain meet. But of course they did meet now and then. The unfortunate evidence of this was there on my very first day in the school, a more-or-less empty one, since for some reason I'd arrived a day early.

I'd wandered round to the 'bogs', a set of lavatories next to the Masterman Library. It was roped off, with one or two official-looking men coming in and out, telling me to move off. Next day the news was quickly on the grapevine. A skivvy had aborted her baby in one of the lavatories, and the culprit was almost certainly one of the senior boys, since he was known for his flirting with the maids and had not returned that term. No more was heard of the incident. It had never happened.

Of course this sort of thing was a problem in the monastic, single-sex school that Columba's was then. For sexual release among urgent young men in the College at that time it was a skivvy (*droit de seigneur*) or one of the junior boys ('Close your eyes and think of England'). I was to learn more of these activities and proclivities later. Meanwhile, on the first weekend, I was to see how the Master Race ruled the school, through its hierarchy of housemasters, prefects, house captains, spies and fifth columnists. And in this Columba's was different from the haphazard drunken order of Major Wormell's Sandford Park; there were many more gauleiters here, better trained and sober, and many more boys to punish – and seduce.

On that first Sunday, when we were free in the afternoon and could roam up the Dublin mountains behind the school, I fell in with two friends, from my time with the Guthries in County Monaghan, already at the school:

Nick Fitzsimon, who had lived at Annaghmakerrig during the war, and John Killen, a doctor's son, who came from nearby. And a fourth new boy, ill fitting like me (indeed he was much older than me – he must have been in his late teens), a large blond Swiss-German youth called Charlie Seltzer. Charlie was the son of a government minister in Switzerland and had done something very wicked at home, and had been quietly exiled to Ireland, to St Columba's, to finish his education, of which he seemed to have had little, his English being sparse and inaccurate. But Charlie did have one thing about him in abundance that Sunday – hard cash. Swiss francs, Irish five-pound notes and a lot of jingling coins. And nothing would do but that we took him to a pub that afternoon.

Nick and John knew the ropes in this matter, how one could take a mountain road up to Lamb Doyle's pub, in those days more or less a she-been, a white-washed cottagey pub where one knocked on the back door if the place was closed and, if one was tall enough and known to the proprietor or the missus as a sensible Columban – that's to say one with money and a head for drink – one was admitted for a pint or two of porter in the back room. Or something stronger, which was Charlie's tipple that Sunday afternoon, whiskey, which, with his Irish fivers, he took to like a Trojan. It was drinks all round.

On returning to the college, Charlie's breath smelt and he was somewhat merry when we got to the cloisters before going in for six o'clock Chapel. A prefect accosted him. Questions were asked. Where had he been drinking? Who had he been with? Charlie, since he was about nineteen and saw Irish pubs just as uncouth cafés which anybody could patronize at any age or time of day, thought he'd done nothing wrong, and apparently gave a straightforward answer – he'd been having a Sunday afternoon drink. To his credit he didn't say who he'd been with. After Chapel, Charlie was reported to his housemaster, G.K. White, to await an appointment with him. We other three kept mum. Unfortunately one of the other masters, Kenny Mills, was driving by and had seen the four of us on the road coming back from the pub. This too was reported to White, who was now happily making devious enquiries into the whole matter. Finally we were all hauled up in front of him. We denied everything. We had simply met Charlie on the road back, had been nowhere near the pub. But of course the road itself was out of bounds. We three were gated. And Charlie was beaten by G.K. He took it in an amused but puzzled spirit, saying to us afterwards, in his guttural Swiss-German accent: 'You Irish, so strange habits – you beat zee men like cattle! For zee having just a dhrink! Ha, ha!'

Charlie was right. It was all a nonsense, but as far as the College authorities were concerned it was a serious nonsense. St Columba's, with its all-seeing housemasters, masters, prefects and house captains, its gatings and birchings, was going to be a tougher proposition than Sandford Park. I had moved from what had been an open prison to one up on the moors.

St Columba's was not a prison in any real sense; we were allowed four exeats each term and we could roam as far as we wanted, among the sheep and gorse bushes, up the mountains behind the school. And some of the masters and senior boys were not gauleiters, but decent men, though they were in a minority. The school was certainly run by the tougher, the misguided and the more devious types. Misguided because, as at Sandford Park, there was a palpable aura at St Columba's then of superior difference from, and indifference towards, the rest of the Irish world around us. Tougher because at St Columba's there were more numerous, arbitrary and usually unjustified punishments – painful beatings, rarely by the masters (that was only for the most serious crimes) but by the house prefects. These young men could simply take the law and the cane into their own hands and, on the say-so of the younger house captains, beat viciously.

Some of these house captains were not to be trusted in their judgments of behaviour; some bore grudges or were in love with junior boys and would have their rivals for the boy beaten for some minor offence. Behind the workaday surface the school rather resembled Florence under the Medicis – the housemasters princes, the prefects and house captains Machiavellis, all consorting, listening, advising, plotting and planning punishments or other subtle retributions. One incident, on my penultimate day at school at the end of the following summer term, illustrates this.

Since exams were over I had gone with Nick Fitzsimon, John Killen and a third boy known as The Horse (for the size of his marriage tackle) down to the village of Dundrum where we had clubbed together and bought a bottle of sickly sweet Cyprus sherry. We drank almost all of it, in ditches, on the way back to school. The bottle disappeared – I assumed one of us had thrown it in the ditch. We all trooped into Chapel at six o'clock. Sometime after Chapel I was told to go and see G.K. White. On his desk when I entered his room was a half-empty bottle. But it wasn't the bottle of Cyprus sherry we had bought in Dundrum. It was Spanish. G.K, tall, gaunt, grey hair *en brosse*, in his long black gown, smoking a cigarette from an elegant amber holder *à la* Noel Coward, said in his high nasal voice, 'This alcoholic beverage, Hone, was found in your dorm locker after Chapel.'

The bottle had clearly been planted in my locker before Chapel, and found afterwards, both times when I wasn't in the dorm.

I said, 'I didn't put it there, Sir. Who found it?' 'The house prefect, Fish, found it there. But that is not the point, Hone. The point is that it was in your dorm locker, so it must have been put there by you, and you must have been drinking from it.' 'No, Sir, I didn't put it there, I don't know who …' White stood up. 'I shall not dispute the matter with you, Hone. You will see the Warden tomorrow morning.'

And so I did, but not until midday when, in the empty school – all the other boys had gone home for the summer holidays, whereas I couldn't leave for some reason until the afternoon – the Warden, the Englishman my grandfather mentions in his letter to Hubert, the Reverend F. Martin Argyle, beat me thoroughly. This beating seemed gratuitous, superfluous, since he knew I was not coming back to the school, and that an hour later I was to leave the place forever.

So who had planted the bottle in my dorm locker? It couldn't have been Nick, or John Killen or The Horse. But there was someone else who might well have done this. I had been having a bad relationship with the Gwynn house captain throughout the summer term, because one of the junior boys in the long Gwynn dorm, an attractive blond boy with his bed next to mine, had come to like me, partly I think because of my cricket prowess with the First XI. Several other seniors fancied him as well, as indeed I did myself in a platonic, romantic way. One of the particular fanciers was the house captain, who had not had any luck with the boy.

I have no certain evidence that the house captain put the bottle in my locker, and had told Fish so as to have me shopped. But as some say of Christ's supposed image on the Turin Shroud, 'If not him, then who?'

'Such, such were the joys' of St Columba's College. Though I shouldn't exaggerate by dwelling too much on the base attributes of the place. There were other, better, aspects to the school.

NINE

Because it so strenuously aimed for conformism in all things St Columba's was a fine breeding ground for rebels. They could sharpen (I was
going to say 'hone') their rebellion there, as I suppose I did. I say 'I suppose' because I didn't consciously rebel. I just simply kept on getting caught,
smoking with Nick Fitzsimon behind the cricket pavilion or whatever. I was
a poor rebel in that way. Certainly I was way behind the elderly irascible science teacher, George Large, a Catholic who had been a senior member of
the old IRA and had used his metallurgic skills to forge a prison key taken
from a wax impression, and so, with a few other desperadoes, had sprung
Éamon de Valera from Lincoln jail – imprisoned there by the hated British after the Easter Rising of 1916. What George Large was doing at this
Protestant imperial school, a symbol of the oppressor in Ireland for many
centuries, I never found out.

But it shows how St Columba's did have an Irish side to it. Ireland was
lurking in the bushes groping with a skivvy, or up at Lamb Doyle's pub – or,
spectacularly, right there in the science lab in the shape of tough little arch-
IRA rebel George Large. He and I didn't hit it off. The sadist Dudgeon had
been science master at Sandford Park. Anything to do with test tubes upset
me, renewed painful memories. George had a habit of suddenly shouting at

me. 'Hone! Will you just do one thing for me? Stand right away from the equipment, back of the class. And stay there.'

Well, that made two rebels, George and me. And there were a few others; Nick and the fine cricketer 'Crooked' Lee, the three of us with our little Woodbine-smoking school behind the cricket pavilion – and particularly Dan Brownlow, carelessly and much more daringly rebellious, an older, elegant and sophisticated Dubliner, a senior who had refused to be considered as a house captain or a prefect and just laughed quietly at school prohibitions. But unlike laughing Charlie Seltzer he was far too clever ever to get caught. Dan led a charmed life at the school. With the connivance of Fred the boiler man he kept a Fiat in the garage next to the boiler room, left the dorm after lights out and drove into town, to The Green Rooster in O'Connell Street – a daring place in the Dublin of the time, since it was open until midnight, and you could meet a girl there and get a mixed grill. What thrills! We few who were in the know admired Dan Brownlow. But for us there were no girls and mixed grills in The Green Rooster – it was Florence under the Medicis and cold spaghetti.

One of the benefits of the school was the fact that the teaching was generally excellent, if you availed yourself of it. The teachers were paid more than in other schools in Ireland, so St Columba's could take the pick of the pedagogic crop from Trinity College. But this was a benefit I didn't make much use of. Apart from English, History and Geography I just couldn't get to grips with any other school work. Maths, Science, Latin, French – I wasn't interested. It all seemed quite pointless. And so I created a record in the school, which I believe stands to this day. I was sent down a form in each of my three terms at St Columba's, from Five A, to Five B, to Shell A, landing up among the real academic dunderheads, decent farmers' sons and such like, where we didn't even have the properly qualified French teacher. We were taken instead by the greatly talented art teacher, the bird's-nest-bearded Oisin Kelly, conscripted for the job. Not so talented at French, at which we were much less talented, he would throw chalk at us, with great accuracy, especially at the ultimate dropouts chuckling in the back row, among whom, of course, I shared a proud place.

What saved me at St Columba's was what had saved me at Sandford

Park: I became tops at sport and, at the senior level, in cricket, athletics, even rugby and tennis. So I had access to some of the privileges that went with this: weekend trips to play cricket at Portora School in the north, and to inter-provincial athletic contests elsewhere in Ireland, where I won the high jump and some sprints, and in the shot putt (thanks to Len Horan at Sandford Park) swept the board and created records. I think I still hold the Columba's record in the seven-pound shot – fifty-six feet, eight inches. I got my colours in athletics and in cricket with the First XI. As at Sandford Park, it created surprise that such a bad lot should excel in this major aspect of public-school life, where a sports star was marked out as one on course for all the other glittering prizes in life. Though in my case there were clearly grave doubts about this.

In the long dining hall, where the housemasters sometimes sat at the head of the table with us at lunch, G.K. White, towards the end of the summer term, asked me what I intended to do when I left the school. 'I think I'll take a rest cure, Sir,' I said. 'Hone, I asked the question seriously. You might consider a serious answer, if you are capable of such.' Since I knew that White's father had been a Dublin bishop, I thought to add insult to injury by pulling his leg again. 'Well actually, Sir, I hope to go abroad – to Africa, the mission fields, and write inspiring articles for *The Church of Ireland Gazette*.' G. K. looked at me sourly. 'Hone, you will go far – downhill.'

White was a curious man. Dry to the point of clinical dehydration, with his superior amused chuckles, his slow and studied beatings. I always assumed he was queer. He may have felt this idea was generally to his disadvantage – for, sensationally, in the year after I left he married the matron and took over the house with her that had been the sanatorium. He stayed on at the school, as teacher and then as one of the Fellows, way into his nineties. *Goodbye, Mr Chips*. But G.K. was not as nice as Mr Chips. He writes to Old Joe towards the end of my final term at the school, in July 1953:

Dear Mr Hone,
Mr Lyon of the Public Schools Appointments Bureau interviewed Joe the other day and talked to me about him afterwards. I have seen Joe about it since and he is quite clear about what Mr Lyon's advice is. I want to let you know briefly about it.

143

He can do nothing about getting him into the film industry (Joe's ambition) and is not optimistic about it. Joe however says he intends to make use of Tyrone Guthrie's introductions to people in England and see if anything comes of it.

Joe mentioned to him that he would like as a second string to get into journalism: with regard to that his advice is that the only hope for him will be to apply to a provincial or local paper (in Cheltenham if they have one) for a start in the humblest capacity ... But there would be no chance for him in that sort of work in London.

Mr Lyon is not keen on the idea of making something out of his cricket: he says there is really nothing in it except for the very good, which Joe is not.

Finally he said that if Joe found later that he wanted to get a job in a commercial firm in England he could apply to their London office: they would interview him there and Mr Lyon is confident that he could get him a start somewhere.

I am glad to be able to tell you that in cricket at least Joe has impressed us by his readiness to discipline himself and to accept discipline. He is the best bowler we have and has had some useful innings as well, and he fields not badly. They say if he had good early coaching he would have been really good; as it is he is good by our standards. He has also distinguished himself in athletics.

I should add that he impressed Mr Lyon very favourably. He found him – contrary to what we had led him to expect – diffident about his prospects. I fear I cannot say anything good about his work. What was it that Scott said of Byron? That he dashed off his poems with 'the easy nonchalance of a nobleman'? Anyhow that appears to be Joe's attitude to the examination papers which he is now facing. If it is all as easy as he thinks it will be, if a lordly assurance will take the place of knowledge based on previous work, then he should impress the examiners favourably. But I fear it may prove otherwise, if my previous experience of these examiners is worth anything. We have done what we could but we have failed to get Joe to work even this term in anything like the way he should; we cannot treat boys of his age as if they were six years younger and jump on them all the time.

All good wishes to you and Mrs Hone and David.

Yours,

George White.

Jump on boys all the time? Indeed. Repressed and frustrated sex was rife at the school, but some boys, at least, were successful with it up the gorsey hills on Sundays before evensong. However, there were some disastrous consequences of these affairs. One of the senior boys shot and killed himself at home over a thwarted relationship with a junior. I've sometimes thought that, since mild ale is provided for sixth formers in some British public schools as an introduction to the real world, discreet (feminine) brothels should have been laid on for the senior boys as well. Less trouble and tragedy, and fewer lives subsequently maimed, would surely have resulted from such an admirable provision. Certainly my own taste was very much for girls, but apart from the skivvies (and I'd seen what could happen there on my first day if you meddled with them) there weren't any at the school. And as G.K. White says, my other tastes were for working in pictures or journalism, or making a career as a professional cricketer. It's clear that Mr Lyon and White held out no hope for me in any of these three occupations, judging my capabilities suitable only for a commercial career – one up from carpentry and bicycle mending at least.

Of the rest, how did my year at St Columba's affect me? Not very much and not very well, apart from increasing my cricket and athletic skills, and giving me the camaraderie of some senior boys in the athletic field such as the Irish schools mile record-breaker Dessie Watt; and David Neligan, famous in his time for the hop, skip and jump, later Irish Ambassador in Paris. Of course, had I gone to the school a few years earlier as I should have done, I might have taken more benefit, academically and otherwise. Or I might simply have suffered many more beatings, and learnt even less.

G.K. White in his housemaster's report after my first term says: 'I am not wholly satisfied with his attitude to the rules, nor do I think he has yet learnt what real work is.' The other masters confirm a poor pupil: 'Weak' in Irish. In Maths: 'Low standard. He does not impress me as someone who is trying very hard.' In George Large's form report: 'I have had to speak to him almost every week for unsatisfactory work.' In History and Geography: 'His standard is not generally high.' Argyle, who taught us Latin, says: 'His standard was, and still is, very low; he has obviously never known how to work at the subject, being rather inclined to go his own way.'

Of course Argyle couldn't have known how I'd achieved Latin honours in the previous Intermediate standard exams at Sandford Park, by courtesy of little Mr Carpenter. Sandford Park was that sort of school; St Columba's maintained loftier standards. But clearly I wasn't up to them. I suppose I was marked indelibly by my Sandford Park years – years of cold and hurt with the only real learning that of deceit and subterfuge, years that marked me out as a sink-or-swim boy.

As I left St Columba's that summer I could see that it was going to be the same again, sink or swim. Well I wanted to swim and, as G.K. White writes to Old Joe, I hoped to swim into the film business. Anyway, I wanted to get away from all the dull twaddle of scholastic learning, away from the beatings and all the footling and pain that had been part of my life in Ireland. I wanted some happy fantasy-reality now, to go to England and rise up into the glamorous firmament of movies, the world of the silver screen and the stars.

But my minders had other less romantic hopes for me as I see in a letter from Hubert to Argyle in the summer of 1953, in the light of this last school report:

Dear Mr Argyle,

We only today got Joe's report, a very bad one, from his grandparents, but Joe has already left to stay with friends in Dublin, so I am afraid the suggestion that he should take some thought about the contents of the report was completely ignored. We had no idea that all had not gone well. Without wanting to be disloyal to our old friends Joe and Vera Hone, I ought to explain that we have this difficulty about his report and anything confidential that is said about Joe every single term. We are not told until we pester to have the report sent to us. This time we were told that a confidential letter from his housemaster was also sent and the Hones told us that this would be enclosed with the report, but it did not come.

Joe Hone senior, when scolded about all this, says he is old and ill and occupied with his literary work and I know this is all true and he means no harm. But the result is that any information that might be applied to Joe's upbringing never reaches those who are more than anyone else in charge of him in the holidays.

I explained to Joe's parents that we should either have to be formal guardians in charge of the child or else simply lodging-house keepers in receipt of a proper fee of 15/- a week as it then was. The signed document agreeing to pay a proper fee was never implemented at all, though Joe senior some time ago raised it to 30/-. I mention all this not to complain, but to explain that while we have very little authority we have a great deal of responsibility for Joe which we don't want to shirk at all. A couple of years ago when Joe's parents asked him over to England at no notice when my wife had arranged all sorts of other things for him in the holidays, I began to think it was all too much of a strain for my wife and that some other arrangement must be made. But no other arrangement is possible; his relations are old or indifferent or, like his parents, very irresponsible. So as we are very fond of him and he of us and considers this place his home, it seems to me that, unsatisfactory as it is, the present arrangement is the best one. But it is very harrowing for my wife as she does not believe that his holidays in England are sufficiently supervised, yet she has no right to complain, and we hear nothing. We have only had about three letters from his parents in fourteen years.

I am sure you will forgive this outburst. Joe has many good qualities and it will be very sad if they are allowed to go to waste. His irresponsibility is very likely hereditary, but I am sure susceptible to some sort of discipline, and influence. He now has, which he hadn't a year ago, companions of his own age, very nice boys in the neighbourhood, and while he is here he never gets into any mischief. But in the ordinary course of events he is very careless and destructive.

He spent a large part of the holidays making an adaptation of a Balzac story on my typewriter for a film script. He was secretive about it, but when he left, characteristically he left it all on the drawing-room floor, and my typewriter was not improved. Yet it struck me that what he had written was very good for his age, very well written and far better typed than this letter is.

I think he has a great capacity for doing, and persevering in doing, anything that interests him personally, but that all his interests lie outside what is usual for his age, I mean his 'intellectual' interests. He is oddly adult, by which I don't mean precocious, but he will talk confidently and not always stupidly about subjects that most children find very boring.

We are all worried about his future. But my view is that he will have no difficulty, too little difficulty, in getting a job, possibly quite well paid, on the strength of his charm, personality and superficial accomplishment, and great assurance. I mean film work or in journalism, as he has a great gift of being liked. He'll get such a job and probably knows instinctively he'll get it whether he passes exams or not, and that very likely is why he isn't bothering about his work or our gloomy predictions about his future if he doesn't work harder. But of course unless he learns self-discipline and consideration for others, journalism and films will be very bad for him, though I think very likely his ultimate goal will lie in that direction. He will want to and be able to express himself more than there is scope for in any usual profession. But I wish before he embarks on journalism or anything of the kind he could take a few years in the merchant service or something of the kind, where he would have to obey orders and stick to a timetable and at the same time see a bit of the world under a certain amount of strict control. I don't think though that the army would be a good idea, though his family might look in that direction because it is cheap and easy to arrange. He did a trial trip on the sea with the Drogheda service to Dieppe (horses) but it was under the wrong conditions and I don't think his dislike of it should be taken as conclusive.

As I have said, anything we advise or work for is liable to be reversed by his parents, but we can't on that account dissociate ourselves from all these plans, and we are very glad in any case that we urged successfully that he should be moved from Sandford Park as he is certainly making more friends at St Columba's and as a boarder at Sandford Park he was too big a fish in too small a pond and apparently did what he liked.

Forgive this very long letter, but we want you to know something of Joe's background. I don't think he has any psychological complications except the obvious ones, that his parents can't bring him up and that he must be embarrassed about this. I have made him understand clearly that this place will always be his home and I am sure he doesn't feel 'unwanted' here, because we do in fact find him a real addition to our household and everybody here is fond of him.

Don't trouble to answer this letter but, if any difficulty should arise, please remember that, though we are not his guardians we will, in point of fact, have to take responsibility for him, if his grandparents die. There seems to be no one else.

Yours sincerely,
Hubert Butler.

Well, a real handful of a letter, interesting in that Hubert has changed his mind about me in several crucial ways, as we shall see. But I must record at once the Reverend F. Martin Argyle's reply:

Dear Mr Butler

Although you told me not to trouble to answer your letter I feel I must thank you on my own account and on that of his Housemaster, Mr G K White, because your letter has been most helpful to us in helping to fill in Joe minor's background. White, of course, knows the family well and knows how difficult, for various reasons, and yet how attractive they are. The trouble is that Joe has come to us very late indeed, and he is here for such a short time. I hope we shall be able to do something for him, though as you say I am afraid we won't make much headway in a direct appeal to him to work at his ordinary school studies for the sake of examination achievement. He is also quite determined not to go into anything like Irish shipping even if he could get in. We both agree with you that he needs something that will continue to provide him with a framework of order and discipline for his life as he is obviously capable of charming his way into something like journalism or films, which would probably be bad for one of his temperament and character. There is no questioning his intelligence. The Balzac incident you quote from the holidays is just the sort of thing I would have expected when his interest is caught and he obviously has a flair for English. Probably the circumstances in his life force him into an independent attitude. He is determined to depend on his own resources and rely on his own judgement, which is understandable in his case. I can only try to be patient while he is here and hope that some of the friends he makes, both amongst the boys and on the staff, will continue the good work you have done for him.

 Many thanks for writing so fully,

Yours sincerely,

F Martin Argyle. Warden.

This letter puts a different complexion on Columba's insofar as Argyle seems to have a good judgement of my character, a humane grasp of my problems, ambitions and abilities; and he certainly hits the mark by saying that, given my disrupted family background, I was determined to rely on my own resources and judgment.

What is curious is that Argyle never showed me these qualities directly. He could only address his understanding to Hubert, and beat me unnecessarily on my last day at the school, which was hardly a humane goodbye. Perhaps it was his British reserve? – and also a sort of academic elitism, so that Argyle could only speak freely and truly of me to Hubert, both of them Oxford classical scholars, but could not speak the same human messages to me. I don't suggest by this that Argyle's and Hubert's harping on discipline, order, exams, concern for others and so on are not important considerations in the running of young lives. They are. What I question is the moral ambivalence in their approach to me, that on the one hand both of them praise my good characteristics but on the other Hubert wants to export me to England and Argyle beats the hell out of me.

There are several other contradictory points in Hubert's letter to Argyle. Hubert, who less than two years before had written to Old Joe that he and Peggy couldn't have me any more at Maidenhall, is now saying that I'm a real addition to the household and that Maidenhall, as he has now told me clearly, is my home. And then he says that he doesn't think I have any 'psychological complications' whereas in the previous letter to Old Joe he says I'm a 'psychological mess' and a few years before he's been agitating with Freudian Dr Eustace about my being in just the same mess, indeed that I may have been born 'morally blind'. Something of a turnabout.

Perhaps, getting older, I was behaving better. Or perhaps Hubert realized that however I was behaving he and Peggy were now finally committed to me, and I to them, for better or worse, and all three of us had better get on and make the best of it.

All the same, despite Hubert's hopes in his letter to Argyle that I find some regular discipline in the services after I left St Columba's, I certainly wasn't going to join the British merchant or any other sort of navy. I'd left St Columba's with only four 'O' levels, English Language and Literature, History and Geography, which weren't going to get me into Balliol. If I'd had any money that summer of 1953 I might well have started dawdling about the Dublin bars, following my father downhill.

Now my aunt Sally and her husband Stanley Cooke-Smith came to the rescue, suggesting that I come to London that autumn of 1953, and stay with them in Hampstead in their attractive Victorian house in Oakhill Park, a woody cul-de-sac off Frognal. Stanley ran an antiquarian and second-hand bookshop, the Beauchamp Bookshop, in South Kensington. He was a charming bespectacled balding man with an untidy moustache: tall, stooped, cadaverous, every inch the Heath Robinson antiquarian, glasses perched on his forehead, studying rare first editions and precious bindings close to his nose. 'Suu-perb!' he would say, contemplating some rare folio.

The idea may have been that I would work in the bookshop, but initially there was no suggestion of this. I was to start at the bottom. So Stanley took me to the Labour Exchange in Westminster on my first day in London and, looking down the Sits. Vac. notices on a big board, he pushed me into a job as a city messenger and post boy at Leon Bros., Stockbrokers, of 4 and 5 Copthall Court, at three pounds a week. It wasn't much like working in the movies. There was the great London fog that winter – you couldn't see more than a few yards ahead – and after the Stock Exchange closed at half past three I groped my way about the city delivering settlement cheques to various other stockbrokers and banks, and then came back, licked the stamps on scores of letters and got the post out.

The office where I worked was literally Dickensian – flaring gas lights, high stools ranged against a long double-sided desk with the other half-dozen clerks perched on either side, the head clerk at the top. It was a silent, fusty place where the only sound was the sudden clicking of the ticker tape or the loud, commanding or sometimes panicky voice of one of the young partners in the next room, often on the telephone to their agent in South Africa where the firm handled mining and diamond shares. 'Buy at the seventeen rands premium offer! Sell at two-and-a-half percent plus on the profit margin!' and so on. Old Joe would have been terrified in the place. It was the sort of office where his São Paulo Tramway shares had gone down the tubes. For lunch, aping a Pooterish city clerk, I had a sandwich and a half of mild ale at a pub round the corner. I can't remember much else, except that I must have acquitted myself well enough with the stockbrokers and with Stanley, who, after my three months in the city, gave me a job in his South Kensington bookshop. I owe him much for that. He put London at my feet.

It was the start of my independence, of another and better education than I'd had at any of my schools: a little more money at the bookshop, three pounds ten shillings a week now, with thirty shillings a week for my keep in Hampstead, and eventually an ex-army BSA 250 motorbike for which I saved up twenty-five pounds. I also decided that living in artistic Hampstead

I should be a painter. So I went into the art shop next to the Everyman Cinema and bought shiny tubes of oil paint, camelhair brushes, an easel and several primed canvases – and painted some dreadful pictures. Luckily I didn't waste any more money on a beret and smock, which I would have bought in the art shop if they'd had such.

Still, as well as painters, Hampstead was for poets. So I took to poetry. And wrote a good deal of romantic stuff with an antique ivory dip pen and silver inkpot, closeted, Chatterton-like, in my heavily curtained bedroom. Some not too bad, I thought, one particularly about a girl I'd met, loved and lost back in Dublin. The last verse was suitably mournful:

> Now all the years in the air
> Are hers for the asking.
> Free as a rumour she may run
> All the lyrical land round in its colour:
> Through twelve shifts of the weather
> Til she come to that place with another,
> Where hills glide and great winds gather,
> There to enchant him with her laughter.

I hadn't forgotten movies. During the next eighteen months I watched nearly everything there was to see at the Everyman, then the best art cinema in London, with two changes of classic films every week (and no Pathé newsreels or Rank travelogues about the Three Counties Fair in Malvern): Eisenstein's *Ivan the Terrible* and *Battleship Potemkin*, and particularly the French classics, Clair's *Sous les Toits de Paris* and *Italian Straw Hat*, Tati's *Monsieur Hulot*, René Clement's *Les Jeux Interdits* and Jacques Becker's *Casque d'Or* with the beautiful Simone Signoret; Renoir's *La Grande Illusion, Une Partie de Campagne* and *The River*; Cocteau's *Les Enfants Terribles* and his *Orphée* – all of which made me fall in love even more with movies.

Meanwhile I thought to learn something about their history, which I did by taking an evening course at the City Literary Institute in 'The Art and History of the Cinema', a series of rather dry theoretical lectures with an exam at the end of the term which I at least passed with honours. I think I knew intuitively – or sensed it from the early Hollywood, helter-skelter one-reelers – that getting into pictures required some daring personal action, like turning up brazenly at the studio gates and asking for a job. Your literally 'broke' into pictures. It was all about chance, energy, personality – and charm no doubt, one of my qualities apparently, which Hubert and others had harped on about, to my detriment. In any case there was no course or exam then that could get you behind a camera.

But now in London I was at least working professionally among books at the bookshop. There were books, books and more books. Buying them on trips with Stanley, selling them, reading, dipping into them, taking Steegmuller's *Life of Flaubert* out to read on a bench by the Natural History Museum. And back in my swagged and sombre Hampstead bedroom, with ivory dip pen and silver inkpot, writing a first short story called 'The Tide' about two children laboriously making a wonderful sandcastle on a beach and being dismayed, forgetting that the tide is coming in to wash it all away. I suppose this was the start of my literary writing, though I didn't think it at the time. I still wanted to get into films, to get my Balzac short story adaptation made into a movie.

What impulse made me take up writing my own fiction? I think, like my pretending to be a painter, with expensive oils and brushes, it fuelled a need to create a fictional life, to get right away from what had pained me in real life. 'We lead lives of selected fiction,' Lawrence Durrell wrote. I had first chosen the life of a Hampstead painter, then a poet, and, failing in those scenarios, I now thought to try that of a Hampstead writer.

At the bookshop I worked in the basement, with Paddy the Irish packer, a delightful Tipperary man, slow and considered in everything, with his neat rolls of twine and reams of brown parcel paper on his bench. But he had one problem (or perhaps it was a virtue). He hated the telephone, and while Stanley was out to lunch, and Paddy sometimes had to hold the fort upstairs, and when the telephone rang … well, one day, coming up from the basement and without his seeing me, I saw him approach the ringing machine, essaying, like a bullfighter, a grab, a tease at the beast, then retreating, then having another go, but still refusing to pick it up, with a final retreat to Stanley's desk where he sat down and looked preoccupied with other more serious matters, while the phone went on ringing.

My main job was typing out the titles, condition and prices of hundreds of second-hand popular novels by authors such as Mazo de la Roche and Howard Fast, on Gestetner waxed paper, then duplicating the pages, stapling them and sending them out to all the public libraries. Upstairs Stanley worked the ancient wooden roll-of-paper till, pocketing his lunch money from it, and once or twice a year he got out a fine printed catalogue of the expensive books, antiquarian and modern first editions, many by Irish writers: Wilde, Yeats, Joyce, and James Stephens's *The Crock of Gold*, in 'near mint condition' I remember, signed by Stephens, priced ten guineas. Cheap at the price, perhaps, for such a fine signed presentation copy.

But Stanley was quite prepared to up the price if he knew a customer wanted a particular book. He had a rich French client in London who collected Proust's first editions, and had all of them, except his first book, *Les Plaisirs et les Jours*, a luxury volume with a foreword by Anatole France and romantic chocolate-box flower illustrations by Proust's friend Madeleine Lemaire.

Stanley bought the book from an extraordinary little man, Jewish and energetic, a Mr Mushlin, a freelance book dealer who would come into the shop without warning and tempt Stanley with his valuable wares, usually author-signed first editions, always in 'Very Fine' or 'Mint' condition, neatly enveloped in cellophane and highly priced. Mushlin had sold Stanley many of the Irish writers' first editions that Stanley specialized in, and now he came up with exactly the book that Stanley's rich French friend wanted: *Les Plaisirs et les Jours*. Apart from a dozen copies on special paper for Proust's intimates, it was one of only a hundred or so copies for the public. It was a heavy art-deco covered coffee-table book, with a selection of Proust's tyro fiction – decadently romantic, snobbish stories about duchesses, countesses and princesses with their gallant young lovers. Highly unrealistic but with all the spawn of Proust's future genius, when he refined his aristocratic idealism about the French *haut monde* into a picture of that society's terrible emotional and physical corruption.

Stanley wasn't greatly interested in Proust's work. It was the writers of the Irish literary renaissance who interested him, and in marrying my aunt Sally, whose father Old Joe had known all the writers of that renaissance and had many letters, papers and signed books from them, Stanley gained a particularly good contact in this field.

Knowing of Stanley's Irish interests, Mr Mushlin also came up with a selection of Joyce's first editions, *Chamber Music*, *Portrait of an Artist*, *Dubliners*, *Pomes Pennyeach*, and of course the prize item, the first edition of *Ulysses*, in 'Fine' condition, one of seven-hundred-and-fifty copies, in its big quarto, Greek-blue cover, with all the French printer's misprints. (Joyce scholars have since identified some of these as intentional – Joyce's intention, not the French printer's mistakes – all wonderful grist for the mill of the Joyce industry.)

The fiftieth anniversary of 'Bloomsday', 6 June 1954, was coming up, so Stanley agreed that I could clear the shop window and display just the five Joyce first editions. I did so, the books neatly spaced out with little notices which I'd typed beneath each of them – just the title, that they were first editions, with the dates and prices. People stopped and looked at the window with interest. But no one came in and bought the books. Stanley had priced the first edition of *Ulysses* at two hundred and fifty pounds, I think, and the other four books at around one hundred pounds each. There were no takers from my splendid window display.

There was one place, though, with more than serious money available for these sorts of books, and Stanley had good connections with this institution, the Ransome Library at the University of Texas, Austin. He sold all five books to them for a thousand pounds, I think. And cheap at the price. The copy of *Ulysses* that he sold then would fetch upwards of fifty thousand pounds today.

The one book (or the unbound pages, which were all there ever was of it) that Mr Mushlin never came up with was the real first edition of *Dubliners*, which my grandfather had at least printed, in 1909, when he started the publishers Maunsel and Co. in the 1900s, and was in the money. He knew Joyce and had corresponded with him in Trieste about publishing the short stories. Unfortunately a page proof got into the hands of the British authorities in Dublin Castle and reading 'Ivy Day in the Committee Room' they considered it disrespectful to King Edward VII, and threatened a libel action if the story was published. My grandfather's partner, a Mr Reynolds from Liverpool, took fright and burnt all the unbound sheets of the book, so that not a single page of this first edition of *Dubliners* has ever come to light. What was my grandfather doing meanwhile? He was taking a leisurely trip, driving from the Holy Land across Persia to Tashkent in an early automobile with a friend (the friend was driving, one hopes) and knew nothing of the book's incineration until his return. Mr Reynolds, though he knew about publishing, was thought generally (except by my grandfather it seems) to have been a man of sharp practice in the business. The story went round later that to start with my grandfather had the money and Reynolds the experience. After the firm collapsed, Reynolds disappeared with most of Old Joe's capital, and their positions were reversed.

Worse still, had my grandfather been on the spot in Dublin he could surely have managed to keep one set of the unbound sheets of *Dubliners*, and Stanley could have sold this unique printing for a small fortune to the University of Texas in the 1950s. My grandfather could have lived in clover for the rest of his life, and not worried about getting me into the merchant navy. Poor Old Joe. He shouldn't have gone to Tashkent.

To some extent, financially, he made up for his loss here with his famous Irish author connections. Stanley, in the mid-1950s, having laboriously catalogued all my grandfather's Yeats papers, comprising scores of letters and all the other papers relevant to his biography of the poet, sold this 'parcel', as Stanley liked to refer to such goods, to the University of Texas, for something in the region of $20,000. Stanley then sold to Texas all Old Joe's George Moore papers, which he'd had in the writing of his biography of Moore, and his book on the family, *The Moores of Moore Hall*, for half the price of the Yeats collection – Moore being lower down on the authorial stock market. (Unfair, I think, as several of Moore's novels, and certainly his three autobiographies, are splendid books, tactfully conceited and exaggerated as the memoirs are.)

I think Stanley took a fifty per cent cut in these sales to Texas, with Old Joe taking the other half, at least a hundred thousand pounds in today's money. But Old Joe continued to play the poor mouth, though now, with the Texas windfall, he needn't have had any more financial mournings over his cheque stubs with the smelly dachshunds on the sofa. Or worries about paying for me, which he was still doing, as I learnt to my surprise years later, paying Sally and Stanley another thirty shillings a week for my keep in Hampstead above my own thirty shillings, which was something none of them mentioned to me. Instead Sally said I was paying too little for my keep and should be paying more. My grandfather was not the only member of his family who was tight with the purse strings, but he was more forthright about his imagined penury, at least with the Butlers. He writes to Peggy, in response to some angry meeting or letter from her or from Hubert at this time in the early 1950s:

My dear Peggy,
Thank you, thank you – but I have never questioned your goodness, or that of Hubert towards Joe. On the contrary, I have acknowledged it with gratitude time and time again. What has annoyed me is that there is no reciprocal re-alisation on the Butler part of the very difficult moral problem with which I have been confronted for years, ever since Nat began to bring children into the world without the means to support them, and then himself became invalid.

My own view has always been that my first economic responsibility is towards Vera and David, then to Nat, and only thirdly to Nat's issue. Actually it has been a mathematical certainty that our spending on capital on two and three above will, if we live, reduce us to penury in a few years time. I do not think therefore that Hubert was justified in calling me 'mean'. 'Immoral' might be truer in the context of encouraging Vera to increase her expenditure on Joe. But perhaps Hubert has an exalted idea of my circumstances? …
Yrs. ever,
Joe.

Perhaps Hubert had got news of the Texas windfall? On the other hand, Old Joe's problems about Nat were surely more financial than moral, in his having to pay for the support of three of his son's children. And he was mean about this. But since they weren't his children surely he had some right to his miserliness in the matter? And Hubert might have seen this in his dealings with Old Joe about me.

There was one other interesting episode in my Beauchamp Bookshop days. Interesting because had the project succeeded, I might have got into movies straight away, though not as a technician, which was what I wanted.

Stanley had seen an advert in the *Telegraph* asking for unknowns, teenagers, to play the part of the young Alexander in an epic Hollywood movie, *Alexander the Great*, which the American director Robert Rossen was casting for. Stanley, all cock-a-hoop, said I must apply for the role at once. I was ideally suited for the part, he thought. But photographs, obviously, were required in the application. So Stanley arranged an appointment with a friend of his, Paul Tanqueray, a society photographer, round the corner in Thurloe Place. I went ahead with the idea, keen to embark on another fictional life, seeing myself now as a movie star.

I turned up at the studio and the society photographer, summing me up appreciatively, asked me to take off my shirt and vest. I stripped to my trousers. I felt he wanted me to take those off as well. He had bright lights and a matt cloth background. Against this, and blinding me with the lights, he asked me to assume various athletic poses, particularly a sort of Charles Atlas pose – biceps and pectorals tensed, hands clasped about my crotch. Suggesting I twist this way and that, he clicked away with enthusiasm.

The photographs were sent off and a week later there was a letter from the producer asking me to come for an appointment with Mr Rossen at the Grosvenor House Hotel on Park Lane. I was dazzled by the meeting in the drawing-room of his suite at the hotel. It was summer and there were a lot of flowers everywhere, and it was all very grand. Fully dressed now, we talked a little, and Mr Rossen was tactful in his enquiries and didn't look me over like raw meat as the society photographer had done. Then he asked me to read from the script, which I did quite reasonably, I felt. After twenty minutes he stood up and shook my hand. Yes, he surely thought well of me for the part. But in the event not quite well enough to cast me as the young Alexander. Perhaps, looking at the photograph [see illustration], my hairstyle was not quite Macedonian enough? The producer wrote a polite letter a week later declining my services. None the less I like to think I was within a hair's breadth of becoming a movie star. In the event Richard Burton played the older Alexander. Who played the young hero? I don't know. I've never seen the movie.

More important to me than books or being a painter, a poet, a writer or a movie star was my first experience of the world of magic make- believe, the professional fantasy life – in this instance the theatre – an experience supplied by Tony Guthrie who, expectedly, was the one person in my family who didn't think my ambitions in that direction were unreal. He was producing *La Traviata* at Covent Garden and later that year he asked me to come round with him and watch rehearsals. We went in through the stage door, and suddenly we were in the great gilt and velvet auditorium, where he took a seat in the stalls with his script, notes and, supplied by his wife Judy, a thermos of tea and a blanket, for it was a chilly day. The artistes, in this case the chorus and small-part players, were assembled on stage, with a man at an upright piano, the repetiteur, at the side of the stage.

Tony was usually much happier directing the chorus, bit-part players and spear carriers in his productions than dealing with the stars, who he thought had a tendency to get above themselves and be tiresome. Having consulted his notes, he stood up, all six foot six of him, and really pelted into the business. He clapped his hands and, with his fierce military smile, said: 'Well, then, are we all assembled? Right, Act One, the intro. And this time, can we have more speed on the tempo?' (Looking at the repetiteur and then round the stage.) 'And MUCH more twirl and swirl from all of you, if you please. This is not the death-bed scene. Not yet. Right?'

Right. The pianist played a faster tempo, the chorus belted into song and started a very vigorous swirl and twirl and Tony went to the back of the stalls to see how it all looked from there; and I watched it all, fascinated. This was the real world, or something very like it, for me. Later Tony told me he'd take me to see his agent the following week, to see what chances, what openings there might be in films for me. I was surely on the first rung of the ladder on my way to the stars.

TEN

I wasn't. There is now a stage demon, wheezy, sleek haired, jaw-crunching, jumping in with a puff of acrid smoke from the wings in the shape of my interfering father, wanting to change everything in my life for the worse. Nat writes to Hubert on 22 November 1954:

Dear Hubert

I hear that you have been recently in London and gather that you have seen Joe. It seems that he is trying to get an Irish passport, and it is possible that for ordinary travel and holiday purposes he might be entitled to one, though not of course without his mother's and my consent. We suspect however that his purpose is to disappear to the continent for a long period (say until he is 27) during a part of which he is liable to military service in this country. His mother and I have been very exercised and anxious in our own minds as to whether we should give this consent for a passport. (We have, of course, been aware that this matter would probably arise).

For different reasons Biddy and I are both against giving our consent; but I feel that perhaps you might think differently and that you might have some arguments on the other side which I ought to take into consideration. I would be grateful in any case if you could let me know how you feel about the problem.

My regards to Peggy,

Yours,
Nat Hone.

5th December. Since writing this letter (and not posting it) I hear that a new bill to be introduced in the present parliamentary session will make 36 (instead of 26) the age of liability to call up. It seems ludicrous that he should be facilitated to play hide and seek with the authorities here for that length of time.

Well, I had no mind to dodge any authorities in Britain, just as I had an even stronger mind not to do any National Service. Though I was born in London, my mother was born in Ireland and my father was certainly Irish, albeit Anglo-Irish-American, and I had spent over fifteen years in Ireland and only a few years in England, and thus so far as I was concerned I owed no military allegiance to Britain. Indeed, with all this parental Irish background, I could certainly have got an Irish passport, as I eventually did. Nor, if I got an Irish passport, had I any intention of running off to the continent for ten years. How my father got this nonsense into his mind I've no idea. But what is clear is that, having abandoned me as a two-year-old, and taken no responsibility for my upbringing later, and having done little or no work himself (least of all in the armed forces) and lived half his life off my mother's earnings, he was now insisting that I take the Queen's shilling. And to ensure that I did so he would deny me an Irish passport, which of course would not just have been available to me for 'holiday and travel purposes' but would have made me an Irish citizen and not therefore liable for military service in Britain, as Nat appreciates without his quite saying so. All this high moral tone of his about my having to take on obligations (which he never did himself) shows, in these circumstances, an extraordinary dictatorial impertinence.

What is perhaps more extraordinary – given that Hubert was a pacifist and a regular subscriber to the *War Registers International* magazine – is his reply to my father, dated the following week, 8 December 1954:

Dear Nat

I quite agree with you and Biddy that it would be a great mistake for Joe to try and dodge the authorities about military service. I was over in London and spoke to him about it all last week, but I found him, as did the Cooke-Smiths, very determined to go his own way, and I'm not sure what impression my arguments made on him.

He has not and does not have any moral scruples against military service. It is merely that he considers it a waste of time and an unnecessary obstacle in the way of his project for a training in film technique.

Personally I don't hold any very strong views about the disciplinary value for Joe of military service. I think he would probably quite enjoy it, being of a convivial turn of mind, but that he's probably right in thinking that the ordinary training of sloping arms and bayoneting sandbags would be a waste of time and not particularly elevating to his character ... So I am not thinking of it in terms of 'DUTY', stern daughter of the voice of God, but as a piece of legislation that Joe can't infringe without disaster to himself and which he had better therefore turn to his own advantage if that is possible ...

With this in mind I made enquiries about an interpreter's course when I was over in London and found out that these did exist within the military framework and also that Joe was ready to be interested in them. One does a few weeks ordinary military or naval service and the rest of the time is spent as an ordinary student of some language that the War Office considers valuable ... The most valued language now of course is Russian, and there is a course at Cambridge under a Professor Hill with whom I have good contacts. I am not sure how easy it is to be taken onto this course. I believe that Joe could, but that he would be much more likely to be taken on if he had already shown an interest and had some knowledge or experience. It's impossible to get into Russia but the day before I left I took him round to the Yugoslav Embassy and found that they were quite willing to consider the idea of an exchange. We would take a Yugoslav boy here for two or three months and Joe would go out there for a corresponding period. The only financial costs would be his fare to and fro ... With some experience of Slav languages and countries behind him he would be in a very strong position to be taken on for this interpreter's course, which would be of permanent value to him, and would rank equally with other forms of military service.

As regards his Irish passport, I certainly think he ought not to be encouraged to take out this simply as a way of dodging his obligations in the country where he works. Yet of course he is Irish, both by parentage and upbringing, and if he feels himself Irish, and is ready to accept some of the obligations and some of the privileges of belonging here, I don't see that he could be refused his passport ...

I hope in the meantime you will give your support to this interpreter's course idea, as frankly it seems to me the best way out. I think it appealed to Joe's imagination and while he wouldn't admit that he was ready to embark on it I felt I had broken down some of his resistance to the whole idea of the two years' service.

I would wait to decide about his passport until you see what his reaction is. I suppose when he gets to twenty-one he will be able to decide his own nationality himself, will he not? – provided the Irish government is willing to admit him to citizenship. So I would be inclined not to make too much of an issue of this, do you not agree?

Good wishes to yourself and Biddy.

Yours,
Hubert.

Another long and thoughtful letter (what a time Hubert spent writing letters on my behalf!). The reason for Hubert's stalling with my father on the Irish passport and citizenship business may be that, with his own linguistic gifts, and his study of Russian at the London School of Slavonic Studies before the war, he hopes that I may follow in his footsteps, and benefit as he did in doing this Russian course with Professor Hill at Cambridge. It doesn't strike him that I had little gift for languages, least of all the difficult Russian language. This Cambridge Russian interpreter's course, as emerged later, was in fact as much for the training of spies as for interpreters, a course which people like Michael Frayn took at the time. I don't suppose that Hubert had any idea then that the course was an entry stage for work in the British Secret Service and that, had I taken it, I might have ended up being shot by the Ruskies against a wall at the back of the Kremlin.

Meanwhile, as well as canvassing Hubert, my father had been agitating about my doing National Service with the one person who had been willing to help get me into the film business, Tony Guthrie. Nat writes to him from Cheltenham:

Dear Mr Guthrie,

I understand through Peggy Butler that my son, Joe, is going to see you about getting a job in the film industry. He is apparently keen to get in on the technical side and possibly has a superficial knowledge of it. I do not wish to put obstacles in his way, nor will I. On the other hand it would be utterly disastrous for him if people to whom you may introduce him were, out of kindness, to say 'Maybe – I'll drop you a line sometime.' He is older in sophistication than his age (sixteen and a half) but younger in learning and discipline. Though he may tell you otherwise he will have to do his National Service in this country if he is going to live here. (He is a British citizen, born in London, and the Irish authorities have refused him an Irish passport).

I think myself that the proper procedure for him is to join the army on a three-year contract, and to pick a trade relevant to the film industry. He would thus learn discipline and technical knowledge which he so far conspicuously lacks.

He would have to add a year to his age to join the army but there is no difficulty about that. If he did this he would be at least a year ahead of the other boys and would have fulfilled his obligation to the State.

Yours sincerely,

Nat Hone.

PS: Of course you will not show, or communicate the contents of this letter to Joe. Though you may send it to Peggy if you think that worth while.

Which Tony duly did, almost immediately as is clear, since he hadn't yet taken me to see his agent:

Dearie,

Thought you'd be interested to see this. I have replied saying, yes, I take his point about Joe doing his National Service, and as regards the film industry have said that the man I'm taking him to see is likely only to offer the most vague general 'advice'. I'll endeavour to make clear to Joe, if not clear already, the difference between this and any concrete offer of work …

Nat's letter to Tony continues his sporadic, cheeky and lying interference in my life. There are three or four examples of this in the letter. First because he says he's not going to put obstacles in the way of my getting into pictures, but then insists that I have to do National Service first, which would be the biggest obstacle to my getting into them. And then there were no National Service courses, apart perhaps in aerial photography, which would help me get into the film industry. He then says that I can lie my way into the army by saying I'm a year older! Well, lying about my age would surely have been tantamount to my lying to the Queen, which might possibly have resulted in my being put in the glasshouse for the duration. And certainly I wasn't going to lie to her, or indeed join her army. Then he says that I'm a British citizen, which I wasn't, and then that the Irish authorities have turned me down for a passport, which they couldn't have done since Nat hadn't as yet given me his consent to apply for one. Nat's whole letter is thus one of devious special pleading to Tony, so to persuade him to get me into the army. What possessed Nat to write such a farrago of fibs? Was he making a very late start in being 'responsible' about me?

In any case Hubert persists with me and with Nat in his idea that I should do my National Service, but first go to Yugoslavia to get the lie of the Slav and Croat land and its language. So Hubert writes to Nat again on the theme late in 1954, in a letter as ambivalent as his previous one to my father:

Dear Nat,

I heard from Joe this morning. He has been round all the various offices enquiring, and I gather that his view is that he would stand a chance of being accepted for the Slav languages course if he had some previous experience but not otherwise.

But if he registered of his own accord as an Irish citizen he would of course be in a much stronger position. As he has not registered already, he would, as an English citizen, start with a black mark against him.

That is why Peggy and I have decided to ask you to support Joe's application for Irish citizenship and I am making it clear to Joe that I am only asking you this on the strict understanding that he registers for military service (or 'volunteers' as the case may be).

I think if he got Irish citizenship as soon as possible he should then go to spend two months in Yugoslavia as I have been able to arrange for him, in Belgrade; then when he comes home he would be in a far better position to impress the authorities ... I have two or three friends who possibly might be influential enough to help, once it appeared that he knew something about the whole business.

I forget if I told you. Zvonimir Petnicki to whom he would go is a school teacher whom I first met in 1934 ... He speaks English perfectly and has latterly been employed as an interpreter for the various Yugoslav delegations abroad and has accompanied them quite often to London, New York and Paris. We would take his boy aged thirteen for a couple of months here to perfect his English as a pay back to them for having Joe. Joe would be staying with Petnicki's wife in Belgrade who I gather looks after the family and is amicably separated from Zvonimir. I liked her very much when I saw her. I have a good many other friends in Belgrade and Zagreb, mainly bourgeois like myself! – but sufficiently varied for Joe to have a wonderful opportunity of learning something about the place. And of course he would have to work hard at learning about the place. I am going to suggest to him that he tries to write about it while he is there and I will make an effort to get his stuff put into shape and printed.

How is his fare to be paid for? That is a problem we'll have to face. As it seems such an opportunity for Joe I am ready to take responsibility for collecting the money which will be at least fifty pounds even if it means sending the hat round among the relations. It will always be something for him to look back on and should be a real education as well as a way out of the present difficulty.

I think a friend of mine is still in the British Embassy in Belgrade. If I find he still is, I will ask him to give an eye to Joe now and again.

Yours ever,

Hubert.

However there was only one problem in the whole scheme, which Hubert doesn't mention. I was all on to go to Yugoslavia and stay with these interesting people, see the sights, learn a bit of the language, broaden my outlook and all that – but I still had absolutely no intention whatever of doing National Service or taking the Russian interpreter's course. Perhaps, for the sake of the Yugoslav trip which I was looking forward to now, I didn't mention this crucial factor to Hubert.

Nat meanwhile writes to me in mid-December 1955:

Dear Joe,

News that I have received from Hubert this morning inclines me to alter my decision about your passport. Subject to one or two conditions I am now prepared to give my support to your application.

The conditions are (1) that you register on the 18th at your local labour exchange (claiming exemption on the grounds of Irish citizenship) and (2) that when your passport is issued it will be held in my custody except at such times as it is required for the purposes of foreign travel. When I have evidence that you have complied with the first condition and that you are agreeable to the second I will give my formal consent to the issue of the passport.

Love from Mummy,

Yours, Daddy.

Another impertinent letter, and pompous in its legalistic, courtroom phraseology. Where did Nat get these phrases from? He may have remembered them from his time in 1930s Dublin, as a supporter of the Irish fascist Blueshirts, shooting the tops off the Brandy and Benedictine bottles in the Wicklow Hotel, when he was probably arrested and 'held in custody' for his bibulous target practice. And he must have unearthed them again so as to impress on me his stern and dutiful interest in my future. And it may have been that he actually thought I would comply with his conditions. In any case there was a delay in the whole passport matter, and Nat writes to Hubert, late in January 1956:

Dear Hubert,

I have been telling Joe ever since your pre-Christmas letter on the subject that I will endorse his application for an Irish passport if he sends me the forms properly completed. I did make and have made the stipulation that he should confirm that he is obtaining the passport for the particular purpose of carrying out your excellent idea. He knows this but we have not had a letter from him yet.

I am grateful to you for all the help you are offering him in this matter and I do hope if it can be arranged he will take proper advantage of your kindness.

His fare to Belgrade could be a difficulty. We are even more hand-to-mouth than usual. (My Mama might cough up his fare – twenty-five pounds return if he goes via Ostend and Salzburg) and I daresay he has some money of his own. An approach from you would, I'm afraid, be more likely to succeed than one from me.

Yrs,

Nat.

Hubert must have made the approach to me, and I must have agreed to Nat's conditions (though I never later fulfilled them) for I got my Irish passport, and the money for the return rail ticket was somehow raised, and Hubert gave me fifty pounds cash for expenses for the two months' visit, along with a small notebook in which he stipulated I must account for every penny of the fifty pounds when I got back. He also gave me half a dozen packets of Players cigarettes and bars of chocolate for me to give to his friends in Zagreb and Belgrade. And several rolls of lavatory paper. Such things were in short supply in Yugoslavia, he told me. And off I went, on my first real trip abroad, eighteen years old and fancy free – with Hubert's cigs and choccies and the fifty pounds of his money.

I can appreciate now, as I didn't then, Hubert's generosity towards me. But I see his careful financial mind too, in giving me the little account book. Hubert was still the pennywise Victorian and I was still the spendthrift, unreliable boy, likely to run amok with his money. It didn't strike him, I suppose, that I might perhaps fiddle my expenses, filling the account book with sensible costs, like Zagreb museum tickets and Serbo-Croatian grammars, when I had spent the money on movies and beer. On the other hand this may have struck him. But he was an honourable man and had the same hopes for others. And so I took the train, several trains, across Europe, and arrived in Zagreb in the summer of 1956.

I first stayed with Dr and Mrs Curcin, old friends of Hubert's, in their large, bright, modern apartment on the hill overlooking the cathedral. Dr Curcin was a great friend and admirer of the famous Yugoslav sculptor, Ivan Mestrovic, then living in America, and the flat was crammed with his work, which Dr Curcin was keeping for him – a petrified forest of heroic statuary, mostly in the Great Mother Earth department.

And it was here, lying out on a steamer chair on the sunny balcony recovering from a bout of 'flu, that I first met Marija, a friend of the Curcins, who happened to visit one morning. Marija was an art student, with long blonde Rapunzel-like rings of braided hair, wound round and round her head, until it formed a honey gold crown on top, a *retroussé* nose, high cheekbones, flawlessly pale skin and a look both virginal and provocative, making haughty distances with her big blue eyes one moment, filling them with scandal and mischief the next.

When I was back on my feet she showed me round the city, particularly the old medieval and baroque town on the hill, where we took the little funicular railway up, buying paper cones of hot chestnuts next to the ticket kiosk at the top, before wandering off along the pastel-washed streets with their sugar-stick churches, candlelit shrines and sudden leafy vistas over the later Hapsburg city far beneath. And it wasn't long before I was pretty well in love with Marija.

One day we learnt that President Tito was due to visit Zagreb, and we went downtown for the great event. Tito arrived in a huge American limousine, at the head of a long motorcade, resplendent in a white suit, streaming through the wildly cheering, waving crowds in Republic Square.

There was genuine delirium and tumult. It was my first taste of what was Yugoslavia's most obvious quality then – a sense of tremendous optimism among the people, a sure belief in their ability to create a new and united country out of that previously so divided and battle-scarred land; to forge a middle way between Marx and capitalism. These were days of hope in Yugoslavia, when young people from all over Europe came out to spend working holidays helping on various construction projects such as the Zagreb-Belgrade motorway. For many at the time Yugoslavia was the promised land, offering a way out of the impasse of conflicting East-West ideologies, a country where communism had a human face. And what with Marija's sensuous company and all the buoyant political enthusiasm of the time, I became a Titoist myself.

In those days, with Yugoslavia's sharply controlled currency and economy, life in Zagreb was ridiculously cheap for a foreigner with sterling to convert into dinars. For the equivalent of ten pence each Marija and I had the best cinema seats, and twice that sum took us out dancing, at the University Club or a student café, with spicy kebabs, wine and accordion music.

We were joined by her friends and I became a part of the city, an almost invisible foreigner (for there were no tourists in the city then), picking up some of the language as the autumn came, leaves falling lemon yellow in the light – embarking on a love affair and a political conversion at the same time, the first very much part of the second.

But this was not quite so as far as Marija was concerned. Neither she nor her parents were Titoists. Quite the opposite. Like the majority in the north they were Catholic and Croatian – and strongly nationalist in the latter cause, for the family had come from the old Hapsburg Catholic bourgeoisie, when Croatia had been a province of the empire and Zagreb had always looked north to Vienna for its religious, intellectual and material sustenance. And even farther north to England. Marija's parents, for instance, when I sometimes went with her in the afternoons to their dark, heavily furnished flat overlooking Strossmayer Square, always served up an English tea with Earl Grey's best.

Thus it was Marx and Cupid rampant, so that at first I wasn't conscious of it at all; I began to deviate from Marija, praising this great new socialist society while she mocked it gently and, when I persisted in my praise, condemned it roundly. 'Everything in Yugoslavia is run by the Serbs,' she told me rather bitterly, out walking one day over the crunchy leaves in the Tuscanatz woods. 'And they have no ambition but to dominate us up here, feed themselves on our wealth and hard work.'

I was unaware then that Marija, like many Croatians, regarded most Serbs, with their Turkish colouring and Orthodox faith, as rough and dangerous peasants – vile bedfellows, forced upon them most recently by Tito and his godless social order. I argued her points like a commissar.

'But Marija – surely you and the Serbs and all the other smaller republics here are in this together: for the sake of national unity, the greater good, sink or swim.' This was my sort of response; hers was of bitter laughter.

'If the Serbs really believed that themselves we wouldn't mind so much. But they don't. They simply want to use this enforced national unity as another opportunity to crush us.'

It finally dawned on me that Marija's antagonism towards communism and the wicked Serbs was rather stronger than her affection for me. The affair waned on her side, and I reacted by trying to save it with more specious Marxist argument – by pointing out to her, among other things, that appropriate emotion between people could only bloom in an appropriate society. For me that autumn love affair depended on the personal and political going hand in hand, and so I persisted in propagating this dubious equation.

Ah, that I might have kept my commissar's mouth shut! It all came to a head one day between us when, passing through the lovely candlelit shrine to the Virgin in the old city gate, I mocked the superstitious, outmoded values perpetuated there, in a world where there was now so obviously a new and caring God, the Socialist God. Such shrines would inevitably disappear, I said, just as nationalist antagonisms would in the coming Balkan millennium. After this spiel Marija was not available for any further political or emotional education.

Shortly afterwards I left for Belgrade, in the wicked south lands of the Serbs. I had already read some of the classic fictional texts on the city and the Balkans – John Buchan, Graham Greene, Eric Ambler, Agatha Christie and others: they evoked a land of rough adventure and revolution, of plum-pudding bombs, the Orient Express and *Stamboul Train*, a land of seedy spies and revolutionaries lurking in third-class carriages, nursing all sorts of mayhem. And wasn't it somewhere down there that the Lady Vanished and Hercule Poirot, waxing his moustaches, pondered the grisly wagon-lits murder? I was looking forward to all this mystery and derring-do. Belgrade at the time, as I saw on my way from the station, still had a lot of shabby Serbo-Turkish wooden houses and old stucco mansions near the centre, just the sort of houses for revolutionary assignations and bomb plots.

There were half a dozen of these houses on the street where my hostess Mrs Petnicki lived, and as the taxi drove along I hoped she might live in one of them. She didn't. She was a thoroughly modern communist woman and lived in a new apartment block at the other end of the street, just round the corner from the parliament building – Mrs Petnicki, wife of Zvonimir, Hubert's Yugoslav diplomat friend, from whom she was separated, living with her teenage son Petar who was to come to Maidenhall later.

Mrs Petnicki, ensconced as she was in her large new flat in a city with great housing shortages, was clearly a favoured member of the Party, and after my conversion to the Titoist cause in Zagreb I should have got on well with her. I didn't. She was a real virago – a small intense short-fused woman, who had been a brave partisan fighter with Tito in the war. I soon realized what the Wehrmacht had had to put up with when, swapping guns for words, she came to deal with me in a series of vehemently executed verbal attacks, ambushes, feigned retreats and vicious counter attacks. A guerrilla war broke out between us, with her son Petar acting as a spy for her.

The *casus belli* lay in the fact that, through other Belgrade friends of Hubert's, I met a number of dissident students – painters, poets and musicians who were not just against Tito but against everyone and everything. They were Serbian anarchists in the great Balkan tradition, these half-dozen Byronic souls and some equally headstrong, dark-haired, arrogantly beautiful girls. Despite my earlier political conversion in Zagreb I soon took to them, attracted by their vagrant spirit, talent, wit and idealism.

It was this that came to infuriate Mrs Petnicki, dedicated hard-line communist that she was. She attacked me, condemning me and my new friends as anti-social, anti-state and enemies of the people. She stormed at me that I was abusing her hospitality, consorting with criminals.

At first, since I'd told her nothing of these new friends, I wondered how she'd found out about them. Things became clear the next day when I spotted Petar, the wily son, following me secretly as I crossed town for one of my 'antisocial' meetings. Pretending ignorance of Petar's tailing me, I stopped at a shop window, watching his reflection in the glass as he paused across the street from me. Then I doubled back, mixing among the crowds in the main Terazije Square, before going in the front door of the old art deco Moskva Hotel and slipping out of the back entrance, losing Petar entirely. That was my first exercise in the art of espionage, mimicking the role of hunted spy. I wasn't unaware that afternoon that, by slipping my tail, I'd lurched into Greene-and-Ambler land, taken a first step into the shadowy world of spies and counter-spies.

A Serbian friend of Hubert's – a Mr Radovic as I'll call him here – the representative of a big western multinational company, had an office in this same Moskva Hotel. Shortly after the incident with Petar I used my introduction to him.

A number of western businesses had offices in the Moskva Hotel – a sort of safe house at the time when Tito's relations with the Soviet Union were going through a very rocky stage and a Soviet takeover was possible. Mr Radovic's suite, reflecting the clout of his company, was spacious, typical of the extravagant but now tawdry décor of the hotel: a flashy suite with Tiffany-style lamps and Balkan-Gothic stained glass windows, rather like an upmarket Turkish brothel.

Mr Radovic, middle-aged, withdrawn, professorial, seemed at odds with these louche chorus-girl surroundings. He took me down to the dining-room, offering me a tasteless lunch of meatballs and watery gravy, eating meagrely himself, diffidently and soberly peering at nothing in particular through heavy-lensed spectacles.

But he was friendly in a punctilious manner, spoke perfect English, and seemed wise and understanding of westerns ways. So I told him of my difficulties with Mrs Petnicki. He commiserated with me tactfully, but offered no other comments or advice. We finished with an inedible Serbian pudding – a prune or two in an *ersatz* chocolate sauce. And that, I thought, was the last of Gospodin Radovic. I resumed my by now very surreptitious meetings with the students.

These devil-may-cares, given the acute housing shortage in Belgrade and their generally anti-social attitudes, had created an extraordinary camp for themselves out of tin huts and sack tents on a marshy spit of land hidden by reeds and willows, by the banks of the Sava river across from the ramparts of the old town. Here they pursued their 'anti-social' activities.

In the daytime, the revolutionary *paysagistes* painted rather conventional views of the willows and the pearl-grey, misty water beyond. At night, in the warm autumn, things were much livelier, the encampment lit by dozens of candles by which some of the new arrivals still painted in the half dark. Indeed one of the students, an emaciated, tow-haired, most morbidly refined Serb, sunken- and wild-eyed, would only paint at night and on only one theme: corpses in open coffins surrounded by keening, witch-like women; macabre studies of orthodox funerals. The others simply chatted, played the mandolin, smoked, drank a little and canoodled in the velvet shadows. It all seemed very daring to me at the time.

Petar still followed me, but I'd become adept at giving him the slip and had told Mrs Petnicki that I was occupying myself daily at the British Council library over Serbo-Croatian grammars, which was partly true. It was here one afternoon that I spied Mr Radovic, fiddling among the books on the far side of the room. I went over, greeting him, and he jumped.

'Ah,' he said, 'I was just looking to see if the new Herman Wouk had arrived, *The Caine Mutiny*. They say it's very good.' The shelf he'd been fingering through contained nothing but non-fiction. He then suggested we walk back together to the Moskva Hotel.

'How are all those wicked student friends of yours?' he enquired lightly as we strolled across the Terazije. 'Fine,' I said. 'Of course they are all artists,' he remarked. 'Or do they talk politics as well?' 'No, not really. Just bohemians.' He seemed disappointed. We were approaching the entrance to the Moskva Hotel when, seeing something or someone at the doorway, Mr Radovic suddenly stopped, taking my hand. 'Do come and have lunch again,' he murmured, before, quite absent-mindedly as it seemed, he noticed the book he'd been carrying in his other hand. 'My goodness,' he said, 'how careless. I took this book away from the Council library without having it checked out.' He passed it to me quickly. 'I have to go, an important appointment. I wonder if you'd be so kind as to take the book back to the library for me? And return it in my name to Mrs Moore. Make sure you say it's from me, won't you?' Then he was off, and I had the book in my hand – a copy of Virginia Woolf's *A Room of One's Own*. It didn't seem his sort of book. I couldn't return it that day, the library being closed. So I took the book down to the charmed encampment among the reeds and willows on the Sava. And there, horror of horrors, I lost it, somewhere in the candlelit dark that evening.

I went back next morning to the Moskva to tell Mr Radovic what had happened with the book, and asked for him at reception. The clerk denied all knowledge of any Mr Radovic living at the hotel, as did the manager when I pressed him. 'No, you are mistaken. There is no such person here, or such a business company either. Try the Balkan Hotel opposite.'

My friend Mr Radovic had become a non-person overnight. I was puzzled. Something was up and it didn't sound good. That evening, when I got back to Mrs Petnicki's flat, still without the book, I knew the worst. I found her with a stolid, grim-faced man. Mrs Petnicki translated his questions to me. 'You have been meeting with a Mr Radovic at the Moskva Hotel?' 'Yes,' I said casually. 'You were seen receiving a book from him yesterday,' she went on. 'What have you done with it? This gentleman requires it.' 'I'm afraid I lost it, careless of me, left it down somewhere.'

She translated this back to the sour-faced man, who posed another loaded question. 'He asks if you lost it down by the river Sava last night, among your friends. You and your other counter-revolutionary friends,' she added ominously.

The fat was in the fire. They shot counter-revolutionaries in communist countries, didn't they? The secret police, and the grim-faced man was surely one of them, were looking for Mr Radovic's Virginia Woolf book, which must have been a code book, the pages marked in some special way, intended for the British Secret Service when it was deposited back with Mrs Moore at the Council library. And I had lost the book, down by the Sava, but clearly neither Mrs Petnicki nor the secret policeman believed this. The code book had been given to me by Mr Radovic, so I was clearly in league with him. We were both counter-revolutionary spies. The man, with Mrs Petnicki, searched my room and didn't find the book. The two of them then talked together. It seemed I was about to be taken off for more severe interrogation. But Mrs Petnicki, who, as a partisan heroine, must have had more clout than the secret policeman, prevailed on him to let me go. After the man had left, she said to me, surprisingly, 'You think you are Jesus Christ! You must leave, tomorrow. At once. You must get out of Yugoslavia at once.' I was very ready to comply.

There was only one problem. To get out of Yugoslavia in those days you needed an exit visa stamped by the police, and in the circumstances they were unlikely to comply. I was trapped. There was only one thing for it. At the time the British represented Irish interests in Yugoslavia, so next morning I packed my suitcase and went straight round to the British Embassy, and explained things to the duty officer, who passed me on to a middle-aged, sandy-haired man, and I told him all that had happened with Mr Radovic, Mrs Petnicki, the secret policeman and the students by the river.

'What was the name of the book that Mr Radovic gave you?' the sandy-haired man asked. 'Virginia Woolf's *A Room of One's Own*,' I said. He nodded. The whole business now seemed to make sense to him. He went into the next office and there was a short murmured talk with someone else. When he returned, he wrote me out a diplomatic *laissez passer* and stamped it with the Royal Arms. I made a diplomatic exit on the Orient Express that same day.

This was my first brush with the secret service world of letter drops, code books, and assignations in Balkan hotels and British Council libraries.

Spotting trouble at the door of the Moskva Hotel, Mr Radovic had unloaded the dangerous book on me and done a runner just in time. I suppose now I ought to have done the Russian interpreter's course at Cambridge and joined the service myself, without the meatballs and ersatz chocolate pud – dry martinis, shaken not stirred, instead.

But I appear to have done nothing on my return to Maidenhall and the Butlers. Indeed it seems I did nothing – at least physically – so successfully that Hubert became alarmed, or annoyed, or both, and wrote to my grand-mother believing me to be suffering from some physical illness. Then he wrote to his own doctor in Dublin, early in January 1956:

Dear O'Brien,

I think Vera Hone will have telephoned you by now about young Joe. I do hope you will be able to see him. I really don't think there is anything wrong with him physically, but his inability to exert himself is so extraordinary that I don't think one can just dispose of it by saying he is lazy. But I won't write you an essay on him here; I enclose two letters I have received about him from his hosts in Yugoslavia, which are more valuable than anything I can say, as I think it fills in the picture. It oughtn't by the way to be at all an ugly picture. Joe has plenty of admirable qualities and we are fond of him here.

I dare say you will conclude that the case is 'psychological', but my wife and I are very unwilling that he should consult a psychologist; it would merely increase that preoccupation with himself which is already considerable. In any case a psychologist would probably only point to various causes for the insta-bility in his background of which we are perfectly aware already, and are deal-ing with as best we can.

If you find there is nothing physically wrong with him you can help him best by assuring him of this very strongly. Several times I have hesitated to urge him to exert himself, sawing logs or something of the kind, because the prospect of having to do this has really almost made him look physically ill! And he argues so convincingly that it would be bad for him that he per-suades us sometimes against our better judgement. There are plenty of ways in which he could entertain himself or make himself useful out of doors, but he has shrunk from them all on his last visit. This was very disappointing to us because we had made a big effort to bring off this Yugoslav trip for him; we have to take two children of his hosts here in exchange and we thought he would make it his duty to see that the experiment justified itself and that he shared some of our bother this end. I incline to think that in the long run he will have profited by it but in the meantime one is more conscious of all the bother and expense it was.

I don't want to persecute him. A friend of mine who is Foreign Editor of *The Manchester Guardian* has asked Joe to try some articles for him on Yugoslavia. And Joe is trying and is plainly quite a good writer who has to take time to think things out, but he is using his preoccupation with his writing as an excuse for avoiding every other obligation. But I promised not to write another essay and here is one!

If you thought this a good idea and could prescribe to him some daily physical regimen, as strenuous as you thought he could manage, we would do our best to see that he carried it out.

Yours sincerely,
Hubert Butler.

I don't think I saw Dr O'Brien. Certainly I can't remember his prescribing me any strenuous 'physical regimen'. Perhaps I became more willing over the log sawing in Maidenhall? Certainly I was making notes for articles on Yugoslavia when I got back – as Hubert was very much encouraging me to write, and I was no doubt preoccupied with this, at the expense of pulling my weight in the household. It's true that I was selfish then in my preoccupations with other aims, mainly at that point trying to get into the picture business. In fact I think my problem with the log sawing was psychological. I didn't like it, and thought I was being press-ganged into ways that had no future for me. As Argyle at St Columba's had earlier pointed out to Hubert, since my Hone family had failed me, and because of the awfulness of Sandford Park and my failure to take much benefit from St Columba's, I was determined to rely on my own resources, to make a life for myself in my own way – which didn't include sawing damp logs. A selfish way no doubt, but I could see no other.

ELEVEN

When I got back from Yugoslavia at the end of 1955, I had my Irish passport. I was an Irish citizen, and so I didn't have to do any square bashing or, indeed, the Russian interpreter's course. Though with my time in Yugoslavia, a fair smattering of Serbo-Croatian and my experiences with the sly Petar and the mysterious Mr Radovic, I was probably well qualified now for entry into the Russian course – and from there, into the British Secret Service.

But the only thing I really wanted was to get into the picture business. For the moment, however, I could see no way in. First of all I needed a union ticket. So I made enquiries, back in London, staying with my aunt Sally and Stanley in Hampstead again, with the Association of Cinematograph Technicians in Soho Square. I had hoped for an appointment with Anthony Asquith, the well-known movie director, then president of the ACT. But for some reason he wasn't available. Instead I saw a minion, a superior Cockney clerk, not unlike Peter Sellers's later incarnation of the finicky shop floor steward in *I'm All Right, Jack*, who made the situation interestingly clear to me: I couldn't join the union without first working in the industry, and I couldn't work in the industry without first getting a union card. As neat a catch as that later Catch 22. This ACT union card became a sort of Holy Grail for me in the next few years.

I was once again at a very loose end. I went over to Dublin to stay with my grandparents, who had moved from their lovely house in the Wicklow mountains to their last residence, an attractive red-brick Victorian town house in Winton Road, just off Leeson Park. My grandfather, with his double specs perched on forehead and nose, smoking and groaning with the dachshunds over his cheque stubs, was not altogether pleased to see me. He doubtless foresaw that, with my out-of-work arrival, I would shortly be a further drain on his bank account. Whether because of this or because he was now genuinely well disposed towards me (or both perhaps) he got me a job.

Old Joe was a friend of Dr Arnold Marsh, the well-known Irish educationist and retired headmaster of Newtown, the notable Quaker School in Waterford, notable for at least one reason in that it was only one of a pair of co-educational schools in Ireland at the time. There were girls at Newtown … Dr Marsh had been asked out of retirement to take charge of the other Quaker co-educational school in Ireland, thirty miles north of Dublin: Drogheda Grammar School, a smaller but equally notable eighteenth-century foundation.

I took the train up to Drogheda for an appointment with Dr Marsh, an appointment, as he had indicated on the telephone, as an English teacher and housemaster with the junior boys. It didn't immediately strike me that with only four 'O' Levels and having left St Columba's in some disgrace only two years before I was ill-qualified for any serious teaching job. Of course in those days, and perhaps especially in Ireland, educational qualifications were not the be-all and end-all of matters scholastic. Indeed, with Mr Carpenter at Sandford Park, I'd had first-hand experience of the sometimes rather happy-go-lucky academic attitude in some Irish schools then. So I hoped that, with a bit of front and a tactful silence about my academic qualifications, I would get by.

Dr Marsh was a busy, genial, lively man in his seventies, with a great frothy shock of white hair and twinkly eyes. We met in his rather chaotic study off the main hall, which was beautifully Georgian, with a stuccoed ceiling and a black and white chequerboard marble floor. The spring term was starting in a week's time and Dr Marsh was busy with a hundred things, papers piled up on his desk, telephone ringing. He made no enquiries into my educational qualifications. Instead he asked what I'd been doing since I'd left St Columba's. I had worked in my uncle's London bookshop, spent two months in Yugoslavia. I had learnt quite a bit of Serbo-Croatian. 'Oh,' he interrupted, 'something of a linguist then?' 'Well, something there, yes.' 'And French, of course, you know French.' 'Well, yes, something there, too.' 'Good. Because I'll need you to teach French to the junior class.' 'Yes, of course.' 'And English, History, Geography – and Latin as well.' 'Latin … I see,' I said, with some doubt.

'But I understand from your grandfather that you got honours in Latin at Sandford Park in your Inter exam?' 'Well, yes, I did.' 'So Latin here will be no trouble for you.' 'No. No. I shouldn't think so.' 'Good. And you'll be housemaster in the junior boys' dorm. Four pounds a week, board and lodging included. Would that suit?' 'Yes. Yes, certainly.'

He stood up. 'Of course there's no corporal punishment here. Just detention now and then, by tending the vegetables or cleaning out the pigsty in the back yard. But there is one thing I'd like to ask of you. Being a co-educational school we sometimes have a little trouble, the older boys and girls …' 'Yes?' I was eager to hear the worst. 'Yes. Holding hands in the corridors. I want you to keep an eye out for that, Joseph. And discourage it.' 'Of course, certainly. Of course.'

Holding hands in the corridors … And no beatings. This was clearly a very much happier situation than at Sandford Park and St Columba's. Here the liberal ethic was being very properly interpreted. Why, I was only to discourage the holding of hands. Dr March gave me my return rail fare – three or four half crowns, I remember, for which he rustled and jangled absent-mindedly about in his pockets, and I took the train back to Dublin in an excellent mood. At eighteen, in the space of a twenty-minute interview, I had graduated scholastically, skipping 'A' Levels and a university degree, to the position of fully fledged teacher and housemaster. G.K. White and the Reverend F. Martin Argyle would have been astonished at my sudden academic rise, and no doubt derisive of Dr Marsh's easy-going recruiting methods.

But neither White nor Argyle was a Quaker. And that was a key point about Dr Marsh – he was a dedicated Quaker, and Quakers took a much more sensible attitude in their dealings with young lives – a kindlier and broader attitude than any of the traditional schools of the time. With the Quakers, book learning and exams were not the main point of school life; the rounded formation of character was more important, the aim to let young lives breathe, in their own way, to their own ends, be it carpentry or bicycle mending. Or, as I came to see at Drogheda Grammar, tending the cabbages in the back garden or cleaning out the pigsty.

Despite such Quaker leniencies in the educational field, it strikes me now, as it must have struck Dr Marsh then, that he was taking a risk in employing someone with no teaching qualifications whatsoever. Of course, he knew my grandfather, who must have vouched for me, but I think the real reason may have been different. Dr Marsh had that supreme teaching qualification: he was a kind man, with a great sympathy for the young, an understanding of where their real gifts lay. Furthermore, he had an intuitive knowledge of what their real problems and hopes were; how they could be unhappy, with a difficult family background, homesickness or whatever; and how their ill-discipline, foolishness or lack of academic interest was often a consequence of this. I think that, given his sharp intuitions, he may have sensed some of these same sympathetic qualities in me, and perhaps he sensed my own schooldays' unhappiness – so that, barely out of school myself, I would be resolutely on the side of the pupils, not the examination boards. Perhaps it's glib to say that Dr Marsh, though very much the busy and efficient headmaster in all matters of school detail, was a child at heart. But I think he was. And I suppose I was too, and he recognized this, and perhaps liked that in me.

But to return to that train journey back to Dublin. Other more realistic and worrying thoughts must have struck me. I had expected to teach only English. Now it was French, History and Geography as well. And Latin … I had certainly jumped a few academic hurdles with startling speed. But in a week's time I was actually going to be in the firing line – confronted by a dozen or so possibly unruly boys and girls, some of whom might know French and Latin better than I did. Still – if I could pretend successively to be a painter, a poet, a writer, a movie star with Mr Rossen and a spy with Mr Radovic, I could equally well pretend to be a schoolteacher. On with the motley!

In the event I found teaching remarkably easy. The pupils were eleven- and twelve-year-olds; a dozen of them, friendly, not unruly, and bright in many ways other than academically. I was brighter than them in that field, except in French and Latin. I got round the French problem by more or less cutting out the grammar altogether and by digging out instead a translation from a book we'd done in Froggy Bertin's Sandford Park French class, *La Belle Nivernaise*, a children's story of a family on a barge on the Nivernais-Rhone canal in the early 1900s. I got more copies of the book in Dublin and distributed them to the children, secreting my English translation I had in the high sloping desk at the end of the long room where we had our lessons. Off we went on every French class, up and down that delightful French canal with the little heroine, chapter by chapter, the pupils stumbling in their English through the French text, me correcting them from my crib. Sometimes, in order to show serious hard work, I would write up sentences on the blackboard in French, and then, with a flourish, the perfect English translation underneath.

I did the same thing with the Latin classes – keeping well clear of the grammar and sticking to the text I knew from little Mr Carpenter's classes at Sandford Park, and accordingly had the hidden crib for Caesar's *Gallic Wars*: 'All Gaul is quartered equally in three parts,' and so forth. When attention flagged I livened up the story by making a drama of it, like Asterix, embroidering the battles with the Gauls, dancing round my desk, with sword and spear play and an imaginary shield. It all went down a treat.

In English I kept clear of Shakespeare, which I'd never managed at school, and instead got them all Penguin copies of *Animal Farm* from which each pupil read a page. We really got into the story of the worthy old workhorse Boxer and the wicked porkers, which I treated straight, as a pure fable, without delving into its political undertones. They hugely enjoyed it.

All except one boy, who didn't enjoy any of the lessons, a tousle-headed, rather grimy boy who sighed and groaned in the back row. I mentioned this problem pupil to Dr Marsh. 'Oh,' he said, 'that's Stephen Pearce. Don't worry – he has no use for book learning. But he's good at lots of other things. Particularly dealing with the pigs in the back yard. That's his passion. Just send him out to the pigs at the start of each class. He'll be more than grateful to you.' Which I duly did.

'All right then, Stephen, off to the pigs!' I said jovially, arriving at each class. And he jumped for joy, running off to tend the pigs. Indeed Stephen was good at other things. He became a very fine and commercially successful potter after he left school. Stephen would likely have been crucified in any other Irish school, by beatings, dull pedants, detention and exams. As it was, left to his own piggy devices and unencumbered by dull scholasticism, he was happy and found himself in his later career. What a very sensible school Drogheda Grammar was.

Upstairs in the junior dorm I had a little room at one end, where I could look along two rows of iron bedsteads, six to either side – just like the dorm in Jean Vigo's movie *Zero de Conduite*. I would patrol the roost of an evening. 'Lights out, boys! And no talking.' 'Please, Sir, can't we have another five minutes?' 'No, Naismith.' 'Oh, please, Sir!' 'Please, Sir – tell us that story you started the other night, the one about the greedy boy who fell into a lake of marshmallows and sticky chocolate.' 'Go on, Sir!' 'Please, Sir!' So I recounted and elaborated on the prize-winning story I'd written for wispy Mr Sheehan's English class at Sandford Park. The lights didn't go out until well after time.

Thinking of *Zero de Conduite* again, I see now how, at Drogheda Grammar, in class and out of it, I was doing more or less exactly what the jolly, waggish, Chaplinesque teacher who followed the woman with nice ankles had been doing in that film. In another way I was aping schoolteacher Kingsley Scott and his Jacques Tati vagaries. I was mimicking school teaching. But I'd no alternative. The pupils enjoyed it, and so did I.

Then, towards the end of term, the great moment came. On a weekend when I was down with my grandparents in Dublin, my grandfather said he'd been chatting to Michael Killanin, the journalist and Irish peer from County Galway, at the Kildare Street Club, and had mentioned that he had a grandson who was keen to work in films; had Michael got any ideas about getting such work? Well, he had. He was producing a film in the west of Ireland, starting that spring, with someone called John Ford directing it. And if I went to the company production office, in the mews behind Michael Killanin's house in Landsdowne Road near the rugby ground, and presented myself to the production manager next Saturday morning, there might be an opening for me of some sort, maybe as an assistant director.

The great John Ford ... I had certainly heard of him, and I soon found out what he was up to in Ireland. He was coming over to repeat (as the producers hoped) the success of *The Quiet Man*, in a trio of films inspired by similarly 'authentic Irish' material: a rebel Civil War story, *The Rising of the Moon*, based on a play by Lady Gregory; a pastoral tragedy about an old Galway poteen maker from a story by Frank O'Connor, *The Majesty of the Law*; and a farce based on Percy French's famous narrow-gauge West Clare Railway, *A Minute's Wait*.

I went round to the mews next Saturday morning only to find a dozen other hopefuls hanging round the back door that led into the production office. The door was locked and repeated knockings led to nothing. I left, until the crowd had disappeared, then returned, shinned up the wall, dropped into the yard and was in the production office. Two or three small smart men in blue suits and rimless specs were barking down the telephone to London and Hollywood. They paused in their machinations, surprised.

'I'm Joe Hone,' I said. 'Lord Killanin sent me. He said if I saw the production manager he might have something on the technical side for me on this film.' Brows beetled. Silence. 'I'm Teddy Joseph, the production manager,' the smallest of the three men finally spoke up acidly. 'How did you get in here?' 'The door was locked, so I shinned up the wall.' Silence again. I supposed this athleticism may have impressed them, showed a proper initiative. 'All right, we do have a job as it happens,' Teddy Joseph said. Within minutes I was offered the post of third assistant director to the Master at a salary of ten pounds a week plus overtime. I had literally broken into movies. Ten days later, the term at Drogheda Grammar having ended, I was with the rest of the unit on the train to Galway.

At this time in the mid-fifties John Ford seemed to have been in pictures forever. His first big film, *The Iron Horse*, he'd made in the mid-twenties, but for ten years before that, with his brother, he'd turned out innumerable two-reelers: Westerns and other frontier films. He was contemporary with all the early greats – D.W. Griffith, Chaplin, Lillian Gish, Mary Pickford – and his later movies, *Stagecoach* particularly, were generally considered among the most notable the cinema had produced. John Ford was a legend.

But in Ireland, as a result of *The Quiet Man* and his Galway ancestry, he was a living God. Ford was deeply if sentimentally fond of Ireland. His ancestors had been famine exiles and, understandably, he regarded Ireland as his own lost estate, feeling its history of British oppression, poverty and suffering as a personal affront that he was duty-bound to commemorate in his work whenever possible – particularly in his Irish films. In the land of his fathers, even more than in Hollywood, he was a man not to be crossed, I was warned; being an Irish Protestant – the faith of the oppressor – I should best keep out of his way. This advice seemed incompatible with my job as one of Ford's assistants, which at that point I naively saw as a business of my looking through the camera and discussing the merits of the view with Ford. I soon learnt otherwise: I was to be the dogsbody of the unit, there to keep the rubbernecks at bay and get the boss a cup of coffee.

The first location on the O'Connor story, *The Majesty of the Law*, was in and around a little thatched cottage near Oughterard in the middle of Galway – a wild and beautiful landscape. We were up early on the first day's shooting: a lovely blue morning in April, the small hills a patchwork of various greens, the skies away to the west moist with running clouds. The light was peculiarly intense, yet varied, such as one only gets on Atlantic coasts, coming and going in brilliant spurts of colour and sudden shadow. John Ford arrived later at the head of a big cavalcade of American cars, completely the star of the show, stepping into what might have been a stage set for his Irish vision – the lone traditional turf-cutter's whitewashed cottage, the green hills of Ireland. Off we went, with Bob Krasker, the Australian cameraman who had photographed *The Third Man*, lining up the first shots with the boss instead of me. All the same, there was no doubt about it, I was in the picture business now. And in at the top with the great John Ford.

So why this long urge to get behind the silver screen? It had started at school when I was ten or eleven, at the Sandford cinema where we boarders were allowed to go to the first house on Saturday nights, but only with Dudgeon's approval of the show and if our conduct during the week had merited this glittering reward. This last proviso explained my somewhat curtailed attendance. All the same I managed to chalk up quite a score of films at the Sandford, different from the weekly Western or gangster movies – films that appealed to me in some deeper way: Johnny McQueen's two-day-long pursuit, betrayal and inevitable death in *Odd Man Out*, Harry Lime's similar nemesis in *The Third Man*, the doomed nature of happiness in *Brief Encounter*. These themes of trust and consequent disaster at the hands of a vindictive or uncomprehending world seemed very relevant to my own family and school circumstances. I fell in love with heroic failure. I came to believe that Martins should never have killed his best friend Harry Lime in the Vienna sewers, and that the girl gives him all he deserves by walking past him in that last long shot in the municipal cemetery about which Graham Greene had such doubts and Carol Reed was so sure of.

I didn't so much identify with the actors or the dialogue as with a film's mood, evoked by the photography, lighting, music, montage, the landscapes and sets. It was these that gripped me, and I wanted to create these technically inspired emotions myself. The real thrill for me often lay in the gaps between the action: the silent evocation of cobwebbed, curtained death-in-life in Miss Havisham's mice-infested, decayed wedding-breakfast salon in Lean's *Great Expectations*, the soundless leaf-falling cemetery road at the end of *The Third Man*, which parts the would-be lovers forever.

These silent scenes struck my heart. I suppose I had come to mistrust words – Dudgeon's words to me at the school, nearly always a prelude to sadistic punishment; the whispered words of my minders behind closed doors which usually heralded some unhappy change for me, being packed off to my real parents in England or to camp with strangers. Words had often been a prelude to pain for me, punishing directions to do something or go somewhere unpleasant. These films, though they dealt in pain and betrayal, justified it, explained it, and of course romanticized it with swelling violins or zither music. I was not alone in my feelings of loss. It was all potently up there on the screen. Like millions of others I found in movies what I lacked, or thought I lacked, in life. I was different only in wanting to control the manufacturer of the drug.

But for the moment, in the wilds of County Galway, I wasn't doing any of this movie creation. The best I could do, when I wasn't keeping the crowds at bay, calling the actors on set and running round on every sort of errand for Ford and the other two assistant directors, was to watch how Ford went about creating these moods.

Ford was tall and thin, almost willowy in an English manner, in loose slacks, with legs that were long and supple as a dancer's. Walking with him didn't result in any vertical movement. He glided along, *High Noon*-fashion, in a white bawneen jacket, yachting pullover, tweed cap, black eye patch, with half a wet cigar rolling in his mouth. He must have been in his mid-sixties at the time: his sight not good, face deeply lined, hands discoloured. But there was an air of concealed alertness about him. His physical approach to anything was direct and full of quiet intent. No gesture was ever aimless or wasted. He handled inanimate objects – his cap, his cigar butt, his big pocket handkerchief – as if they were alive, small animals in his hands. He surveyed a landscape or a space on the set with his one good eye with a studied amusement or satisfaction, as if his visual impairment was a special advantage allowing him to see things hidden to normal vision. He passed through the physical world singling out and naming its virtues, as an archaeologist will detect and unearth a whole civilization beneath a desert. Ford had that gift, of making everything that happened in the moment important, as he did in his movies. You saw and heard things you'd never noticed or heard before.

All of this, though, I learnt much later. My first day with Ford brought other more obvious lessons. Ford, in common with other energetic directors from the old pioneering days such as Howard Hawks, had a rough and ready sense of humour, a broad locker-room wit, which he often employed for professional purposes, to draw a performance from an awkward actor or 'blood' some junior technician. These little slapstick performances of his occurred quite frequently during the next three months, a play within the play, during which everyone held their breath – for, if they did not promote smiles, they usually brought tears instead. I was the first to inspire one of these show-stopping theatricals.

Rain had driven us all into the big marquee near the cottage for lunch an hour early, and I had taken it upon myself, as assistant to the Master, to remain outside, peering at the bruised sky, waiting for a break in the clouds. When this came, I went inside and sidled up to Ford like a toastmaster.

He was at the head of the top table, in the middle of a long story about the Old IRA – a lord at a feudal banquet, dispensing largesse to fifty or so of his minions. At what I, wrongly, took to be a break in the story, I whispered to him: 'It's brightening, Sir. I think we can start filming again now.' There was silence. Ford turned and studied me very seriously for a moment. Then he put away his plate and got to his feet. He reached for his cap and started to fiddle with it in a humble way. 'I'm afraid,' he said to the assembly, 'you'll have to leave your dinners. Back to work. My assistant here tells me there's been a break in the weather.' Most people had started to move before Ford, with much amusement, sat down again and the others resumed their seats. It was a bad moment. But he had done me a service, in tempering my enthusiasm. I was less free with my advice to Ford afterwards.

One learnt most from Ford not by talking to him (nearly always a hair-raising experience) but by watching how he looked at the set or a landscape, pondering how he was going to move his actors in or against it. For his greatest gift was his ability to narrate visually: to place and relate people unerringly – in their homesteads, barracks, their landscape, whatever; and giving them an identity, not through dialogue (which he kept to a minimum in his films), but by recreating their emotional history in their movements, gestures, customs, songs and dances, or anything else that displayed their physical link with life. His vision, from a lone horseman in Monument Valley to the mechanics of bridling a horse, was so accurate that you were convinced of an absolutely authentic spirit of person and place. He caught the essence of the matter; and the hell with the facts. Indeed, latterly Ford could not see well at all. He never looked through the viewfinder or watched the daily rushes, and he rarely looked at the script. It seems that what he'd long ago learnt to do was to mount the whole film in his head, shot by shot, then link the story closely with the location, get his stock company of actors together, and then have someone come in and photograph the result. The only piece of film lore I ever heard pass his lips was: 'Everything's all right with a picture so long as the audience isn't conscious of the machine.'

All that spring we filmed throughout the west of Ireland, each week or so moving on to a new location: in Galway town and Limerick, at Lough

Cutra Castle near Lady Gregory's ruined home at Coole Park, and finally at Kilkee, a little seaside resort on the Atlantic, the terminus for Percy French's famous West Clare Railway. Location shooting is a caravan that packs up each evening when the light goes yellow – the modern version of the old travelling circus, complete with temperamental fat ladies, strong men, performing animals and dangerous high-wire acts. And like a circus our unit died each night in a hundred anonymous hotel bedrooms, and had to re-assert its corporate identity every day anew. Sometimes, hanging around in the rain on blank days, one doubted that the co-operative will would ever return to start the circus up again.

Ford would confine himself to his hotel bedroom, incommunicado, with his box of Havana cigars that Ernie O'Malley, his sidekick and Old IRA friend, carried about with him. The production manager and the accountants shouted long distance on the telephone, or loomed ominously in the lobby; actors wandered about brokenly, all got up and nowhere to go; the electricians and lower orders played cards and covertly drank stout by the neck behind the mobile generator. The one thing Ford (a Trojan on the bottle himself when he wasn't filming) vehemently prohibited on loca-tion was drink, a diktat which did not go down well with some of the Irish actors. Only one of them, the famous Irish comedian and panto star Jimmy O'Dea, had the better of Ford over this, in a scene I witnessed that would have been a pearl in any of Ford's films. O'Dea, a rubicund pixie of a fellow hardly five feet tall, was having a quiet bottle of stout in the back bar of the hotel after his first day's work when Ford – all six-foot-two of him, glower-ing, cap pulled down over his ears – surprised him, saying: 'Now Jimmy, let's start the way we mean to go on. Put that drink down.' O'Dea's nose rose a fraction over the bar as he fed himself some more liquid. 'I will not,' he said. 'Me time's me own, after business hours.' 'That's enough now, Jimmy. I'll send you back to Dublin.' 'Right you are. Just say the word.' O'Dea held his ground and Ford retired. O'Dea had his glass of stout every evening. Ford could be matched, but you had to be Jimmy O'Dea to do it.

When we got to film in Galway town, in an alleyway near the river, Ford was setting up a scene outside a murky doorway in the pouring rain – the rain supplied by the town watering cart (cameraman Bob Krasker was very keen on town watering carts and big ten-kilowatt arc lights behind the corner, with which he'd so brilliantly evoked ruined Vienna in *The Third Man*). This was a scene in which an IRA man, keeping watch outside the door, was to walk across the alley, look both ways and return. No dialogue. For some reason there wasn't a bit-part actor available for this role, and Ford approached me. 'All right, Hone, you're the right size and suitably suspicious-looking. Get to make-up. And wardrobe – they'll have a dirty trench coat and a slouch hat for you.' 'Make-up, Mr Ford? A trench coat?' I was astonished. 'You heard what I said.' 'To act, you mean?' 'Yes, to act, Hone – the IRA man.' 'Yes, Mr Ford, of course.'

Heart thumping furiously I went off to make-up, then wardrobe. My goodness, this was surely going to be my real break in pictures – as a movie actor, such as Robert Rossen, casting for *Alexander the Great*, had not allowed me. But Ford had seen the light and was now about to employ my hidden dramatic gifts. He'd be the making of me – as a new Montgomery Clift or a young Bogart, or at least as a member of his stock company back in Hollywood.

All togged up, the slouch hat at a rakish angle, I got into position by the doorway. 'Right, we'll rehearse it,' Ford said. 'Quiet, everybody!' one of the assistants shouted. 'You just walk out the doorway, Hone, look both ways, cross the alley, then walk back.' We rehearsed it, satisfactorily it seemed. 'Okay, QUIET! We're shooting,' the first assistant yelled. The arc lights fizzed into brilliant light, the town watering cart, attached to several sprinklers over the alley, started to spurt, the camera crew went into their preparatory litany: 'Turn over … speed … mark it!' and the clapper boy came out with his board. 'Scene 78, take one!' CLAP! Dead silence, except for the gentle rain. I slouched off across the alley, Bogart fashion, but halfway across I realized I was supposed to have looked both ways before I set out. Or was I? I stopped, undecided. 'CUT!' yelled Ford. 'I'm sorry, Mr Ford – am I to look both ways at the doorway, or halfway across?' 'Either will do, Hone. Either,' he said dryly. 'Okay, we're going again. First positions!' the assistant cried. And I went back to the doorway. On the next take I looked both ways at the doorway, but thought to embellish my performance by looking both ways halfway across as well. 'CUT!' yelled

Ford. 'Once is enough with the looks, Hone. You're not watching a tennis match.' Another take. And this time I noticed the rain had increased. I could hardly see where I was going. I stopped again, nearly bumping into the camera. 'I'm sorry, Mr Ford … I couldn't see …' Ford was on his feet now. 'You know something, Hone? You're more fucking trouble than John Wayne. Okay, let's go again.'

We did another take and this time the rain was belting down from the sprinklers. 'That's better, Hone,' Ford said. 'But we'll do it one more time, just to make sure.' I did it again, and now the rain was really soaking me as I crossed the alley. But Ford was finally pleased. 'Okay, cut – and print it!' he growled. I came over to him, a drowned rat. Wet cigar rolling in his lips, Ford was smiling. Everyone was smiling behind the camera. Everyone was happy. Clearly I'd given a show-stopping performance. And of course I saw now why Ford had increased the rain on each take. I'd come to see already on the film how Ford provoked, 'blooded' young actors to get a really edgy performance out of them, and he'd been 'watering' me to get the same effect.

But then the doubt. I suddenly realized, with the smiles all round, and the laughs now, that Ford had been playing an elaborate practical joke on me, turning up the rain intentionally on each take so that I'd get absolutely soaked. I had to face it then – I wasn't going to make it as a new Montgomery Clift. Though it seemed to me I'd made a damn good try at taking over from Humphrey Bogart.

The final two weeks' filming in Kilkee of Percy French's railway farce, *A Minute's Wait*, were lovely days. We went out every morning on the old West Clare narrow-gauge railway, which was being closed down after we left, filming along the line – the squat Puffing Billy engine shrieking and bellowing for the last time across the stony landscape of West Clare, two canary-coloured wooden carriages full of yelling actors, the guard's van packed with cameras and picnic lunches. At Kilkee there were scenes of slapstick and Irish railway blarney: porters falling over themselves, farmers' wives losing all their chickens, lovers' tiffs, a lot of drinking and 'Are you right there, Michael, are you right?' sung in the station bar. This blunt knockabout Irish comedy was very much to Ford's taste, and he filmed it with relish and fluency, like a man interpreting a happy dream for the fiftieth time.

On the last evening Ford suddenly arrived at the smallest of the three Kilkee hotels where I and the other junior technicians were quartered. We were just starting a chicken dinner, and he asked if he could join us. And then he did an unexpected thing. 'What about some wine?' he asked the waitress. 'Red or white?' she said, thinking her description detailed and the choice lavish. But Ford seemed to know about wine and together we went down to the cellars, where we found racks of wine and some fine vintages. In Irish provincial hotels there was an idea that the fresher the wine the better, like milk, and so this old wine had lain there for decades. I remember we had two bottles of fine old Paulliac claret at the hotel's usual price for any bottle of wine, seven and sixpence – about forty pence now.

But what I most remember was Ford raising his eye patch in the bad light of the cellar and scrutinizing the labels, fingering the old bottles. There was nothing of the wine snob in his gestures: for him these bottles were beautiful objects, and the wine inside was even more to be honoured – an elixir, full of old custom, toil and taste, part of a precise landscape, some great vineyard in the south. He might just as well have been handling a finely-balanced revolver or stroking the flanks of a proud cavalry horse. And that was what I learnt most from Ford – to forget all the machinery of the cinema, the scripts, lights, the mechanical tricks; the only real trick was to get out into the world and look at things properly and handle them well.

Hubert, meanwhile, wasn't greatly pleased with my new movie career. After the filming was over, and in the light of a piece in the *Irish Times* by a journalist, Leslie Deakin, about my working with Ford, Hubert writes, in the latter part of a letter, to my grandfather in the summer of 1957:

> I dare say Leslie Deakin's rather fanciful account of Joe in the *Irish Times* will have annoyed you by its inaccuracies rather than pleased you by its praise. I think he may prove a creditable grandchild to you and he the one with the least stable background. Pamela ['*Mary Poppins*'] Travers has committed herself to Camillus, and I understand that the other two [*Geraldine and Antony*]have had some money left them.
>
> Joe dropped in here with Bob French and Leslie Deakin who may well be the source of most of the flattering inaccuracies about Joe that appear in the press. Leslie Deakin is a bustling, talkative, go-getting character and at present

seems to be pushing Joe hard along in the usual good-hearted, vulgar cinema, theatre-television-BBC way of doing these things. We think it frightful but it appears to be universal, and Joe I think has an inner integrity which will survive these ghastly orgies of nonsense.

A little severe, but Hubert didn't understand films, and didn't like them. On the very few occasions he went to the pictures with us as children – to *The Wizard of Oz* I remember – he would call out loudly in the middle of some scene: 'Who's that girl? How did she get there?' 'Shhssh! Shhssh, Hubert!' No, Hubert wasn't a movie man. But why be so hard on the movie and theatre business? After all his brother-in-law, famous theatre director Tony Guthrie, was in something of the same vulgar line of country. Hubert himself, in the early thirties, had made one of the best translations of *The Cherry Orchard*, which Tony produced at the Old Vic with Charles Laughton, Ursula Jeans, Roger Livesy, Marius Goring, James Mason and other rogues and vagabonds. So Hubert must have had some theatrical experience, although it was to do with Chekhov's great play, not with the sentimental goings-on of Judy Garland in *The Wizard of Oz* – or with John Ford, equally sentimental, back on the 'oul sod' in County Galway. But I think the main reason for Hubert's resistance to my career in the picture business was that, with my 'fatal charm', it would be very bad for me – as emerges in the earlier part of the same letter to my grandfather:

Dear Joe,

Peggy and I have just been revising our extremely unimportant wills (we leave everything more or less to Julia) and think, though our motive may irritate you a bit, that we ought to tell you that we find with a good deal of sadness that we won't be able to leave anything of consequence to Joe. We are enquiring if one of us could take out a small life insurance on his behalf but it would amount to very little, just an indication that he had not been forgotten and we shall leave him a few personal things and that is all.

Well, we don't know and you had much better not tell us – it is no business of ours – if you or Vera are leaving anything to Joe; we only want you to know that we can't, though if by some highly improbable event we did come in for money, we should try and do something for him. He has behaved very well to us, and though he has a very difficult and talented temperament and is, both in his virtues and his vices, totally unlike either of our families, I think it unlikely that we shall quarrel with him or feel anything but affection and interest in him and his concerns.

He has, of course, no notion yet about saving money and if we were able to leave him anything we would tie it up well so that he could not touch the capital; he is getting a good deal more sensible, but he is obviously finding it pretty hard to cope with the fatal gift of charm, which he shares with most of his family. Those who are fascinated by him have allowed him to get away with far too much and he seldom seems to leave a place for the next without a great many loose ends and an atmosphere of spiritual untidiness. But many of his faults may be due to his lack of a secure background. So don't let him irritate you …

So there we have it – that fatal charm again, harped on like the words of a Cole Porter song. I certainly wasn't aware at the time that I had any fatal charm. But I knew very well that if I was to get into pictures I would have to summon up a good deal of front and brashness.

Finally, of course, there is the money business again between Hubert and my grandfather. It was good of Hubert to put his cards on the table about this, in saying he couldn't leave me anything – which as well as this information was also clearly an indirect way of saying to Old Joe that he should leave me something: which Old Joe must indeed have been irritated by, for he didn't leave me a penny. Probably just as well. With that fatal charm I'd likely have blown it all in a month with call girls and pink Champagne.

TWELVE

When Ford's travelling circus finally packed up in Kilkee I was at another loose end. Of course I wanted to go on working in the picture business in London; but one of the British technicians in Galway had confirmed what I'd been told before, that without an ACT union card I'd never get any film work in England, that I'd only been employed with Ford in Ireland as a special concession because I was a friend of Lord Killanin, the producer.

This was bad news. So before the unit disbanded I plucked up courage and asked Ford what I might do to further my career as a mechanic behind the silver screen. He raised his eye patch and looked at me doubtfully. Then he smiled. 'I'll tell you what, Hone. Go see an old friend of mine in London, the Irish director Brian Hurst. He'll probably have some ideas for someone like you ...' He rolled the wet cigar about his lips some more and smiled again. I couldn't see what he was smiling about, I'd never heard of this director Hurst. Ford gave me his phone number.

So it was back to London, staying with my aunt and uncle Sally and Stanley, up in Hampstead. On a morning a few days later I called Mr Hurst. 'Hullo-o-o ...' a deep seductive voice with a touch of Irish brogue answered. But then the tone changed. 'Who dat? Who dat there?' he went on. The accent was bright West Indian now. 'Ah … I'm Joe Hone. A friend of John Ford's. I've been working on a picture with him in Galway, and he gave me your name and said I should call you, that you might have some ideas about how I could get into pictures over here, and …' 'Come right on round, Joe Hone. Have a drink. I'm about to have a glass of the Old Widow – Champagne to you.' 'Come over now?' It was ten in the morning. 'Of course, if you want to get into pictures, no time to waste. 24 Grosvenor Crescent Mews, Belgravia.' He emphasized the 'Belgravia' in a mock-posh voice.

All this was a bit strange. An Irishman, mimicking a West Indian, drinking Champagne at ten in the morning? But I went right round. I now had to make another break into pictures, and this sounded an easier way than having to climb over a high wall.

The small mews house was at the end of a cul-de-sac behind St George's Hospital, with an alleyway leading off at the end to the Grenadier pub and Knightsbridge. An athletic young man in a striped matelot T-shirt, holding a dishcloth, opened the door. 'Mr Hurst – be with you in a minute,' he said abruptly, leaving me, clearly annoyed at something. I went inside, straight into a large gloomy living room, lit only by a big front window and a sunlit skylight far above, giving a spotlight effect on the floor beneath.

I wandered round hesitantly. There were some very good pictures on the wall – I recognised a blue period Picasso and what looked like a Monet, and a Russian icon above the empty fireplace. A long scruffy sofa, a big record player, some books and Modigliani-like sculptures. But the room was dominated by a huge Elizabethan-style high-backed armchair, covered in a Turkish kilim, set next an ancient electric fire. A rather decrepit, threadbare air to everything.

I heard a lavatory flush, turned, and there was Mr Hurst, doing up his flies, moving from the shadows, pausing in the skylight spotlight, so that I saw him clearly now. In his late fifties, I thought, a big man, robust, a flow of white hair over a well-fleshed face, intense twinkly blue eyes, a wry smile. He was wearing an Aran-knit cardigan with well-cut slacks. He came across the room, a gliding walk, looking at me, very relaxed. We shook hands. A graceful gesture. He had fine hands. Then he made for the big armchair, collapsed, took out an asthma inhaler, and drew on it deeply.

When he had recovered, he said: 'Get him, that one …', speaking of the athletic youth who had let me in. 'Doing his Bette Davis act. Getting above his station. Supposed to cook and clean for me. Now he thinks he's my live-in lover. Not that I don't fancy him. But there's a limit with servants.'

I perched on the sofa. 'Yes. Yes, of course.' I was rather nervous. I hadn't expected this sort of talk. Hurst took another go at his inhaler, put it down. 'Not a lot of good.' Then he spoke up loudly in an imperious voice. 'Charles!' he shouted. Then he turned to me, sotto voce. 'He likes to be called Charles … Charles! If you've got over your pet, bring in that Champagne. And the Guinness. Did you hear me, Charles? We have a visitor from Ireland, Mr Hone.' 'Yes, I heard you … coming.' Petulant.

He came in with two large fluted glasses, a bottle of iced Veuve Clic-quot and one of Guinness. He popped the Champagne and the Guinness, mixed the foaming drinks together in the glasses, then handed me one. Hurst raised his glass, tasted it with relish. 'See, I've gone native this morn-ing, with my Aran knit and the Guinness. But with the Old Widow to go with it. Eases the start of the day, don't you find?' 'Well, yes. Yes …' I sipped my black velvet. 'It's not the alcohol I like – just the taste. So,' he went on. 'You were working with Jack Ford in Galway?' 'Yes.' He raised his glass again, speaking softly now, the Irish burr more pronounced. 'Well, here's to you, Jack. "May the road rise to meet you, and your shadow never get longer."' Another go at his drink. 'Jack Ford likes this. Pretends he's only a hard liquor man, knows nothing about wine. In fact he knows plenty about wine.' 'Yes, I know.' And I told Mr Hurst about our last night at the hotel in Kilkee and how I'd gone down to the cellar with Ford and how he'd looked at all the bottles and labels like an expert. 'That's Jack all right. Expert on drink, till it comes out his ears.' 'Of course not when he's filming,' I said, the puritan know-all about Mr Ford now. 'No, not when he's shooting … And he doesn't go whoring then either.' 'Whoring?' I was surprised.

'You thought he was an innocent that way, did you?' 'Well, yes. I mean no. I …' 'You were right first time. He is an innocent, and makes sure he keeps it that way, and he's made some great pictures that way, too. But he can't handle real life – has to play the tough guy there, all those locker-room jokes. Backslapping, booze and fearful of women. I tried to wean him off that. In the thirties he was over here preparing *The Informer*, we went to Paris one weekend. I'd lived there, learning to paint in the old days. I took him to a brothel I knew. Nice girls but rather cramped accommodation. We had to share a room. I looked round after a bit, and there he was happily sawing away like a lumberjack. He turned and said "Pleasant, isn't it?"'

'I see. I rather got the impression he was very much the good Catholic Irishman.' 'He is, but only when he goes to Mass – and confession.' Hurst gave a wicked smile then, so, encouraged, I went into my movie-buff mode. 'Whoring, yes,' I said, and continued sagely, 'and of course he does treat women badly in his pictures. That long scene in *The Quiet Man*, when John Wayne manhandles Maureen O'Hara for about five minutes, dragging her across that field. And I saw him do just the same sort of thing with a young actress out at Kilkee station. Punishing the woman.' 'You're right, Jack puts himself across very much as a man's man. And he is – he fancies men and fears women. Only feels safe with them when he's 'blooding' them on the set – or screwing them.'

'I'd no idea ...'

'Of course, as a wicked Protestant from the black north, it's never been a problem for me – with men or women; though I've since taken a reserve position in the faith. I'm Catholic now. For my sins. Better chance of redemption there. "Be Prepared," I say. I was a boy scout, up in the north. Scoutmaster had his way with me. I should have thanked him.'

'I see.'

'And now you want to get into pictures?' 'Yes, but I can't get a union card.' He raised his glass. 'We'll see what we can do about that.' And that was the start of a long and lucky, often funny and usually happy friendship with Brian Desmond Hurst.

Brian was the most genial rogue I've ever met – a wit, joker, splendid raconteur, widely talented and generous, a storyteller, a fantasist. That was the key to him. He lived on a different plane to most of us. Waking up every morning he saw the day ahead as an exciting draft script that he would flesh out according to his whims, depending on who telephoned or who turned up. The day in any case would be lived from the commanding heights in his battle against the mundane, against the dull and the dreary who would be routed and victory celebrated in a dozen surprising ways, the script produced in full colour, with every kind of droll or saucy performance, and with no expense spared.

But as in Ford, his best friend, there was a brutal streak in Brian – partly his nature and partly because he was a movie director of the old school. This brutality could suddenly explode in work or play, with producers, actors, his boyfriends or with others, high or low, for Brian was a real 'dukes to dustmen' man. He could be cruelly rude and dismissive with anyone, just as he could charm them off the trees with a flow of Celtic poetry and blarney.

He was gay of course, though not in the least effeminate. As he'd intimated to me at our first meeting, he liked – indeed, as I afterwards learnt, had loved – women as much as men, though latterly he'd concentrated on 'the younger man'. He rarely flaunted his sexuality, but he never hid it. And this was risky at a time when you could be jailed as a practising homosexual, as his friend Lord Montagu had been just before I'd met Brian. Jailed or much more likely blackmailed, as some of his friends were then. To be clearly homosexual wasn't the easiest way to get to make pictures at the time either, particularly with the puritan Lord Rank, nominally head of the Rank Organization out at Pinewood, for whom Brian made most of his last films. But Brian didn't give a damn. As far as the police were concerned he led a charmed life in his excursions picking up guardsmen in Hyde Park and round at the Grenadier pub. Of course he fancied young policemen, too, and I imagine had come to arrangements with some of them in the Chelsea force, so that he wouldn't be bothered by the law. He was part of the rich rough-trade gay London mafia of the time, with the difference that Brian was openly happy in that world while most of the others weren't. 'I am as God made me,' he once told Lord Rank, when his Lordship had popped an awkward question to him about him 'proclivities'.

That was another big factor in Brian's life – God, and most particularly St Teresa of Lisieux, whom he had made his patron saint. I used to wonder how, in all conscience, Brian could square his promiscuous gay sex life with his Catholic beliefs and his passionate veneration of this good woman. I think Brian knew that, if his conscience was bad, he would always be forgiven by the saint, through his prayers to her, and by big whacks of cash and confession when he went to her cathedral in Lisieux, as he often did. St Teresa watched over his future, his movie work and everything else, guiding him along all the right paths. 'For He shall give His angels charge over thee to keep thee in all thy days …' was one of his favourite quotes from the Psalms.

Though I think the real reason for Brian's happy-go-lucky, the hell-with-it attitude to life was that as an eighteen-year-old soldier with the Royal Irish Rifles at Gallipoli he had faced and suffered far more than most men, even in war, from the appalling carnage there and the terrible deaths of his comrades, so that any problems or setbacks – the dross of real life that might beset him afterwards – would be of no real consequence. He had survived the very worst at Gallipoli. So it was to be Champagne in the morning and a bottle or two of brown ale for the guardsmen at night. I was to learn later of his time in the army. In the meantime he took me under his wing and in the next ten years or so that I lived for a time in his mews house and went abroad with him, he never laid a finger on me.

He came to refer to me in company as his Irish 'nephew'. This wasn't so that I wouldn't be embarrassed with him and his queer company. I think Brian needed a pretend nephew as a familial stay in his later life: all his own family, including his brothers and sisters from his youth in Belfast, having died or lost touch with him at that point, apart from his adored and very wealthy older sister Patricia who lived next to the Dorchester Hotel. I was a pretend nephew – or indeed a pretend son. I think he felt something of that for me, knowing, as he came to, of my own broken family background. However, some years later he told me he had a son, a married, very conventional and now middle-aged engineer in Canada, the product of an affair with a French-Canadian girl he had loved years before in Paris. Though the son visited Brian at long intervals, coming via Dublin with presents of Aran-knit cardigans and sides of smoked salmon, I never met him. But then again, this man, conventional and very distant, didn't sound like Brian's son. Was he actually his son? There was always room for doubt in anything Brian told you about himself. As with Ford, it was the story that counted, and the hell with the facts.

But Brian was as good as his word about getting me into pictures in London. A week or so later he told me to report to a friend of his, the production manager on a movie being made out at Elstree, by the Associated British Picture Corporation. This was a Boulting brothers comedy with Ian Carmichael, *Brothers in Law*. So for the first time I walked into a movie studio – through the arched studio gates, towards the big sound stages, with an acidy smell of pear-drops and shaved pine in the air from the cutting rooms and carpenters' shops. Brian had got me a job as a runner at six pounds a week, a sort of fourth assistant director in fact but non-union grade, most menial of studio jobs. Did that matter? Not a whit. I was in the picture business proper now.

I'd come in at the tail end of *Brothers in Law*, and being nervous, and not knowing what might be required of me, I lurked in the shadows of the sound stage with the electricians, waiting for a call to work. There were few calls. I didn't do much running. But the next picture I was assigned to at Elstree was very different, a big technicolour American movie, *The Little Hut*, directed by Mark Robson with Ava Gardner, Stewart Granger, David Niven and an Italian heart-throb of the time, Walter Chiari. This was an adaptation of a long-running French stage play, set on a desert island with Gardner and Granger as the two shipwrecked passengers and a third, their very British manservant, David Niven – and a fourth, lover-boy Chiari. The whole desert island and the palm-leafed huts were set up on the main sound stage, against a huge blue-sky backdrop, the set blazing with tropical sun under a great cluster of arc lights. Now I had more work to do, calling the actors on set when they were ready to shoot.

Granger and Niven were easy to deal with, professionals. There were never any problems when I called them. But Chiari and Ava Gardner were usually difficult. Ava, one of the biggest Hollywood stars of the time, was tardy on call each time I went to knock on her caravan door. One day she was late in answering my knock. Finally she appeared, very scanty in her grass skirt and bodice – more scanty than usual.

'Miss Gardner, Mr Robson is waiting on the set for you.' Standing on the threshold she smiled, looking at me with her huge dark liquid eyes. 'Don't call me "Miss Gardner" – call me honey …' she said sweetly. I could just see inside the caravan. Walter Chiari, upgraded now to Ava's toy-boy lover, was sitting on the sofabed, dishevelled and looking rather pleased with himself, a bottle of whiskey open on the table beside him. He was lighting a cigarette. It seemed clear to me it was a post-coitum cigarette. Cigarettes, whiskey, and wild, wild women. I was really in the picture business now.

My next picture at Elstree, *Interpol*, directed by John Gilling, was even more engaging for me – an international thriller romp, with location shooting and starring two splendid heavies, the great biblical muscle man Victor Mature and Anita (*La Dolce Vita*) Ekberg – real blonde bomber class, with such a sensuously extended pair of bristols that she could have felt her way in the dark with them. And Trevor Howard, wry, dry, and weatherbeaten. On this picture I had more to do, mostly ministering to Mature and Howard, both of whom were partial to the bottle, so that I had difficulty unsticking them from it when I went to call them. They were a sexy, genial and convivial trio.

Miss Ekberg never called me honey but when I went to call her in her dressing room I usually got a good look at the fabulous body, often *déshabillé*, getting up the lacy scaffolding on her bosoms. She, with her attendants, took hours to get ready for each set-up, and to my pleasure I would have to go repeatedly to try and rootle her out of the dressing room. She could see me in the mirror when I came to call her, and would look up at my reflection. 'Coming … I'm coming!' she would call out with a petulant pout, giving a last bouncy test to the bosom scaffolding. What a thrill!

Later we went on location to the London docks for two weeks, to shoot in an old warehouse and on a Yugoslav tramp steamer on which Mature and Howard at once struck up a bibulous friendship with the Serbian captain. Instead of whiskey it was slivovitz time now and the two actors, while waiting to be called, more or less camped out with the captain on the bridge of the steamer. I would find the three of them fairly well oiled, playing at driving the ship, with Mature at the wheel and Howard shouting commands: 'Hard a port, me hearty!' 'Steady as she goes …' 'England expects!' 'Engage the enemy more closely!' and finally 'Splice the mainbrace!' with a rollicking footloose return to the slivovitz to do just that.

I was interested to see that, old pros that they were, none of this boozing affected their performances at all. It seemed to put a nice quizzical edge on Howard's grizzled performance as the British Interpol man. Mature, as his American counterpart, was particularly impressive and sure-footed when he got to the warehouse set, where, in a long reverse tracking take, he had to run hither and thither over the wide space, stopping and starting, glaring this way and that with his gun. And having rehearsed it he did all the complex manoeuvrings in one take. I was on good terms with Mature by then, so I asked him how he'd managed to act it out so skilfully. 'It's not acting, Joe. It's all about hitting your marks.' 'Your marks?' 'Yes, all those little bits of wood nailed down over the warehouse floor – I hit them with the toe of my shoe each time I get up to them, know where I am and where to stop for the camera then. Acting?' he said dismissively. 'It's hitting your marks that really counts in this business.' Indeed Victor couldn't act, except in three modes. His most usual one was a rush to camera, when he would jerk to a stop and give a fierce strangulated grimace in close up as if he was about to do battle with the Gorgon in a biblical epic, when in fact it was supposed to be a sexy look aimed at Miss Ekberg on the reverse shot. His other mode was a rock-faced, narrow-eyed, motionless, Moses-on-the-mountain look. And his third was a leery smile, which, in his floppy suit, tousled brilliantined hair, open collar and loose tie, suggested he'd just been bedding a woman in a crummy motel. But none of this much mattered in this pretty third-rate movie. In fact his hammy acting gave the picture a splendidly lurid quality where you watched his glaring face, beefy charges and gyrations with fascination. Mature was a very nice man. Indeed, in the right hands, he did come to act in more than three modes – very creditably and entertainingly, when Vittorio de Sica took him in hand years later in Mature's last picture, *After the Fox*.

At the end of *Interpol* loose ends loomed again. I was still living with my aunt and uncle in Hampstead, but I spent more time now down at Grosvenor Crescent Mews with Brian, meeting his extraordinary entourage of hangers-on and visitors, endlessly varied. A new 'slave' would appear on the scene every few weeks, to cook and clean, and other handy work no doubt upstairs in Brian's bedroom; actors – famous and unknown, straight and bent – would arrive at all hours, to talk serious work for some film Brian was hoping to make, or to talk and play with less serious ends in view; Michael Redgrave and strapping guardsmen from the Knightsbridge barracks, cockney conmen and famous east-end villains, prissy male models and limp-wristed women's hat makers, trendy new directors or technicians from his old movies down on their luck who would get a fiver or two from Brian on the way out, and other film friends rocketing on the way up such as Terence Young, who was soon to embark on directing all the early James Bond films. All men, of course, but all meat and drink for Brian, or rather smoked salmon, scrambled eggs and Champagne for Brian and his posh friends, with brown ale and bread-and-cheese for the guardsmen and lower orders out in the kitchen, which was the standard fare in the house.

But there were a few women visitors. His old friends Hermione Gingold and Siobhan McKenna and the odd young woman or two, whom Brian laid on for his straight men. Including me, when he more or less put me still a virgin into bed in the spare bedroom with a lovely bohemian Australian girl, Rita. I have more than getting into pictures to thank Brian for.

At other times, when there were just a few of us, Brian would embark on one of his stories, fact or fiction, one hardly ever knew, of how he met Ford in Hollywood: 'I didn't meet him at the studios. I'd no interest in pictures then. I was going round the world, with a rich Russian countess I'd met. Staying at the Beverly Wilshire. Met him in the revolving doors – he was pushing out of the lobby and I was pushing in. But he was pushing the wrong way – Jack always had poor eyesight. So I swore at him through the glass, and he swore back, a string of Irish curses from both of us. Got to be friends at once. I had a big open Buick and I drove Jack out to the studios, told him I was a painter. "Well, come along in then," he said, "and paint something for me." So I did, some phoney Bavarian murals for the picture he was going to make, Four Sons. After that I did more painting and set designs for him. Became best friends.'

There was never a dull moment at number 24. One evening, halfway through a carefully crafted story about staying at Castle Leslie in Ireland where a fabulous naked youth had emerged from his bedroom wardrobe, we heard screams from the next-door mews house and a rattle on Brian's window. 'Oh, don't worry,' Brian said. 'It's just Tony's girlfriend – Tony's trying to kill himself again.' Brian let a distraught young woman in. 'No, it's really serious this time, Brian. Come quickly.' Brian went rather wearily next door and I followed. This was Tony Wright (known as 'Tony Wrong'), a beefy blond Rank star, musclebound and hammy, who had figured in quite a few Rank tough-guy B-pictures, but who had felt recently that he wasn't getting his due with serious pictures out at Pinewood. He had taken to bouts of pretend suicide with his girlfriend. But this time it was almost for real. We found him on the floor of the living room, laid out motionless, looking very pale. 'He's had half a bottle of aspirin this time, Brian!' Brian knelt over him, took his pulse, stripped open his shirt and listened to his heart. 'Well, it's still ticking. Just …' He looked up at the girlfriend. 'Got a stomach pump here?' he asked her casually. 'Of course I haven't got a bloody stomach pump here!' 'With Tony in these moods … should keep one handy.' He turned to me. 'Run round to St George's, Joe. Get an ambulance.' The hospital was just round the corner and Tony Wright-and-Wrong was saved.

Apart from Champagne breakfasts and sides of smoked salmon from Harrods, Brian was a big spender on other items: a lovely navy-blue open-topped Bentley in a garage round the corner, evenings at Les Ambassadeurs, an exclusive dinner and gambling club off Park Lane, and fivers all round to old and new boyfriends. Since he wasn't at that point making a film, I wondered where all his ready cash came from.

'Come,' he said one afternoon. 'We'll go call on my sister Pat.' He took the Russian icon of Saint Bridget off the wall and we were soon cruising round the park in the open Bentley, with Brian, white hair aflow in the wind, summing up the talent on the pavement as we passed. 'My passion wagon,' Brian said of the car. 'I have lots of luck with it. George Cukor was over here to prepare *Les Girls* and wanted to buy it off me thinking he'd have the same sort of luck with it. George is somewhat small – in height, not the other way. I said "But George, your feet won't reach the pedals." "Never mind, Brian. I'll just have it stopped here in the park and wait in it."'

Patricia had an apartment in Dean's Yard, a cul-de-sac next to the Dorchester. We went upstairs and she opened the door. She was a generously built, elderly, white-haired woman in flowing, flower-patterned Indian-style robes and turned-up Turkish slippers, living in a small apartment crammed with antique furniture, porcelain and other glittery objets d'art.

'This is Joe Hone, my "nephew".' 'Indeed …' She eyed me without favour. 'Oh, no – he's kosher. Won't steal the silver. Friend of Jack Ford, worked with him in Ireland.' 'That's no great recommendation. As it wasn't for you. It's a pity you ever met Ford. You could have been a good painter.' 'I am a good painter. See, I brought you my Saint Bridget. You said your shares weren't prospering. We'll say a few prayers to her.'

Patricia continued to eye me sourly. She brought me over to the mantelpiece. There were two beautiful blue-patterned Chinese lacquer vases at either end. 'Smell them,' she said. 'Each of them.' I smelt each of them. Both exuded a strong musky odour, with violets, peaches, I didn't know what. There was nothing inside the vases. I told her what they smelt of. She turned to Brian. 'Well, he's all right then.' Brian explained to me. 'Very few people can smell anything in those vases. Absolutely nothing. So you're all right.'

After some desultory chatter between the two of them, Pat said 'All right, Brian, I know what you want.' She went to a fine inlaid French escritoire, opened a drawer, took out a cheque book, wrote a cheque and handed it to him. He pocketed it without looking at it. Then Pat said, 'Brian, I'm worried about you.' She returned to the escritoire, got out a pack of Tarot cards, sat down with Brian at a small table and laid the cards out. They gazed at them intently. After pondering things for a while Pat said, 'They look all right. I see good things coming for you, Brian.' 'What's he like?'

Brother and sister lived by signs, by Tarot cards and by prayers to Saint Bridget and Saint Teresa. Pat, by such devotions and second sight Brian told me, had shared quite a fortune on the stock market, which she had played with an old friend of hers, Harry de Vere Clifton, an eccentric Lancashire millionaire aristocrat who owned half of Blackpool. It was from his sister Pat that Brian got his ready cash, when he wasn't extracting money from Lord Rank. It was from Harry Clifton that Brian got the money to make his first movie back in the early thirties, Synge's *Riders to the Sea*, filmed on a wild Atlantic beach in the west of Ireland. 'He wrote me out a cheque for three thousand pounds on the back of a Goldflake cigarette packet. My bank manager called me next morning. "Is this cheque all right, Mr Hurst?" "It would be all right for a thousand times as much," I told him.'

Luck of the Irish. And Brian had bucketfuls of it. Which was another reason why he took life easy: 'She bade me take life easy, as the leaves grow on the tree.' 'Down by the Sally Gardens' was one of Brian's favourite Irish ballads which he sang rather nicely of an evening over the Champagne.

When I had finished with *Interpol,* Brian got me a job as a runner with the Rank Organization out in Pinewood. He was preparing a big picture there himself, *Dangerous Exile,* a story of the young Dauphin in the tower after the revolution; a big technicolour costume drama with a huge budget for the time, close to £400,000, and elaborate sets to be built on a huge sound stage and the back lot, featuring big stars of the time – Louis Jourdan (just finished on *Gigi* with Maurice Chevalier) and Belinda Lee, another blonde bombshell from the Rank charm school, and other fine British character actors. Now Brian cut out the Champagne breakfasts and the brown-ale boys. This was serious business, the most expensive film Rank had ever made. He was up and out at Pinewood by eight. Now there was a different side to him – the professional, hard-headed movie maker.

At Pinewood I was assigned to a group of runners, half a dozen young men, anxious like me to get a union ticket and a real job as an assistant director. At the time, in what turned out to be the last years of Rank's production-line picture making, there were six or eight films in production when I arrived. It must have been a bit like Hollywood in the old days – the whole studio alive with the bustle of all sorts of movie making, hundreds of actors and technicians wandering or running about the place, the clatter of movieolas from the cutting rooms, great plaster sets being constructed in the carpenter's shop, skips of lavish period costumes from Nathans being taken round every day to Wardrobe.

Brian took me out to Pinewood on my first day in his splendid open-topped Bentley. I suggested he might drop me some way down the road from the studio gates, not to make it seem too obvious that I was one of his 'boys'. 'Certainly not,' he said. 'I don't give a fuck what they think – of you or me.' And we sailed through the studio gates, the gatemen opening the barrier and saluting Brian smartly.

I was first attached as a runner to a Norman Wisdom farce, and I really ran now, from the production office up and down the long corridors where the stars' dressing rooms were, to and from the sound stage and then, late in the afternoon, collecting the scores of call sheets for the next day's work and delivering them all round the place. This wasn't the most interesting sort of movie work for me. 'That doesn't matter,' Brian told me sharply one evening on the way back to London. 'For you, you should learn much more from bad pictures than good ones.'

The next picture I ran on, *Windom's Way*, was much better, directed by Ronnie Neame with Peter Finch as the doctor out in the Malayan jungle, the whole bamboo, palm-tree jungle, dispensary, cabins and a small lake all built out on the back lot. Finch was reaching the height of his fine movie acting – very masculine, but subtle and immensely capable in his technique; and highly intelligent, always getting something unexpected and original out of often dull parts. Aside from his professional skill, off duty he was a real card – witty, incisive and something of a drinker when he liked a bit of a lark. I would sometimes have to call him in the bigwigs' panelled dining-room and bar. I once found him at the bar, well away with the Irish actor Jack McGowran, whom I knew; a marvellous slip of a man with a fabulously mobile rubber face, and afterwards the great interpreter of Beckett's plays. Finch knew that Jackie was in need of any extra movie money he could get, so he said to me: 'Now listen, Joe, I want to see if we can get Jackie out on the lot after lunch, as one of the Malayan coolies. Ideal casting.' 'But I think Jackie is on another picture.' 'Doesn't matter. Take him to Wardrobe, get him into a sarong, then make-up with a good dark daub of Lichener Number Five all over – and Ronnie won't know he wasn't born and bred in Kuala Lumpur.' 'Yes, Mr Finch ...' It didn't quite work out like that, but no matter. Finch was the splendid matter then. And so was Jackie McGowran.

Brian then started shooting his *Dangerous Exile* epic, which I wasn't assigned to having been moved to another picture, another expensive costume epic, Ralph Thomas's *A Tale of Two Cities*, with Dirk Bogarde. But I would sneak onto the *Exile* set and watch Brian at work. The interiors, of the palace at Versailles and such like, were vast and elaborate. The movie shot in full Panavision technicolour so that the dozens of big arc lights blazed with such heat that when they were turned off after each set-up the sound stage doors had to be opened to let in the air. I arrived one afternoon to get a glimpse of what Brian had told me was to be one of the major sequences, in the palace ballroom, where there was to be a ball, with scores of extras and playback music, where Belinda Lee was to be filmed on a camera crane coming down a long curved staircase before she mixed graciously with the bewigged and pantalooned guests in the ballroom.

When I got on the set it was dark. Nothing was happening. Shooting had stopped for the day. Brian told me the story that night. 'You see, to save money, they only built one staircase for the grand descent, when, as it turned out, they should have built two – on either side of the ballroom, because craning down on the one staircase meant shooting Belinda on her bad profile, and she wouldn't have this, threw a tantrum, sulked. So I said to the designer: "Well, we'll just have to build another staircase on the other side, so we can crane down on Belinda's good profile. Meanwhile we'll move onto the dungeons in the Bastille set." But meanwhile Earl (Earl St John, the head of production at the studios then) heard what was happening, called me in and exploded. "You can't build another staircase, Brian!" "Oh, come on, Earl," I told him, "it's flesh and blood against just a bit of wood and plaster." "Goddamn it, Brian," he said, "it's another two thousand pounds against an overrun budget already. Couldn't you have Belinda walk down the staircase some other way?" "You mean backwards?" "Well, no, but sideways maybe?"

'We're building another staircase …' Brian ended the story with one of his wicked smiles.

THIRTEEN

aving been a runner at Pinewood for six months, and still seeing no
chance of getting a union ticket, I decided to try and work in the picture business in France, by first studying movie making properly at the only
school for this sort of learning at the time – IDHEC, the Institut de Haute
École Cinématographique, run by the veteran director Marcel L'Herbier in
Paris. But despite several letters of application, recommendations from Brian
and an interview with one of the staff in Paris I failed to get in, and my lack
of any proper French was one reason. Froggy Bertin's French classes hadn't
done me any good, or rather I hadn't bothered to learn much from them.

However, there was another, and perhaps broader education waiting for
me in Paris with Brian, with whom, when he was finished with *Exile*, I went
over to Paris several times, staying either at the Crillon or the Hôtel Raphael, then a most distinguished and discreet hotel off the Etoile. Though
there was no need for discretion as far as Brian and I were concerned – we
always had separate bedrooms.

Brian had many good French friends, particularly the actor-director
Gerard Oury, a man-about-town and boulevardier with the boys. With him
and others we went out on the town, to the Crazy Horse Saloon, then the
most sophisticated and daring of nude-show night clubs – and to drinks

with a finicky little snitch of a man, a queery-boots French marquis (known as 'la Marquise') in his beautiful seventeenth-century *hôtel particulier* on the left bank. The marquis owned a vineyard near Bordeaux. In his seventies, he was dressed immaculately *à l'Anglaise*, Saville Row and Jermyn Street, perfect English, a French aristo of the old school. We met in his palatial *salon*, a long room with rows of tall windows to one side, filled with gilt and marquetry Louis XIV furnishings with several huge armchairs by a dead fireplace. A Vietnamese servant, white-jacketed and gloved, served us vintage Champagne. Brian owed the marquis some favours, apparently, and was doing a little pimping for him in return.

'So you have someone special for me this time, Brian?' the Marquise asked, all eager. 'Yes, he works in Harrods. The fish counter. Simon. Special. And reliable, won't steal the silver. Real gentleman's gentleman. He's looking for work in Paris, with someone ... sympathetic. I can send him over.' 'I'd like that, except ... the fish counter?' 'Oh, don't worry about that, he's scrupulously clean. They're fussy about that sort of thing in Harrods.' I think the favours that la Marquise had done Brian earlier on his Paris visits, and was to do again that evening, were to advance him good whacks of cash-in-hand in return for Brian's flesh-in-hand arrangements for him.

In any case Brian always had big bundles of thousand-franc notes on him in Paris and we would go on, with Gerard Oury and others, to Allard, the small old brass and velvet restaurant on the rue St André des Arts, where Brian knew the head waiter and had his usual dishes – foie gras, then delicate lamb chops in a fennel sauce or with redcurrant jelly, a lemon sorbet and a ripe camembert to finish. And then the wine. 'Old Clos de Vougeout is the best here,' Brian told us that first evening in the restaurant. But this Burgundy wasn't available and the wine waiter brought a Premier Cru Margaux for Brian's inspection instead. 'Oh, that'll do,' he said. 'That'll do.' This was his standard reply in life or in a restaurant when offered something even better than what he'd first expected or ordered.

The next day we went to see what for Brian was the best, the most beautiful sight in Paris, the stained glass windows at Sainte-Chapelle. 'Always answers my prayers,' he told me on the way over the river to the chapel. And indeed he did pray sometime after we'd arrived, at the marvellous, rose-gold, ethereal windows in the upper chapel, standing head bowed, very much the seeming penitent.

Afterwards he said: 'Real Choir of Angels stuff, isn't it? In the late twenties, when I first saw these windows, I was living with a woman – a good woman, but she didn't appreciate them. But I was so excited by them I couldn't think of anything else, couldn't sleep. Painted versions of the windows all night back at my studio, slept in an armchair and when I woke next morning she'd upped and gone.' 'Were you in love with her?' He thought a moment, then said, 'Yes, I was.' 'I'm sorry.' 'Yeats's "Perfection of the life, or of the work?"' he said. 'I was going for the great work then, when I should have taken up with her properly, even married her. But what does it matter …' He turned, and hands on hips, very upright, strolled away in his leisurely John Wayne-style walk into the blaze of coloured afternoon light from the windows.

There were other equally illuminating moments for me with Brian in France in the autumn of 1956. One of Brian's Paris friends was the American Cynda Glen who years before had come to Paris to pursue her talent as a show dancer, had met Erich von Stroheim and had later become his companion at the Von's chateau out at Maurepas, a village twenty-five miles south-west of Paris. The great Erich von Stroheim, of *Greed*, *Queen Kelly* and Renoir's *La Grande Illusion*.

This last film, and Stroheim's performance as the Prussian officer, the brutish-looking, neck-braced but sensitive First World War prison camp commandant, had moved me as much as any film when I'd seen it at the Everyman in Hampstead. And now Brian, offhand, said he was going out to see Cynda and her friend the Von and would I like to come too? Well, I would. And I did.

We were staying at the Raphael, and Brian, who never visited people in less than his Bentley, hired a chauffeured Cadillac and off we went that autumn day out to Maurepas. The château, behind high walls and elm trees at the edge of the village, was hardly that, more a Gothic Charles Adamish villa. The old master, then in his last months, was upstairs, bedridden. Cynda Glen met us in the salon. She was a wonderfully vibrant little woman, in her late fifties, red-haired, quick eyes, funny, sassy, subtle, provocative, but with an underlying toughness. The salon was extraordinary. It was a setting straight out of one of von Stroheim's extravagant 1920s silent epics: a large, dark, tatty room crammed with decrepit furnishings, a vast grand piano, Prussian sabres on the walls, pistols and spurs, a great dusty ship's lantern hanging from the ceiling, frayed carpets, together with a lot of knick-knacks everywhere, ashtrays in the shape of stirrups, a high-backed brass-studded Spanish saddle on a wooden horse, Hollywood photographs all over the piano, silver cigarette boxes engraved with messages from Douglas Fairbanks and Gloria Swanson. But the *pièce de résistance* in this old movie set were the ducks – a little flock, tame and vociferous, wandering in and out, pecking at the piano legs and relieving themselves happily on the Turkish carpets while we sipped Kir Royal.

Brian asked me to wait while he went upstairs with Cynda to see how things were with the Von. I went outside, and walked down the gardens, along a back drive towards a little gate lodge. It was a dank, misty autumn afternoon and the cotton wool mist swirled around me as I passed a series of rotting parallel bars and hand swings in the gloom, von Stroheim's old exercise yard.

The gate lodge was deserted, locked in front, but a door round the back was ajar. I peered in, and went inside. It had been adapted long before as a cutting room. There was a rusty movieola on a bench and cans of his old nitrate films piled up beneath it. On one wall were various notices, mementoes from other cutting rooms and sound stages, in Paris, Hollywood, Berlin: 'Silence – Le Rouge Est Mis!' 'No Smoking!' 'C'est Interdit de ...' 'Verboten ...' On the opposite wall were pale photographs with scrawled signatures: D.W. Griffith, Mary Pickford, Chaplin. A room beyond was filled with other tatty bits and pieces from von Stroheim's movie career: cabin trunks bursting with old props, scripts and call sheets. In corners lay larger objects: a twisted First World War aircraft propeller, a German army commandant's uniform and a collection of stiffened corsets and neck braces, all from *La Grande Illusion* no doubt. Elsewhere lay a wardrobe of gilded jackets and cloaks, a spiked Prussian helmet, sabres, jodhpurs, riding boots, the buckles tarnished, the leather green with damp – the romantic, violent detritus of von Stroheim's life, half fact, half fiction. The Von's life was fading back at the château, and so was his fiction here in the gate lodge – in the cans of nitrate film scattered about, together with the sabres, jodhpurs and corsets, all imperceptibly decaying, the autumn mist seeping through the cracked windows.

Later Cynda brought me up to see the Von. He lay flat out in a small austere bedroom, beneath a blackened crucifix, a shrunken figure with a strangely innocent face, a shadow Prussian officer, where the child had now indeed become father to the man, a white sheet tucked right up under his chin like a great nursery bib. But his eyes were alight, filled with glittery life, unblinking, fascinated by something, gazing straight upwards as if at some last, extravagant, perfectly imagined, uncut epic of his being projected on the ceiling.

Then, as I was quietly introduced, Cynda said I was working in pictures and hoped to be a director and the shrivelled bullet head turned towards me. A momentary glance, then a finger raised for an instant above the sheet: a blessing in disguise, I thought, recommending me to that thronging celluloid world I was entering and he was about to leave forever.

Towards the end of that year I was back running around Pinewood again and no nearer getting a union ticket. But then in the spring of 1957, luck came my way again. At the time Rank was extending their production empire overseas and had opened up an operation in Paris, financing French movies. Brian heard about this and talking to the right people in Pinewood, got me a job as a runner on the first of these Rank-financed pictures: a James Hadley Chase thriller, *Retour de Manivelle – Kickback –* being shot on location along the Riviera and at the old Studios de la Victorine in Nice. Apart from board and lodging the job was unpaid, but Brian said he'd send me out a few thousand francs now and then, which he did.

The unit was already down in Nice and I was to join them. I expected a long slog on a slow train south. But those were still the big free-spending days in movies. And since Rank were paying the costs anyway, the French production manager, when I met him in Paris, gave me a ticket for Le Train Bleu – which was why the following day I was on the all-first-class silver bullet approaching Lyon at ninety miles an hour, getting in to Nice just before six o'clock, and taking a taxi to the Hotel Negresco where the unit was staying. In fact they weren't there that evening – they were out night shooting somewhere, and I missed them again next morning when they'd left early. Something of a panic then. Where was I to go? But a few minutes later a chauffeur approached me deferentially in the hotel lobby. 'Monsieur Hone? Your car is ready.' And I was taken out along the coast road in a big American limo to the location, Edouard de Rothschild's sensational villa and exotic glass-walled gardens perched right on the tip of St Jean Cap Ferrat.

Here, expecting to start my most menial tasks as a runner, I was treated instead with unexpected deference, offered a canvas chair by one of the assistants and given a front-row view of the first set-up; Daniel Gélin, as the crooked chauffeur in the story, pulling up repeatedly in an elegant old Rolls Royce in front of the even more elegant villa. It was some days before I managed to play any active part in the production – keeping the crowds away, calling the actors and so on. And when I started to do this the reaction to my labours was one of surprise and mistrust.

Eventually, I discovered why. The French lighting cameraman – a wry, withdrawn, amused soul, fluent in English when he wasn't pondering the sun and the clouds through a smoked eye-glass – told me the producers believed I was a spy, sent out directly by Lord Rank himself, assigned to the unit in the guise of assistant, but in fact sent down here to see that milord's money wasn't being squandered on fripperies and extravagances.

Of course, a film unit in those days, especially on location, drew its life's blood from just such excess, and *Retour de Manivelle* was no exception. It was an expensive production in any case, with a three-month schedule, extensive locations and studio sets, and with Michèle Morgan – then France's number one female box-office draw – as co-star with Gélin, together with a number of other major French and German actors. And all devoted to this trivial *série noire* thriller, a serpentine but banal tale of murder, blackmail and double-dealing. Claude Charbrol might have made something of it all. But this, in 1957, was just before the onset of the French New Wave, when the industry in France, fatigued after its long brilliance, was settling for less, with Hollywood gangster imitations, costume romps, theatrical adaptations and general run-of-the-mill bourgeois-titillating pap.

The director, Denys de La Patellière – a quick-thinking, tubby, pipe-clenching little man in a suede jacket – did his best with the rigmarole of a script, transforming many of the trite scenes and much of the flat, tough-guy dialogue with deft invention, encouraging the actors to play against the lines, promoting ironies, games between the players, which were never in the script to begin with.

As for me these flaws in the movie didn't matter at all. Here I was, working in the illustrious French cinema, on location around Eden Roc or at Rothschild's villa all day, in a back room of the fabled Negresco by night, with several months of the same to come, in the company of the very approachable Gélin and the less approachable, and therefore the more idolized, Michèle Morgan. She was the ultimate in ever-cool suavity: the palest honey blonde hair, arctic blue eyes, bamboo thin, in drifting white voile dresses – an ice maiden in those voluptuous southern airs.

They were halcyon days of wine and roses: but above all sharing in that completely engrossing, adrenalin-pumping business that is movie-making. We were playing God with life, which is the heart of feature making: the setting up and then filming, with vast concentration, care and expense, a succession of quite unrelated images that one day will cohere in the editing room, displaying their secret design. But first trapping those vivid, free-floating images – the lovely old Rolls driven over a cliff and spinning down the rocks into the turquoise sea near Antibes (this piece of extravagance would have given milord Rank a real fit); Gélin, in just his underpants, gingerly climbing into bed with the similarly clad maid – the sheet pulled up slowly over their heads, leaving provocatively moving shapes against the camera; the grizzly, time-stopping alibi ploy of the murdered body put in a deep freeze, then unfrozen weeks later, and murdered again.

These seemingly incoherent parts – the common currency of the garish *série noire* thriller – were here transformed into something possibly of vital import, the birth of quite a different story, which, in the haphazard blessings of the celluloid recording angel, might transcend the banal genre. Here was the magic that, as we stood behind the camera, took us all away from every other concern. Intent, gazing into a circle of dazzling light, we were all celebrants in a mysterious rite, where time, stuttering through a little mechanical gate, was snatched from oblivion and trapped forever.

On most days, at the end of shooting, the unit was treated to aperitifs by the producer, director or one of the stars. Glasses were set out on trestle tables, pastis and vermouth stuffed into buckets of ice. And it was during one of these little herb-and-aniseed get-togethers, when we were filming back at the Victorine studios, that Gélin, knowing I was Irish, told me of another Irishman (indeed he had gone to St Columba's College), the silent movie director Rex Ingram, who had created these studios and made them famous back in the mid-twenties. I hadn't heard of the man.

'But you've heard of his movie, *The Four Horsemen of the Apocalypse*, of Rudolph Valentino and Ramon Novarro,' he went on. I had. 'Ingram made them both famous in the Hollywood silent days. Then he had a row with MGM, came out to Nice and set up the Victorine studios here, and made a silent epic called *Mare Nostrum*. He was a great silent director, a "primitive", a friend of Griffith and von Stroheim. But a much more mysterious figure. The prints of most of his movies never survived. And nor did he as a director. Disappeared when sound arrived. Never made another picture.'

Gélin finished his pastis. 'Come along and take a look at this guy working on the lot outside.' I followed him onto the back lot, where another company was setting up some night shooting, on a ghastly ultra-modern suburban street set, with an even uglier, futuristic plasterboard house dominating one end of it, and two cold round upper windows, like eyes, staring down at one. A beanpole of a man, with a pipe, a pork pie hat and a mac that was far too short for him, was pondering this monstrous house, seeming to relish its horrors, rehearsing beneath the ten-kilowatt arc lights. Jacques Tati was putting the finishing touches to his film *Mon Oncle*.

'Look at him,' Gélin said. 'Tati's really another great silent director. Like Rex Ingram. Another primitive. No dialogue. Can't be doing with words.'

A little later they started to shoot. '*Dégagez le champ! Silence partout!*' The clapper board snapped and Tati cagily embarked on some manically comic business with secateurs. Against the side wall of the house, having earlier broken one branch of a very neatly espaliered tree, he was trying to even it up – by cutting the opposite branch. After making things even more unbalanced he had to cut another branch, then a third and a fourth, ending up by ruining the whole tree.

Silence. Just the faint hiss of burning carbon from the arc lights, a vague whirr from the peering camera; and beyond, an ever-more-agitated, wildly stabbing figure, pipe rampant, pork pie hat askew, doing battle with the ever-diminishing tree. That magic again, taking shape in the silence. An epiphany beyond words. The silence was golden.

Afterwards, when I was back in Hampstead staying with my aunt and uncle, Sally and Stanley, there was a letter waiting for me from my father, dated earlier that year of 1957:

Dear Joe

We are writing to you to wish you many happy returns on your 20th birthday. I am sorry that we did not write to you at Christmas – we were upset that we did not know where you were and we had a difficult and awkward Christmas ourselves. Your letter at Christmas was most enjoyable, though I did not think much of the card! Save your money and don't buy any more of these pseudo-intellectual nonsenses in future! I hear you are on the Riviera at the moment and I congratulate you on a good deal more common sense (and perhaps ability and application) than I have ever had.

Your mother would appreciate it, indeed she would be very happy, if, on your various travels you could find time to come and visit us. We still patronise the Restoration Inn and Gina sends you birthday greetings. We have it in mind to hire a boat in Devon or Cornwall next July for a couple of weeks – let us know if you would like to be in on it.

I have been building a road for the past six weeks – a risky occupation in view of the old health – and my associate, whom you don't know, seems to have played naughtily with the payments on account so that I have got nothing out of it and am very angry. Fortunately the slate down the road is still good!

Love, Daddy.

A letter far from the hectoring, legalistic tone of his earlier letters to me. And there is his health again, now apparently very dodgy. So what on earth was he doing building a road for six weeks? Looking at the letter now, the biro handwriting almost as fresh as if it had been written yesterday – this letter with its rather stilted phrases, my father's admission of his lack of common sense, ability and application, his suggesting that I might take some pleasure with them on a holiday boat down in the southwest (which we never did), and his hope that I should visit my mother meanwhile in Cheltenham – I feel a real sadness for Nat.

Is there guilt here, for the way he's behaved to my mother and to me over the years? And a glimmer of hope that he might set things to rights with my mother and me by having us all on board together for a jolly family boating trip in the summer? As my grandfather remarked in an earlier letter to Hubert, Nat's was a tragic life. It needn't have been, since, apart from his fabled charm, he had other more reliable gifts and many opportunities to promote them happily and successfully. But it was a silver-spoon life early on, and it was this spoon that choked him later. So he ended up with a rogue pal on a road-building job, but with the slate still good down at the Restoration Inn and Peter's Bar.

Towards the end though he had to forsake the beer and all the bars. Falling ill with a recurrence of his tuberculosis, and then cancer of his remaining lung, he returned to Dublin a year later, and died in the Jesuit nursing home in Leeson Street, with half bottles of Champagne and oxygen to see him out. My mother was with him over all his last days, and Nat was converted at last to the true faith by the Catholic Archbishop of Dublin, Dr McQuaid, in the nursing home. If Nat started off his life with a silver spoon in his mouth, and spent most of it drinking the bitter, he ended up with the wafer and wine, the Body and Blood of Christ on his tongue – his slate wiped clean, I hope. I came over to Dublin, and visited him in the nursing home. He was drifting in and out of consciousness and barely spoke, absorbed in his dying. I went to see him the next day and he was dead. My mother had been with him all night. He was stiff and chilly-looking on the bed, a dull, distant expression on his thin features, the sheet pulled up to his stubbled chin. My mother kissed him gently on the forehead, and we left. I was still working at Pinewood, so I went back to England at once. I didn't stay for the funeral. I should have done, as a support for my mother at least. But the truth was that I ran out on it all, unable to face the fact that I should have felt some real emotion for both of them, and didn't.

Biddy died five years later, of womb cancer in a Bath hospital. In the last months of her life she had gone to live in Chippenham with one of her sisters. Before that she had lived alone in small damp flats in Cheltenham and in the village of Winchcombe in the hills outside the town, where I stayed with her for a few days now and then while she was still working as a filing clerk with Walker Crossweller. She had good friends in Chelten-ham, but I should have gone to see her more often, and I feel guilty about that too.

Yet what she had lost with me, by allowing me to be packed off to Dublin twenty years before, I was never able to regain with her. My mother remained for me a rather distant, distressed relation. Her life was as sad as Nat's. She would certainly have been better off leaving Nat permanently, when she would surely have found a much more secure and congenial rela-tionship with another man. She and Nat had something special between them from the start – their trump, their only card: they were nearly always lovers, physically and emotionally, to Nat's end and hers, for, apart from her fling with Ian McCorkadale, she never had serious eyes for any other man but him. That's the best I can say of them.

But to resume my own life at the time. When *Retour de Manivelle* was finished, there were no more Rank movies for me in France. So having returned to London, and by courtesy of Brian again, I went back to Pine-wood as a runner. Brian was preparing another picture there. But I was just an eight-pound-a-week dogsbody again, and it seemed that was all I was ever likely to be in the movie business, the union ticket as far away as ever.

Then came a further lucky break. I was assigned as runner to another Rank technicolour costume epic, *The Gypsy and the Gentleman*, with the Aus-tralian actor Keith Michell as the gentleman and Melina Mercouri as the gypsy. And what a gypsy she was! I'd seen her already in the Greek movie *Stella* at the Everyman cinema in Hampstead, this sexy, slinky, husky-voiced woman with the huge dark eyes, and here she was, at my visual disposal at least, when I went to call her in her dressing room. She was quite out of the ordinary run of movie stars: those smouldering eyes, ironic, provocative, funny, highly intelligent. How such a little-known and unconventional for-eign actress (so different from any of Pinewood's charm school girls) came to be in one of Rank's big pictures I've no idea.

However, the real surprise was that Mercouri (and Michell, an equally intelligent, if more quietly pitched actor) had been teamed up with director Joseph Losey on the picture. Losey, one of the best and most politically com-mitted American directors, had fallen foul of the McCarthyite communist witch hunts in 1950s Hollywood, was compelled to leave America and had come to work in London a few years before. Since he'd been blacklisted in Hollywood, he'd had to make his first two pictures in England, *The Sleeping Tiger* and *The Intimate Stranger*, under assumed names. Though he had no real affiliations with the communist party now (if he'd ever had), he must have been seen as something of a Red in the British film industry. And so again it was all the more unexpected that he should be given a big picture to make by the politically correct and wary John Davis, head of the studios at Pinewood, and his boss the very Christian Lord Rank. But so it was. So, by chance, I was assigned as runner on the movie.

The script, and the picture as it turned out, was a rigmarole of boozy bucks and bosomy barmaids, the last sort of movie that Losey, who had made classic dark and violent thrillers in Hollywood (*The Prowler* and *M*), might have been expected to be interested in. The reason was simple, though: Losey badly needed the work, any kind of movie work.

Initially, I knew little or nothing of Losey's American background or his movies. What I first saw of him on the set was a tense, middle-aged, perpetually harassed man, pretty well at sea with this Regency melodrama. But what I also saw was how good he was with the crew and the actors – quiet, precise and easy in his directions to the former and never giving more than a few small tips to the latter. I saw how imaginative and painstaking he was with his set-ups, some of them elaborate, where he filmed the master shots in long tracking takes. He knew exactly what he was doing technically. He had, too, that special gift in movie making – the ability to see what could be developed in a script, with an actor, or in a set-up, camera movement, or in the editing to create a sudden frisson, that unexpected 'moment of illumination' in his pictures. Like Ford he was speedy and economic in his shooting, with little wasted footage, so that he was furious with the slowness of the British lighting gaffers and electricians, who always had to pull the switches and break for tea and bacon butties, just as Joe had finally got a shot lined up and the actors ready.

One of the first elaborate studio set-ups and long tracking takes involved a group of bucks at a wild country fair where, with a big crowd of drunken bucolics, the gentleman met the gypsy, and where the main business of the scene was the catching, for various wagers, of a greased piglet. Needless to say (never act with animals or children), nearly everything that could go wrong did. The greased piglet, under the bright lights, became meltingly slippery, then squealingly hysterical and uncatchable. It ran about madly, in and out of shot, snouting the electricians beyond the camera, before galloping off round the sound stage. Or it was momentarily caught by one or other or all of the bucks. But so pugnacious did piglet become that it floored the Regency rakes, or pulled them along the grease-sodden floor, ruining their foppish costumes. Panic and pandemonium as the shot had to be taken again and again. For Losey all this overblown malarkey must have been a sore trial, work very far removed from his chilling minimalist direction of *The Prowler* and *M*. But he stuck to it gamely.

Other than lurking about, watching the shooting and waiting to call someone or other to the set, I had little to do with Losey to begin with. But one day he stopped me outside the production office. 'I hear you've been working in France, on some French pictures, so you speak French?' I nodded, since I did speak French quite well by then. 'Well, I wonder if you could help me out? I have a French guy coming to interview me tomorrow, for a movie magazine over in Paris, *Cahiers du Cinéma*. Would you look after him until I can get to see him? Give him a coffee or a drink.' And this I did. After this I was closer to Losey and he called me Joe and I called him Joe, and we became good friends, both personally and professionally. When we'd both left Pinewood, I went location hunting and working on scripts with him, on *The Criminal* and *King and Country*, his First World War picture with Dirk Bogarde and Tom Courtney.

But this work was after a crisis on *Gypsy*. Halfway through the shooting Joe had had a serious run-in with John Davis about something; the script or the sets, or the budget, I think. Davis decided that, apart from possibly being a Red, Joe was a difficult arty bugger, and was about to fire him. Luckily, Brian – who had already met Joe, liked him and what he'd heard about his earlier pictures – was at Pinewood preparing another movie. (Brian had a three-picture deal with Rank at the time.) Learning of the trouble, Brian went to see Davis and said he shouldn't fire Joe. He was a good director. And if he did – well, Brian thought that might be awkward: he mightn't care to go on working for Rank. Besides there would be bad publicity when the news got into the papers, as Brian implied it would, through him, of how Joe had been victimized for no good reason by the supposedly charitable Lord Rank. Joe wasn't fired.

This was another quixotic act of Brian's, calling Davis's bluff, since Davis, big cheese movie mogul that he was, might well have fired both of them. And at the rate Brian spent money he probably needed Rank's cash more than Joe did. But then, as I knew already from Brian's business with Earl St John over the ballroom staircase and Belinda Lee's bad profile, Brian had a way of dealing with movie moguls, with a mix of cajoling blarney and subtle threat. I wasn't the only one who benefited from Brian's generosity.

So at Pinewood, in meeting Joe, the long train of luck held for me again – from climbing a high wall in Dublin to thus meeting Ford, and through him Brian, to Brian getting me into French movies, so that Joe asked me to help him with the *Cahiers du Cinéma* interview, which was how I got to know and work for him afterwards. If luck is a pre-condition of success in life, and especially in the picture business, then I had full measure of it. Luck, and a bit of assumed front and brashness. The way things were going for me at the time, with all this lucky influence on my side – why, I might have made it as a movie director in a few years time. Ah, but that elusive ACT union ticket …

But it wasn't the union ticket. I knew in my heart I was never going to make it as a movie director. I didn't have the self-confidence, or the tough guts needed for the job, and doubted I would ever have the technical skills either to control the camera work, the actors, the set-ups, the editing or handle a film unit generally. And I think I knew then, in those last Pine-wood days, that I would have to head off in some other direction. I had no idea where.

FOURTEEN

So it was back to Dublin, staying with my grandparents again in Winton Road. My grandfather didn't moan about my unemployed arrival.
Approaching eighty (he died a year later), I think he was tiring of life generally, and certainly of all the Little Joe problems. Since I had some money
saved from my curtailed movie career, I didn't have to put the bite on him
financially and kept out of his way. I went downtown most days to see
friends, and a friend I bumped into outside the gates of Trinity College one
afternoon was a teacher I'd worked with at Drogheda Grammar School two
years before, Alec Reid, who had taught English and French to the older
pupils there.

Alec was a remarkable man – early forties, small, portly, albino, pink-
cheeked, badly sighted, academically gifted, witty and passionate about theatre. Heroically, he treated his physical disadvantages as if they simply didn't
exist. He had come over to Dublin some years before, with his attractive
English wife. I don't know why the Reids had come to Ireland. Perhaps Alec
thought his offbeat character, his interest in theatre (he later wrote one of
the best books about Sam Beckett's work) and his generally droll characteristics would be viewed more sympathetically in Dublin than in England,
as indeed they were, in a city well used to brilliant eccentrics. His friends,

and his students particularly, liked him and appreciated his conceits. In his oddities he became more Irish than the Irish themselves.

In any case he got two days a week teaching up in Drogheda, a junior lectureship in English in Trinity, and was taken on by *The Irish Times* as a second-string theatre critic and third leader writer, writing witty or cleverly inconsequential pieces once or twice a week. Alec, by the time I got back to Dublin, was a well-known figure, strolling around Trinity with his rolling sailor's gait, newspapers, exam papers and God knows what other papers coming out of every pocket, heavy magnifying specs jammed sideways on his nose, a row of pens in the top pocket of his tight-fitting, rather food-spattered tweed jacket. A Heath Robinson professor.

That afternoon, stopping me outside Trinity front gates, he said casually, as if we'd met the day before: 'Ah, Joe, just the man I wanted to see. I'm sure you'd like to go to Egypt.' This was the last thing I was sure I would like to do just then. 'I'm recruiting English teachers,' Alec went on merrily, wagging one of his pens at me. 'For the ex-British schools in Cairo and Alex. The British have all been chucked out of Egypt, of course. But the Colonel is keen to keep these schools going as they were – with Irish teachers.' 'The Colonel?' I asked. 'Why, Colonel Nasser of course.' 'I see,' I said. 'Yes, I've been in touch with him – he's been in touch with the College here, and I'm to drum up a score of likely pedagogues. Their Minister of Education, Dr Khaki, is to be here next week, for interviews. Come along and see him – you'll like it out there.' 'Yes, but, well, I only have four 'O' Levels ...' 'Oh, that won't matter, not in Egypt now. As long as you speak English they won't worry about qualifications. And I'll vouch for you. You were good with teaching the boys at Drogheda Grammar. You come along next week and see Dr Khaki. I'll have primed him about you. Nothing to worry about. You'll like it out there.'

So, since I'd nothing better to do and my money was almost gone, I turned up outside an office of the Trinity English department, along with some other unlikely interviewees, waiting to see Alec and Dr Khaki. As Alec had promised, the interview went without a hitch. Dr Khaki, a big bear of a man, asked no questions about my educational qualifications. It was clear that I'd taught at Drogheda Grammar – and spoke English – and that was enough. The interview was brief, almost hurried, and I was offered a job at one of the four ex-British schools in Egypt, board and lodging, a year's contract at thirty pounds a month, a return flight and a fifteen pounds advance for travelling expenses.

Well, this was luck again. For although I didn't know it at the time, my year in Egypt was the making of me: not as a painter, poet, actor, or movie maker as I had hoped to be, but as a novelist, which I'd never thought to be at all. And here I see how I should properly thank my grandfather for all this change and bounty that came to me in my late teens – my grandfather on whom I think I've been a bit hard so far. For it was Old Joe, knowing Dr Marsh, who had got me the job at Drogheda Grammar, and who after-wards, knowing Lord Killanin, had brought me my first work in movies with Ford. And through Ford I had met Brian Hurst, who had got me into pictures in London and Nice, and so I had learnt to speak French, and thus came to know Joe Losey properly at Pinewood and later do some movie scripting with him.

My grandfather's final gift to me was that at Drogheda I had met Alec Reid, who, because of this meeting, had stopped me outside the front gates of Trinity a year later and enticed me to Egypt. So that although my grand-father originally wanted to get shot of me, to pack me off to the merchant navy or the Hong Kong police, the fact is that it was he who led me to all the exciting paths I first took in life. For it was my year as a schoolteacher in Egypt in 1958 and 1959 that brought me ten years later to write fiction, since it was in Cairo that I found the bizarre characters, situations and the setting for my first novel, *The Private Sector*. 'A man goes into Egypt and is changed forever.' And so it was.

But that's another story, of the year I taught in Egypt, and afterwards worked in publishing (another job my grandfather arranged for me through his friend Rupert Hart-Davis), then worked in theatre, managing John Ryan's Envoy Productions in Dublin and later with Joan Littlewood in Stratford East, then as a Talks Producer with BBC radio, before I joined the United Nations Secretariat in New York in 1967; and, for the next thirty years, settled in the Cotswolds with my family, working as a freelance broad-caster with the BBC, doing talks from outlandish parts of Africa, India and

South East Asia, as well as writing my novels and travel books. Altogether another story. This one should properly end with my childhood and youth, because it's a story as much about my minders as it is about me.

And besides, after I went away to Egypt the letters about me in the discovered Little Joe file pretty well come to an end. Though in another file of my own there are many subsequent letters to me from Peggy and Hubert and others, but they are no longer in the 'minding' form. For better or worse I was Big Joe now.

No, the question here, on the evidence of the many earlier letters about me, has been about whether my minders may have harmed more than helped me in my growing up; about whether I was by nature, or simply by being abandoned by my parents, a most difficult, selfish, troublesome, thieving boy. However, the Butlers particularly succeeded in launching me on what turned out to be a largely happy and reasonably successful life. More importantly, because of their early love and concern and the familial confidence they gave me through bringing me up at Maidenhall, they set me on my own secure familial road – marriage and with splendid children and grandchildren.

What of my minders and mentors, of Peggy and Hubert, my grand-parents, real parents, my aunt Sally and husband Stanley, Tony Guthrie and Kingsley Scott? What happened to them? And what of my siblings, those other six orphans of the storm? Of my minders and mentors, all except Kingsley have died.

My grandfather was the first to die in March 1959. I was teaching in Egypt then and only heard several weeks later that he had died of pneu-monia. And of worry and sadness? I think so. His had been a life that had started with every advantage, coming from a well-off and cultured Dublin background, where he had shown great intellectual and cricketing promise at Wellington and Cambridge, promise amply fulfilled in his early maturity, playing cricket for County Wicklow (he was good enough, so his friend Sam Beckett told me, to have played for the Gentlemen of Ireland, as Sam himself had done), writing half-a-dozen acclaimed biographies and all sorts of reviews and articles for George Russell's *Irish Statesman*, *The London Mercury* and the *TLS*.

Later he lived in one of the two fine Hone family houses in Killiney, on the coast, south of Dublin. He was a man of wide and fascinating friendships – with Joyce, Yeats, George Moore, Max Beerbohm, Augustus John, the poets d'Annunzio and Frédéric Mistral and many others; above all a man lucky enough to marry a good and beautiful American woman, Vera.

But all this bounty had latterly eroded for Old Joe, starting with the financial depression of the early 1930s and his increasing problems with Nat, which turned my grandfather into a fusspot: nervous, panicky, feverishly listing his declining assets on the backs of old envelopes.

His was rather the story of many well-to-do Edwardian gentlemen who, having been given a large sum of inherited capital in the early 1900s, lived well on it thereafter, but on an ever-reducing interest, since such gentlemen rarely had to earn money.

In my grandfather's case he couldn't have earned money in any ordinary way of life, at least. He might have continued to work in publishing, or taken on some undemanding academic job, or earned money from his books. But his books on philosophers, on Swift and his biographies on Yeats and George Moore, were not the sort to spin any real money for him, and early on he had lost half his shirt in publishing with the dubious Mr Reynolds from Liverpool.

I think a major factor in Old Joe's life was that he had an underlying melancholic nature. So when things started to go downhill for him financially in the early thirties, these glooms reared up for him and he came to fear the worst; fears which my father's difficult, spendthrift behaviour at Oxford and in Dublin throughout the 1930s amply confirmed for him. Eventually Old Joe had not the fizz to get himself out of his glooms. A lazy man, as he admitted in one of his letters to Hubert, his mind cloud high among even loftier philosophies.

With me he was always very ready to come down to earth, in the blunt matter of pounds, shillings and pence. In a drawer at Maidenhall, some years ago, I found a letter he'd written him to me while I was in Dudgeon's dreadful Sandford Park. Old Joe's worried spirit rises up at me forcefully as I type the letter out now:

Dear Little Joe

I am not satisfied with the reports I get from your school. You will have to work much harder, and also get over your untidiness and carelessness, or I shall have to remove you to a much severer school. In the last account I had there was a charge of £2.11.0 for school books and I wrote to ask Mr Dudgeon what happened to the books when you had done with them. Now I write to tell you that these books are my property and that you must keep them in good condition, so that when they are no longer needed by you, they can be disposed of to the other boys coming along and the amount credited to me. I forbid you to sell them yourself. Mr Dudgeon tells me you are very careless about your books.

It is essential that you learn habits of industry and tidiness, for you will have to begin to make your own living in a few years time and no one will want to give employment to an idle and careless young man. You must not think that you will have me, or the Butlers, or your parents to fall back on for your support.

I shall come to see you presently and expect to find you in a sensible frame of mind about these matters and to get a better report from Mr Dudgeon. If I do not, I shall have to consider sending you to a house where you will have to work to make up for lost time.

Yrs, J. Hone.

This is a typical letter of my grandfather's. He seems blind to the fact (though his friend the poet Austen Clarke had already told him) that Sandford Park was a dreadful place, so my learning 'habits of industry and tidiness' – indeed my learning anything there – was unlikely under Dudgeon's beady, sadistic gaze. Instead my grandfather worries about the future resale of my tattered old copies of Durrell & Fawdry's *Mathematics* and Kennedy's *Latin Grammar*. On the other hand, to excuse my grandfather's miserly, threatening attitude in the letter, he was an old and put-upon man at the time, with little direct and no legal responsibility for me.

One can go on endlessly with caveats and excuses for someone's behaviour. The fact is people have a bias in their temperament towards one characteristic or another, and Old Joe's leaning allowed him to keep his hand well away from his pocket. And since, before his death in 1959, he left an estate valued at nearly forty thousand pounds (maybe ten times that in today's money) he might have extracted some more ready cash from the estate before he died and been less parsimonious with himself and with Vera.

Vera hung on for nearly ten years after my grandfather's death, first in the Dublin house at Winton Road, then, through the good offices of the Butlers, as a paying guest with the local rector, Canon Smyth and his wife, in Kells near Maidenhall, where she lived in the front room of the large, gloomy and chilly rectory. Finally, when she could no longer look after herself, she came to a small nursing home run by kind nuns near the seafront south of Dublin in Blackrock, where her son David and his wife Rosemary, not far away, paid her every attention. I saw Vera rarely, living as I was then with my wife Jacky in London and then New York. But that Vera was a kind and generous woman there is no doubt, bailing Nat out with secret cheques and parcels of old clothes and shoes, and me, now and then, with very welcome cheques before I had regular work as a producer with the BBC in 1963.

I've wondered what she thought about after Old Joe's death – pondering things in those long years in the isolated rectory, legs crossed like a contortionist's, in a chair against the small fire: the high cheekbones gone skeletal, one finger pensively against her lips, cigarette smoke swirling around from the drafty windows. Dreams of a long-ago woman? Beautiful, innocent, but confident: and so commemorated by the painter Orpen in half a dozen wonderful portraits. A young woman, orphaned, but taken to *Belle Époque* Paris by the famous actress, her rich aunt Julia Marlowe, to Maxims no doubt, and the opera, and to buy huge flowery hats and fashionable clothes on the rue St Honoré. And meeting the gauntly handsome young Joe there; and a few years later married with a curtain ring bought from a local haberdashers by Beatty Glenavy, to seal their secret eight-in-the-morning wedding in a suburban Dublin church.

Her early years have the air of a glittering romantic novel. Latterly, the book became tattered and tarnished, in large part I think by the endlessly worrying antics of her eldest son, my father Nat. Nat become the prodigal son who only returned home for another pair of old shoes, a mackintosh of his father's and the cash to get him back as soon as possible on the mail boat to England. All this must have been a long depressing horror for Vera. Though again, one might make some excuses for Nat in that he was stricken by TB just before the war and even in this he was given the best chance of recovery by his aunt Julia, who arranged and paid for him to go to a Swiss sanatorium high up in the mountains in 1939. My uncle David sent me a letter from aunt Julia to Vera some years ago. It's evidence of how, with her money and influence, she tried to set Nat to rights – a chance which he didn't make best use of:

Hotel Beau-Rivage, Lausanne. 17 September, 1939.

Dear Vera,

I enclose a first letter from Nat. He seems content with all the arrangements we have made for him. We have sent him the money which he will send to Rome for his new passport. The Irish Legation is doing this for him – and he will be relieved to have this new passport so he can move about when the time comes as he desires. No doubt he has already written to you about everything. He seemed content and even pleased altogether with his prospects and his ability to get well. He has a strong belief that he will get well and he must be encouraged in that belief. The doctor says he may never be quite robust as before but will be able to do office work at least. Don't worry about him. He can come and see me whenever he likes for a day or two – which prospect seemed to encourage him too.

Love to you and Sally and David and Joe. I understand your problems. I know you will be able to manage them. Patience and endurance will do much and you have both shown yourselves equal to these necessities before, and will do so again.

Yours affectionately,
Julia.

It's indicative of Nat's hypocrisy that he gets an Irish passport, but strenuously denies me one fifteen years later, thus forcing me (as he hopes) to do military service in Britain. And Nat did get well. Well enough, on his return to Biddy in England, to father another four children, without having a penny to support them, and so abandon them.

And what of my aunt Sally and her bookshop husband Stanley? My saviours when I'd left St Columba's College in 1953 with no prospects, when they gave me a room in their Hampstead house, a start in the world with work (and an education) in Stanley's Beauchamp Bookshop. Stanley lived until the early 1990s. He had a dodgy heart, greatly improved by a bypass operation, which gave him renewed vigour for three or four years. But his heart finally did for him while he was doing the washing up with Sally one evening. He might have preferred to go out inspecting a rare old vellum-bound volume, though there is surely more merit in going out after helping your wife with a dishcloth. And this end was appropriate, for Stanley was a classic homebody, loved his pipe-and-slippers comforts, his food, his wine and his wife.

Sally lived on for nearly ten years, alone in the Hampstead flat they'd moved to, then up to a small restored alms house in Derbyshire near her daughter Susan and her family who paid her every attention. Finally, when she could no longer cope by herself, she went to a care home nearby. I drove up to see her quite often in her last years. She became progressively more muddled, annoyed and panic-stricken. I asked her several times (as I had before when she was entirely clear-headed) about her wartime work as a cipher clerk at Bletchley Park; but her lips remained sealed. In her cloudy mind now, where only old memories held any sway, the war was still on. I like to think that sometimes she remembered the war and took pride in recalling her time back in that Nissen hut at Bletchley, helping decode the German Enigma naval messages of U-boat dispositions in the Atlantic, thus saving vital Allied armament supplies and fuel tankers from America, struggling across storm-tossed seas, as her own mind was then. Sally had done the state some service, and the same and more for me. Like Stanley, when she died she was cremated, and her ashes joined his in the graveyard of Hampstead parish church, a church she had loved.

Hubert died in January 1991, as old as the century; a long life that would have been longer but for a botched prostate operation in a Dublin hospital where, after he was left waiting for several hours on a trolley outside the operating theatre, the anaesthetic wore off halfway through the proce-dure, waking him, screaming in pain. A subsequent operation left him in discomfort and further pain, with catheters and rubber bags for the rest of his life; a situation he bore with his usual uncomplaining stoicism. Back at

Maidenhall he wrote as much as he could under the circumstances, rewriting or expanding earlier magazine articles about the Balkans, the Holocaust and Irish History, published in three collections by the Lilliput Press in Mullingar and Dublin. A fourth and last volume of his essays, *In the Land of Nod*, appeared after his death in 1995.

In preparing these collections he was helped as always by Peggy, with editing by Antony Farrell of Lilliput. Antony first came across essays by Hubert in old magazines in the early 1980s and was so taken by them that he'd gone down to Maidenhall to meet Hubert and subsequently helped him unearth and edit scores of his forgotten articles. Lilliput published the first volume, *Escape from the Anthill*, in 1985.

This collection was widely and enthusiastically reviewed in Ireland, and the three subsequent volumes found much wider acclaim, with publication in England, North America and France. There were literary prizes and other public attentions from all sides. Hubert, in the last five years of his life, having been a largely unknown and then an almost forgotten literary figure in Ireland, became famous, mentioned as one with Swift, Chekhov and Orwell. As Neal Acherson wrote of him: 'His fame began to spread across his native Ireland and then across the world. But by the time of his death, readers throughout Europe and America were asking in amazement why he had not been part of their common culture before.'

All this formed a wonderful late renaissance – for Hubert, his family, friends and readers. He took the acclaim, this sudden late and loud justification of all his old social and religious writings about Ireland, and his explosive unearthings about the bloody fate of Balkan and other minorities during the war, in essays, articles and letters to *The Irish Times*, which the public had previously ignored or sneered at, or for which he'd been vilified – Hubert took his fame as he'd taken most things in his life, without fuss, never saying (though I hope he thought it) that it was no more than his due. A few years before he died he asked me to be his literary executor. I was no longer irresponsible Little Joe.

But the story of my association, for the span of this memoir, should stay with my Little Joe times with him. Here, as with my grandfather, Hubert seems to have somewhat failed to find any reasonable answer to my problems, in that he sees only drastic solutions to them – by farming me out once more, in effect abandoning me, as my parents had done.

A letter from him, in the Little Joe file, is written to an old friend, Bob French, dated 26 January 1950, when I was almost thirteen:

Dear Bob

Peggy says I should not bother you but I am taking the risk. It is about Little Joe Hone. You know his background and some of his problems. And you have an interest in homeless people. We undertook some years ago to look after him till his parents took over, but underlined a hundred times that under no circumstances could we share responsibility for him with Nat and Biddy. In the past two years they have been seeing a good deal of him, we less. For Joe's sake we wished the break to be as gradual as possible, but break there must be.

Now it has been decided, wisely I think, to send Joe to school in England. It will mean however that unless some family in England can, in his holidays, be persuaded to take the same interest in him that we have taken here, he will be dependent on Nat and Biddy. Do you know of any such family or can you suggest how they can be found?

I don't think it will be wholly to Joe's disadvantage if we fade out of the picture, except as friends. Our household isn't the right one for him, even if we had the right to decide anything about him. Peggy has however taken enormous pains with him (so have I for that matter) and he has had a good start. But now that he is older we begin to fear things will go wrong. Also we have done our bit. We are busy people with many problems of our own and he is in no way our responsibility as was made clear to us from the start.

This sounds cold hearted, but we shall always feel warmly towards Little Joe himself, and will co-operate to secure a good arrangement for his future. Any family, who would look after him, would have to have a guarantee of non-interference from Nat and Biddy, such as we failed to secure. I believe under pressure from me and the grandparents they might give this.

Do, Bob, give your mind to this problem, exasperating as you may find it and don't hold it against me that I have asked you ... He is lively and intelligent and has great charm. He is very easily influenced for good or bad and worth influencing ... I have no doubt that there are many families who would be glad to give him a home, problems and all. But how does one find them?

There is no reply in the file to this letter, though I'm sure Bob French sent one – he was a conscientious man – probably saying he had no real ideas about farming-out families in England, since two months later there is a further letter from Hubert, on the same family-searching theme, to his friend Alan Cameron, Elizabeth Bowen's husband:

April 10th 1950.

Dear Alan

This is a supplement to my letter to Elizabeth to catch a later post – about Joe. Peggy and I would be most grateful if you would find out what hope he has of getting Joe into Ardingley. From your accounts it would suit him admirably. You know his circumstances. He is now 13, has been with us continuously until about three years ago. Since then his parents, who live in Battersea, have had him for occasional holidays, and as it has become quite impossible for us to share responsibility for him with them we are looking around for some other arrangement.

We do not think his parents are at all likely to be able to look after him permanently – they have five other children, none of whom they have been able to bring up themselves. I think I can find a family in Sussex, who would look after him in the holidays, and we believe it would be better for him to be in England on a new basis. There are no boys around here of his own age and I believe English circumstances would suit him better. I would get from his parents some 'non-intervention' or 'qualified intervention' pact. His grandparents pay for his schooling, so they have bargaining power and would take my advice.

Joe is a very lively intelligent boy, well-grown and highly social. It seems to be probable that he has inherited more than a share of the great family talents. As you know they've been artists, actors, writers in the family for several generations, some of rare quality.

I think Joe's main failings, his instability of temperament, his rather predatory, egotistic nature, are at least partly due to his sense of insecurity. I offered to be his guardian but his parents did not wish to surrender any control – with the result that he probably has the feeling that he belongs nowhere. We shall always, of course, befriend him, wherever he is.

Love to you both again,
Hubert.

Despite Hubert's avowal of continuing friendly relations with me, there is an air of subdued desperation in these letters – to get me off the Butlers' hands. This keenness is surely evidenced by his writing a very favourable prospectus of my characteristics for possible buyers – 'a well-grown' boy and so on. He might well be preparing to auction me, as one would a bullock or a slave. There is no reply from Alan Cameron to Hubert's last letter, nor any other mention of either Ardingley (whatever sort of school or institution that was), or of any family in Sussex that Hubert thinks he can send me to. And no mention was ever made to me at the time of my being packed off to any new school or family in England. I would have remembered if there had been; I would have been devastated. Did Hubert really think I would go happily to some institution or strange family in England?

What I do remember is that – as a way of gradually withdrawing from me, no doubt – when I was in my early teens, the Butlers went for holidays to Switzerland and Normandy, and I wasn't included, but sent to my grand-parents instead. At that point I was still marooned at Sandford Park, under the ever-watchful whacker Dudgeon. Along with my grandfather, Hubert doesn't see that many of my problems then arose not so much from my not knowing where I belonged (as far as I was concerned I belonged totally to the Butlers and Maidenhall), but from the horrors of Sandford Park, from which I should have been removed long before.

There are other anomalies in Hubert's attitude towards me in these two letters. If he saw me and my family as artistically gifted, might he not also have seen that, given this sort of inherited sensitivity, I was likely to suffer more than other boys from this sudden transplantation he is propos-ing for me? As a market gardener he would have known the damage con-sequent on uprooting a long-established plant from one soil and moving it abroad to a totally different earth; so it was optimistic of him to think I would flourish with some unknown family in England. In fact I don't think he believed this; in face of his problems with me he just wanted to believe it. I think he, and certainly Peggy, must have known how much such a removal would have hurt me.

In any case might he not have considered less drastic answers to my problems? By arranging, for example, for me to go as a boarder to Newtown, the liberal co-educational Quaker school in Waterford where, with pretty girls to hand, my problems might have been substantially eased. Like my grandfather over my schoolbooks, Hubert tends to get into a confused tizzy about me. For example, he has often said in his letters that my problems are largely due to my 'insecurity'. Yet here he is proposing a much greater insecurity for me, overseas, in some institution or with a totally strange family.

Hubert's now-and-then contradictory and insensitive attitudes towards me may well stem from his own sometimes unhappy childhood, about which, in all his many writings, he wrote very little. The most spectacularly unhappy time for him, as he has written, was when, aged seven, he thought his parents had literally given him away to his prep school, Bigshotte Reyles, in Berkshire: undoubtedly a traumatic transplantation for him where, during his first term, he wandered round gawping, unable to speak, and had twice bitten off the top of Matron's thermometer.

This early experience of desertion came, I suspect, to chill Hubert's adult emotions as well, so that he found it difficult to deal with me in simpler human terms, and saw the answer to my problems, ironically, only in trying to organize another exile for me. Hubert, in these two letters, seems to have forgotten the abandonment that I had suffered with my parents, and is intent here on repeating this himself by exiling me a second time. In the event I wasn't sent away to England and Maidenhall remained my home. But it was clearly a damn close-run thing for me in the early 1950s.

Later, in 1969 when Jacky and I and our daughter Lucy left New York and came to live in the Cotswolds, I had a much easier relationship with Hubert in my many subsequent visits to Maidenhall, both with the family and alone. I think he was as surprised as I was that I'd come to make my living out of my novels. It wasn't that we were writers together now, sharing ideas, thinking of similar themes – our writing being so very different. But that I had survived all the rocky shoals of my childhood, which must have pleased him, and Peggy, and survived in a literary, rather than in just a workaday, nine-to-five manner. I sent them my novels as they appeared, and in starting to read one of a pair, *The Sixth Directorate*, Hubert writes to me in June 1975:

My Dear Joe,

You will wonder why I didn't thank you ages ago for your two books, particularly the one dedicated to HM and SM (which flattered us and pleased us enormously). The reason is an embarrassing one and I hoped if I waited a few days it would not be necessary to give it – but not so! I was reading it with great pleasure and admiration – and suddenly it DISAPPEARED. We have hunted on every shelf, under every bed and sofa, even in spare rooms, in case some guest had taken it up, but not a trace. Peggy had it in the porch and then withdrew to bed with a sprained ankle and, as we didn't lend it or have any guest who would pinch it, we can only assume that some tinker (they are encamped at MacDonald's) took it because of its bright cover. We're getting another copy of course, but even if, as we hope, you put in the nice inscription when you come over, it won't be quite the same. We're mad about it at intervals. Pace round goggling at the shelves.

You are quite right, it isn't my style of book, (Nor is *Paradise Lost, Pilgrim's Progress* or ANY modern poet) but after the first chapter I was delighted with it. It fitted in with my mood of the moment, of looking forward to several peaceful evenings with it. As always your writing is exceedingly good and I kept meeting happy images and turns of phrase that enchanted me. What astonished me too was your knowledge and confident familiarity with subjects and places that you must have met or visited in dream or imagination. I don't remember, for instance, that you were ever in Russia. Or were you? How otherwise, though, can you reproduce so well the streets of Moscow or Leningrad, the remote forests and changes of atmosphere – even if you had been there. I think I'd have noticed anything desperately phoney but didn't. However, I'll be reading the whole book soon and will say no more now …

Love to yourself and family,
Hubert.

I had never been to Russia at that point. I was writing a novel, and so had researched and invented all that I needed of the country. But Hubert spoke Russian, had lived in Moscow and Leningrad, and had travelled the country before the war. So this was valued praise.

What he doesn't say in the letter is that without the sense of the great importance of books I had from him and his large library at Maidenhall, I'd probably never have become an author. My upbringing in a house with a large library, with Hubert always writing and reading, was for me, by some curious process of osmosis, part of my coming to write books myself.

There is, in this letter, a typically Butlerian – but also a nicely Tolstoyan or Chekhovian – picture of life at Maidenhall: the tinkers are camped beyond the lawn, and one of them, sneaking up to the porch, and magpie-like, attracted by the bright cover of my book, has pinched it – Peggy in bed with a sprained ankle and Hubert in the drawing-room, only yards away from the porch window, but who has seen nothing of the tinker, deep in thought, pondering a cryptic Serbo-Croatian text.

Hubert, with pneumonia, went to Auteven Hospital in Kilkenny and died there in early January 1991. I was there for the funeral. The hearse, in Irish custom, stopped on the empty winter road in front of Maidenhall for a full minute, so that the dead could take a last look at the house and lands that had been theirs. For Hubert, Maidenhall and its lands had been at the heart of his life and work. I read the lesson at the packed church, 'Once we saw through a glass darkly, but now we see face to face ...'

Peggy didn't come to the funeral, staying in the drawing-room with an old friend. She hated all the fuss and dreary pomp of funerals. Above all, she told me once, she hated the fraud of false green nylon grass covering the excavated grave soil, which had become the fashion at funerals by then: 'The vegetable garden would do me, among the cabbages,' she said.

Peggy's turn, not for the Maidenhall cabbage patch but for the fake green grass at Ennisnag church next to Hubert, was not to come for another five years. Five years through which, though painfully arthritic and largely wheelchair-bound, she soldiered on. More than that, with a freedom from her long concerns about Hubert, she drew together all the strands of her warrior nature – in his service, through the promotion of his work.

And also in my service, with her continued if sometimes bossy and argumentative concern for me, combined with her very real love in many letters between us and during my many subsequent visits to Maidenhall. In chilled winters, daffodil springs, orange autumns, when sometimes, alone together in the silent house with my butter-cooked omelette suppers on trays in the drawing-room, we had perhaps the unspoken feeling, the need to feel at least, that she was my mother and I her son.

FIFTEEN

Peggy would have liked more children of her own. As things turned out she had lots more of them, as paying guests at Maidenhall (for they ran the big house then as a paying concern) throughout the 1940s and 1950s. They came as a very varied mix: as brothers, the two Fitzsimon boys, Christopher and Nicky, and the two l'Estranges, Larry and John, and the two Bruns from Paris, Marc and Richard; or as a group with the four delightful Harrison sisters, or as brother and sister, Eleanor and Tommy Arkell, and the five half-Russian Lieven children – Michael, Chai, Dominic, Elena and the youngest, Anatol – the last a fine writer and journalist on Russian themes, the others all formidable academics.

Many other children and teenagers came to stay at Maidenhall, Irish, British, French, German, Yugoslav, Swiss on exchange visits or to learn English. Some were refugees from the war, or detached children, their parents overseas serving the remnants of empire, and some few from broken homes as I had come from. And I, in the pecking order, just below Julia, was keen to keep my status up, and so resented these new arrivals as interlopers and went out into the bamboos of an evening with my defective Diana air rifle and did them imaginary damage.

Peggy was a great organizer and taskmaster. This was a problem for some of us children at Maidenhall: her brusque commands and reprimands, the constant jobs and errands she sent us on, fetching something for her, dealing with the animals, picking the daffodils and fruit. Most of the children took to these jobs happily, a few with only fair good will. Yet there was one who was mutinous. I sulked, stole the chocolates, hid in the hayloft or up a tree in the windcharger field. Peggy checked on you if you dawdled over or postponed the set tasks – or, indeed, if you disappeared. One was rarely out of earshot of her high piercing voice: 'Joe? Joe? Jo-o-oseph?' A voice that could be heard way out of the house, beyond the hayloft and up to the woods. Peggy's commands and scoldings were always a problem for me.

Not that there was the slightest air of Maidenhall being a House of Correction (such as my grandfather was threatening to send me to). It was a happy, very active, purposeful place and Maidenhall is still the beautiful house it always was (though much improved materially), happily run by Julia and her husband Dick Crampton, and by their daughter Suzanna when her parents are back at their other home in Charlottesville, Virginia.

Many of these children have returned to visit in their later life, and so have I. But I, no doubt, was more difficult than them in those childhood days. And I clearly remained unpromising, since Peggy's scoldings went on way into my adult life. In 1959, when I was twenty-two, I was in Ireland with Joe Losey and his wife Patricia, helping Joe scout possible prison locations for his movie *The Criminal*. The three of us spent a relaxed two days at Maidenhall. But Peggy writes to me afterwards:

Joe darling,
We are planning to turn your room into a bathroom, so come soon and help us over arrangements. We had very nice bread and butter letters from both Loseys – please note neither too busy to be polite! A moral there, I think, for you – a postcard takes little time and less money and would have made all the difference in nice feeling both to your Granny and us. It is something you must be more grown-up about – if you are to be treated on the level of an adult you must behave like one. Either one is forced to regard you as still a schoolboy, rapacious and irresponsible but so inexperienced all is automatically forgiven, OR as an adult but a boor … Won't refer to this again.
Love from us both, PXX

I was sad about losing my bedroom for a new bathroom. But fair enough about the thank-you note. I should have written one, as the Loseys had. I have few excuses, except that the Loseys had a house in Knightsbridge and a secretary to take dictated letters. I had no fixed abode. I was trying to make a go of it in the big city arts world, in theatre or the movies, where any opportunity offered in these fields had to be taken – yes, rapaciously. I had hardly any money and was camping on friends' floors and so forth. I wonder if Peggy quite understood my precarious circumstances then.

I was living from hand to mouth, trying to rustle up any kind of job or money, going to and fro between Dublin and London, as manager of the Envoy Theatre Company in Dublin, a job with Harrods in their second-hand book department and other temporary winter work with Heywood Hill in their Curzon Street bookshop cataloguing their rare books. Or work with Joan Littlewood out at Stratford East, building the sets with Sean Kenny for Behan's *The Hostage*, and afterwards managing a season there with a Pinter play and one of our Dublin musicals, *Glory Be!* I was in a survival tizzy then, pretty well blind to anything but where I was to find the next meal or five-pound note. I had little time for sending thank-you notes.

I should have made the time, however, to send one. What I question now is the harshness of her words in the letter: 'an irresponsible schoolboy … a boor'. Equally I see now that Peggy was right in her criticisms of me. 'Manners Maketh Man.'

Would she have been less critical of me if I had been her son? No, Peggy could sometimes be very critical of everybody – relations, friends or anybody else conveniently to hand. She would have criticized me whether she'd been my mother or not, and one may well learn more from harsh criticism than from motherly love. 'Faithful are the wounds of a friend,' Peggy used to say to me, after a few good dagger thrusts. I think I would have preferred the fidelity of motherly love, although that, from my real mother Biddy with her make-do attitudes, might, given my own some-what similar temperament, have done me no good at all. In any case, in the matter of familial support I was out on my own now, sailing in what seemed to me a very frail craft, far from port in choppy waters with no visible landfall.

John Mortimer, in his splendid memoir *Clinging to the Wreckage*, takes his title from the advice of a yachting friend: 'When your boat sinks, cling to the wreckage – then someone will come out and rescue you. Don't try and swim for it. You'll drown.' Mortimer clearly didn't take this advice: he has swum out manfully all his life, through every sort of stormy weather, waving not drowning. For me it was the opposite. I wasn't going to cling to the wreckage. I'd seen the devils in the shipwreck of my own family. It was the deep blue sea for me.

But Peggy's many letters to me over the years were always much more loving than critical. I have quoted few of them here because they were almost entirely newsy – of her and Hubert's doings at Maidenhall. I had the great good luck to share so many of their doings at the big house. I also had their love, and returned it. It was a frustrated love for all three of us, but it might have been a love in full measure had I been their real son, although real sons often have a more difficult relationship with their parents than I had with Peggy and Hubert. As it was I had some of the worst and most of the best of Peggy. She was a remarkable woman with an extraordinary mix of often contradictory characteristics: loudly energetic but a rapt and silent music lover; forthright but sometimes buttoned up; realistic, intuitive; rudely acerbic but genuinely kind. She exercised her art into old age, not with earlier so accomplished oil paintings, but with witty drawings, cartoons and poems, published together in a late book, *They Speak for Themselves*. Indomitable.

She died in Auteven Hospital in Kilkenny in December 1996, aged ninety-one. She had been in the hospital several times during the previous eighteen months, with serious complaints, and I had been over to see her at Auteven and at Maidenhall when, tough as she was, she had emerged each time from the hospital. This time it seemed she really was going, and I came over to see her again. I rather failed her and went to see her once in the hospital, and then again when she was only half conscious. I held her hand for a few minutes, smiled, and there was a vague smile back. Then I left her in the hands of her real family, her daughter and grandchildren. I went out on the town in Kilkenny and then straight back home. The fact was I couldn't face her death. Sheer funk; an unresolved problem that made me shy away from her death, as I'd sometimes shied away from her in life. It was a sort of emotional reserve that had started many years before, when I'd first come to Maidenhall as a three-year-old and my parents had refused my adoption with the Butlers, which had resulted in my confused feelings towards her, a cauterised emotion between us – for Peggy wanting a son in someone who wasn't her son; for me, loving feelings I couldn't fully express because I knew she wasn't my real mother. Circumstances stood in our way. We had always been stymied in our emotions for each other.

And what of the dramatic mentor of my early life, Tony Guthrie? He had died years before in May 1971, of a heart attack one morning while opening the post in his study at Annaghmakerrig. It's an apocryphal story that opening his annual income tax demand killed him. With his Scots background he was careful with money and always paid his dues. But in matters that took his fancy he could spend lavishly. This he did in the mid-1960s with the creation and costly financing of a jam factory in the old station yard of Newbliss, the local village five miles from Annaghmakerrig. This seemed to him an admirable philanthropic and economic plan, giving work for the unemployed villagers and the depressed local farmers of the time. The farmers would grow the soft fruit and the villagers would happily sweat in the factory over the boiling vats and jam jars. Indeed Irish Farm-house Preserves did well for a few years, the company making excellent organic raspberry, strawberry and blackcurrant jam. The account at the local bank, though, showed an increasing overdraft. To keep the company afloat, Tony abandoned most of his theatre work and took to the more imme-diately lucrative but physically punishing American lecture circuit, giving witty and inspiring talks from Berkeley to Boston for most of the year, and pouring the dollars straight back into the jam factory. Yet still the overdraft increased. The enterprise collapsed with debts of half a million.

There was much searching for answers as to what had gone wrong. Had Tony just been naive about local rural conditions? A dreamer among the raspberry canes and strawberry beds? Naive and theatrical, hoping to pro-duce a local Carmen in a jam instead of a cigarette factory? Yes, in part. In fact the real reason for the collapse was simpler, and devastating for Tony. The local factory manager, in whom Tony had put all his trust and money, had had both hands in the till almost from the start of the enterprise. It was

Tony's discovery of this, and the exhaustion of his long months of lecturing in the States, which must have stopped his heart.

This was not the only heartache for Tony and his relations. In his will he had left the house, with nearly all its contents, the lake and all the land to the steward, Seamus McGorman, in the innocent salt-of-the-earth belief that this local farmer who had worked the Annaghmakerrig estate for twenty years should therefore have the whole place on Tony's death. This was a bombshell for Peggy and Hubert when they learnt of his extraordinary decision. Annaghmakerrig – family home of Peggy's mother, Norah Power's – had become Peggy's family home after the death of her father Dr Guthrie in 1929, and the remaining three Guthries had moved there from Tunbridge Wells. Before that Annaghmakerrig had been Tony's and Peggy's holiday home, and so was filled for Peggy with indelible happy associations, and memories, of her mother, of her and Tony's old and greatly loved nanny Becky (who still lived there way up until the 1960s), of the family servants, estate workers, neighbours, and of the lake, furniture and family portraits – all that gave heart to the beautiful place. Peggy loved Annaghmakerrig probably more than Tony did.

I may be wrong, though. Tony had ambivalent feelings about Annaghmakerig. He loved it too, though there was a sadness in his love, evident in the interview I did with him up at the house for the BBC just two weeks before he died. I asked him what Annaghmakerrig meant to him:

'We're still here because we're very fond of the place. It has all sorts of associations for us. And we like being here. And I think it important, if you can, to have associations with the locality, and if possible some kind of attachment to some part of the world that you regard as home. I think there's a very great danger, in cities particularly and in the modern economy, of more and more people becoming virtually rootless. Whereas if you've been in a locality, as we have here, for quite a number of generations, you grow up with the neighbours. The old neighbours are now my contemporaries. I knew their parents, they knew mine. I know their children and their grandchildren.' 'You never felt of the place here as a burden then?' 'No, I've never felt that. I do find it expensive. But I'd rather be spending the money this way than going to the races.' 'Do you think that having this house in the background of your professional life – which of course has been led nearly always overseas – has this helped your professional life, in the sense that at the back of you there was this house?' 'Joe, I couldn't answer that. I simply don't know. It's given me a feeling of continuity and that I'm working for something rather – as I think – more important than just getting on, or making money. If we had children it would be easy to understand, but since we haven't and whatever has gone on here will end with us, well, then perhaps it is all rather sentimental and irrational.'

The key words – 'If we had children …' then Tony would have surely loved the house without irrational sentimentality and of course would never have given the whole place over to the steward. But as things were and as he says, having clearly decided on this, it 'will end with us'. It very nearly did.

Since they had no children, Tony had years before offered the house to Julia, his niece. But he didn't confirm this offer, knowing that Julia would inherit Maidenhall and would have enough on her hands looking after this other big house. All the Butlers then assumed that Tony, in time, would make a will allowing for some other sensible public use for the place after his death. Or if not, then, on the terms of Mrs Guthrie's will, the house should be sold and the proceeds divided equally between Tony and Peggy. None of this was to be.

The steward was to have it, lock, stock and barrel. And since he would be quite unable to keep up Annaghmakerrig, he would have the roof off in no time, to avoid paying rates. This whole business over the future of Annaghmakerrig created a breach and a great sadness between Tony and Peggy and Hubert.

In the event, Hubert asked Julia – then married to Dick Crampton and living in New York – to talk to her godmother, Pamela (Mary Poppins) Travers. Pamela was then lecturing at a Radcliffe College in Boston. He suggested Julia and Tony (also in New York then) see Pamela in the hopes she might move Tony towards some sensible ideas about the future of the house. Tony agreed and he and Julia flew up to Boston for a meeting. Pamela told Tony at once that giving the whole place over to the steward was crazy. Instead, since she had experience of Yaddoo and several other artists' colonies in America, she suggested that he turn Annaghmakerrig into an artists' residence, first making the house at least over to the Irish State.

Tony took this advice. Julia, particularly, did the leg work in gathering information and telling Tony how artists' colonies were run in America, how the residents should at all meet informally at least once a day for an evening meal. So Tony changed his will at the last moment, and left the house (but none of the land which was still to go to the steward) to the Irish Minister of Finance as a residence for artists.

Hubert writes to me in July 1971, some months after Tony's death:

My dear Joe

Not much news from Annaghmakerrig. Judy has bronchitis but has guests … Peggy hates to talk of it all and so do I. We seem to have wasted much thought and even tears on it, not because we were greedy or litigious, but because AK is such a beautiful place where many were and still could be happy and it has been treated as though it was a theatrical prop made of cardboard. There has been an enormous amount in the press and on TV about the gift to the Minister of Finance, but I am dead certain that the Minister won't accept it when in due course Judy dies and it becomes available. If Seamus has the garden and the lake and all those at AK merely have access, there will be no security against development … and I do not see how Seamus could farm it profitably, as it has never been self-supporting.

Such muddle would seem to me inconceivable were it not for the jam factory's collapse … its management has been incompetent beyond belief. Tony had been working himself to death for it, pouring money from these last lecture tours, and keeping it alive this way … It is horribly painful to write like this since Tony was a very old friend, my oldest, and a near genius. But he had a totally blind spot about Ireland, understood nothing whatever about it, and thought that the swift decisions, the rapid intuitions and ruthless judgement could work in Ireland as well as on the stage and could be compensation for the knowledge that long and often disillusioning co-habitation with one's countrymen can bring …

Surely Tony's solicitors gave him appallingly bad advice or rather refrained from giving him good advice … They were all dazzled by Tony and hesitated to criticise him. What will happen after the Minister has refused it? It will go to Belfast University who, if they have any sense, will buy out Seamus and sell the place to Cyrus J Featherbaum of Minnesota …

Love to you all, H.

Hubert told me later that he thought Tony had simply had an *Après-moi le déluge* brainstorm about the whole business. But his remark that Tony had been treating Annaghmakerrig as a cardboard theatrical prop is equally true. Consciously or unconsciously I think Tony was directing *The Guthrie Inheritance*, his last great production. This might have been expected (though no less hurtful to his relatives), since theatrical drama had been at the heart of his life for fifty years. And drama for Tony always had to be unexpected, irreverent, a totally new slant on the text: umbrellas over Ophelia's grave, an updated *Troilus*, set among the rival protagonists in a Ruritanian world of swirling dancers, gold-braided uniforms, Lehar and Old Vienna. His dealings over the future of Annaghmakerrig, whether he knew it or not, fulfilled many of his theatrical precepts: 'Discomfit the fuddy-duddies!' 'Set the cat among the pigeons!' 'Nothing boring!' 'Astonish us in the morning!' as he told an actor who was being a bit dull about things in the afternoon. Well, astonish everybody he did in his will, not least the steward, who, I'm sure, couldn't have believed his luck in inheriting five hundred acres.

As things turned out the Minister of Finance did accept the house, and passed it on to the Irish and Northern Irish Arts Councils who have administered Annaghmakerrig successfully for the last twenty-five years as a residence for artists. The only problem was that all the land, the gardens and lawn, right up to the front doorstep, remained with the steward who thereafter had the Arts Councils over a barrel: the house was effectively inoperable without the grounds immediately surrounding it. As far as Seamus MacGorman was concerned it was pigs in the parlour – or get your cheque books out. The Arts Councils took the latter course, and vast sums of money had eventually to be paid to Seamus for the land – money which, of course, would have been far better spent nurturing budding artists. So in the end *The Guthrie Inheritance* was by far Tony's most expensive production. But then, in his theatre work and in himself, he was always a man of the most expansive, unexpected and generous vision …

I often stayed with Tony and Judy at Annaghmakerrig in my lean years in the late 1950s and early 1960s, working on scripts for Joe Losey and working for Tony too. He was a great admirer of *Tarry Flynn*, an early novel by the poet Patrick Kavanagh, set in Paddy's homelands twenty-five miles east of Annaghmakerrig. We talked about filming it. 'We'll do it as a drama-documentary,' he said. 'With the local people there. And you'll do a script.' I did a draft treatment and he paid me fifty pounds.

The film was never made. Staying with him a few months later I showed him another movie synopsis of mine, for a rather bigger movie – an epic indeed, *Joseph and his Brothers*, set among Irish emigrants in mid-nineteenth-century New York. This project took his fancy, as anything large scale and biblical usually did. 'And I tell you what,' he said with that sudden military twinkle in his eyes, 'We'll need to raise quite a bit of cash for this one – so we'll get Richard Burton to play Joseph.' 'But I thought you didn't care for working with big movie stars, Tony?' 'Oh, in this case we'll make an exception. Besides, Burton used to be a fine stage actor.' He paid me another fifty pounds and I started work on a final script. This film was never made either. No matter. It was Tony's gesture – and the money – that mattered to me then, and he knew that. Tony was the great bohemian. He knew all the risks for anyone taking up work in the precarious world of theatre and movies, he saw that I was eager to take these risks, and he encouraged me, as Joe Losey was doing. They encouraged me again, in 1962, when they acted as referees when I applied for a job as a talks producer in BBC radio. I gave them both credit for the success of my application over some hundreds of other applicants as I heard later.

Given all that had happened between Tony and Peggy, from great love to appalled dismay at his behaviour over the house, Tony's funeral was going to be painful for Peggy. But she had to go. Hubert stayed behind, possibly because the whole Annaghmakerrig business had soured things so much for him with Tony. So Peggy and I drove up from Kilkenny to the house, then crawled along behind Judy's car for the long slow two miles to the isolated hilltop church, with its circling beech trees budding in the spring wind. There were crowds in the porch and outside right onto the road. Inside, the roof was raised: 'Abide With Me', 'Onwards Christian Soldiers'. Tony loved these old, tub-thumping Victorian hymns – the organ bellowing out evangelical tunes that I had sung with him and the family years before in the same church. This was his final curtain, and he might have been producing the show himself, like the last night of the Proms. 'Rise above!' 'On, on!' Indeed the service was so much him, so much was his presence felt, that, turning and looking along the Guthrie pew, I was surprised to see he wasn't there.

Judy hung on, ill and depressed, for only another year at Annaghmak-errig before she died. She was lost without Tony, as my mother was lost without Nat, whose death I've described earlier, but a native Irish toughness allowed Biddy to survive Nat by four years.

In the early sixties Biddy had left Cheltenham and gone to live with a younger sister, married to an older man, a solicitor, I think, in a lace-curtained suburban house in Chippenham, Wiltshire, where I went to see her several times. She was vague and restless, these were not quite her sort of people though they were looking after her with kindness, if not with any great sympathy. She was not their sort of person. Biddy became ill and a few months later she was admitted to Bath General Hospital where she died within a week, in the summer of 1963, of womb cancer. I heard of her death from her sister. I didn't go to her funeral. Why didn't I? I think it was a feeling that I didn't want to pay final tribute to a mother who, very good and loving as she was in other ways, had never been a mother to me.

Before her move to Chippenham I had gone down to see her quite often in Cheltenham while she was still working for Walker Crossweller as a filing clerk at eleven pounds a week. She was living alone in a damp dark basement flat in Wellington Square, where I camped for the night on the sofa. We went out, together, to a Chinese restaurant nearby or with some of her old friends still in the town, to Peter's Bar and the Restoration Inn. She was cheerful then, but I found empty half bottles of gin and cider flagons beneath the kitchen sink, which explained why: she drugged herself at nights and at weekends. And there were fresh bottles and flagons that she had bought for us both of us when I arrived so in the evenings we didn't have to talk of things that were painful. The fact, for example, that she and Nat had abandoned seven children, one after the other, more or less every year from 1937 to 1944.

Biddy had wanted to be buried with Nat, in Dublin. So I arranged for her to be flown over to Dublin, where she had her wish at Deansgrange cemetery. 'In death they were not divided.' Though poetic biblical phrases are hardly appropriate. Hers had been an unhappy life, redeemed only by her love for an impossible man. But does such love redeem us? Or demean us? Put it another way – my mother accepted her fate with Nat, as we seven abandoned children were left to accept ours with strangers.

So what of my other six brothers and sisters, Geraldine, Antony, Camillus, Sheelagh, Michael and Patrick? I was brought up as a Protestant, on my father's side of the Dublin Hone family, while Geraldine and Antony, who came after me, were brought up by Biddy's parents, the Catholic Anthonys, in their small cottage in Piltown, south Kilkenny. Though our grandmother, Mrs Anthony, was a kind, caring and good woman, they both had a much rougher time than I did, in fairly impoverished rural circumstances, going to the local Catholic national school, short of clothes and shoes and with several other aunts and uncles living there and further relations crowding in and out – so that the two of them were pretty well waifs by the fireside.

However, being Catholic rather saved Geraldine and Antony some years later. Our rich Hone cousin, Evie Hone, the famous stained-glass artist who had created the new east window at Eton College chapel, and who had become a Catholic convert in the 1920s, heard of their plight and arranged to pay for their education and holiday board, via a handsome sum administered by the archbishop of Dublin, Dr McQuaid. So they both went to the best Dublin Catholic boarding schools and afterwards to University College, where they took good degrees, in English and Economics. Evie also left them six thousand pounds each to see them on their way in the world. Geraldine made good use of the money when she married a fellow student, Brian McSwiney, who had done very well with a law degree. They bought a house in Dublin with her money, which laid a good foundation for them and their two children, Myles and Morgan. The marriage came apart later and Geraldine afterwards worked in the art world, for Christies in Dublin and latterly as the successful painter that she remains today.

Antony on the other hand sadly let the money go to his head, literally, with an attachment to the bottle. He married, in England, the actress Frances White, with whom he had a bright daughter, Katherine, who, like Nat and Camillus, went to New College, Oxford. Unlike both of them she graduated with honours in Maths and is now a professor of the subject at Brunel University. However, after Antony's marriage broke up he apparently slid downhill. He had literary gifts and worked on these sporadically, but without publishing success, so that he took to odd jobs, worked as a milk-man for a time, I heard, and afterwards for an insurance company in Surrey. He was chesty and never very strong. He was the twin of Camillus, whom the unmarried, childless Pamela Travers had adopted in Dublin in 1940. Biddy had landed the two babies on my grandfather in Killiney a month or so before Pamela arrived on the scene, and Old Joe, anxious to get rid of the squirming bundles as soon as possible, had said to her, 'Take two, they're small.' She didn't. She took the stronger-looking one, Camillus, who wasn't crying when she saw them first. But she also chose Camillus on the advice of an astrologer in California who, having pondered the twins' birthsigns and timings, firmly recommended she take Camillus and not Antony.

Antony died in 2005, of pneumonia and cancer in a Surrey hospital. His was the saddest of all my siblings' lives, I think. One reason for this was that, more than Geraldine and I, he was deeply unsettled by the abandonment by his real parents and by the discovery, when it came, that Pamela had chosen his twin over him. Antony, with this ache in his heart, was unable ever to get to grips with his life and to make something of it. He reminded me of Stephen Dedalus in Joyce's *Ulysses*, the ever-wandering poet in search of a father. He was a real victim of Nat and Biddy's fecklessness.

But in 1958 Antony tried to come to terms with his abandonment and perhaps set his disquiet at some rest. He had known about his twin Camil-lus and feeling, understandably, that he'd like to meet him, that this might help him find some anchor in his life, had found out where Camillus and Pamela lived in Chelsea and had turned up on their doorstep, announcing to Camillus, who opened the door, 'I'm your twin brother.'

Sensation! Camillus had no idea he had a twin brother. Pamela had never told him. Indeed she had originally told Camillus nothing of his real family, saying that his father had been a colonial sugar planter who had died of a fever. In fact Pamela was thinking of her own father here, who had been a sugar planter in Australia and had then been a bank manager up-country before being demoted to a clerk in another bank. Mr Banks in *Mary Poppins* is surely an idealized version of her father, a longed-for conventional pater-familias since, in reality, her father had died suddenly when she was seven, after a long association with the bottle. Mary Poppins didn't so much come down to earth beneath a parrot-headed umbrella, but as an improving fiction straight out of her own disrupted childhood.

And Pamela's fictional gifts encouraged her to invent in reality, so that Camillus only discovered who he really was in his early teens, when he had found his old ration book in a drawer with the name HONE–TRAVERS on it. Who was the Hone?

When he met his twin Antony, the plot thickened, or rather liquefied, for the two of them at once set out on the town, for some days, around the Chelsea pubs. Pamela was not amused. She had had difficulties enough already with Camillus, largely no doubt consequent on her inventing a father for him and not telling him who he really was. To have told the truth might have made things easier for both of them.

The truth, however, never had a very firm root in Pamela's nature. As with Tony Guthrie letting drama leak into his real life over Annaghmakerrig, Pamela had let fantasy flood into hers and, like Tony, she had some very good reasons. Pamela, first and foremost, was a fairytale storyteller, a fantasist to the tip of Mary Poppins's parrot-headed umbrella. Like her creation, Pamela's imagination took her on fabulous aerial journeys, to the stars and down over London town, landing with her cornucopia of a carpet bag to look after the eager but unsettled Banks children. Like Carroll with Alice and Barrie with Peter Pan, Pamela found herself in possession of a universal figure, a magic nanny who has roused the wonder and delight of generations of children. The problem was that Pamela had not the nannying and mothering skills of her creation. Rather the opposite. She had her cake with Mary Poppins and wanted to eat it – with Camillus. As a letter from her to Hubert in January 1959 shows, her life with Camillus was no fairy-tale.

My dear Hubert,

I brooded long on your letter and was indeed grateful for all the details. And today came Joe's letter, which pleased me very much for it was so mannerly and manly. At first I want to say that I think Camillus's problems are far and away more serious than those you tell me as regards the others, for in addition to all the boasting, 'plushiness' you speak of in Joe, C (at times) has a complete disbelief … in everything …

His present attitude towards the world is one of cynicism – taken up in order that the world might reject him and therefore give him the opportunity of wholeheartedly rejecting it … Today I have been in bed, tired and not well and he came in and talked – I am the only person he really opens up to and then it is to pour out all his negative stuff. This is part of his cruelty, but I feel I must bear it with him for it is backed with unhappiness. He said 'The best thing you could have done was to write to m'tutor and say you were not prepared to pay any more fees and then I needn't go back to Oxford.' I protested that it was not right for me to do that – that he was again leaning on me to live his life for him, that if he really wished that he himself must write. But he would not face that. And went on to ask what was the use of it, he wasn't interested in life there, what indeed was the use of anything, life had no meaning, etc., etc.

I spoke of National Service and he said that although the ten weeks square bashing might be hard – after that he would probably like it. 'Why hard? You know I live in myself, nothing touches me, what does it matter if it is hard? I wouldn't notice it!' Etc. etc. I put up the constructive thing and he cleverly demolishes it. But he knows that in hurting me he is really hurting himself and so do I, and I suffer for him …

My heart aches over him … I read him large chunks of your letter, also Joe's. He said he was quite willing to meet the others … And there is something else that must be clear to all the children – C. is legally adopted. This, unlike marriage, is something that cannot be undone … It will be clear to the others that he is my son. C gets very annoyed if anybody speaks to him of me as 'Pamela' instead of 'your mother'. Somewhere he values this. He says again and again to me 'Well, I'm your son and you've got to bear with it!' and he knows I do not want anything else.

He, as well as I, didn't think highly of Antony's behaviour last year … I will write to Joe and ask him to come and see me. In any case I would much like to meet him, especially if he wants to be a writer … As to the suggestion that C should see Nat, he was not enthusiastic … Biddy would be the worst shock, I think, for C loves children and home and homey things and is always appalled at people hurting children. But Biddy will lie herself out of it all …

Another problem – the three that came after him. He knows about them but I do not know if the others do and they are bound to find out. Indeed, probably best, for then they will not wonder why only C was adopted, though in fact they have all been cast out and I don't want C to feel alone in it … He

254

will not share himself, nor make a real relationship anywhere ... and I put this down to his parents' early rejection, which I have worked for nearly 20 years to make up to him. What he suffers, I suffer double ... I think he has the stuff in him, but not the application. If he could only find something that seemed to him worthwhile. Till recently, it was money, but that seems to be waning ... He has a £150 a year allowance, which must cover clothes, or some of them, but he goes about with holes in his shoes and uncut hair ... At the moment I am letting it be so, in the hope that he will learn. I have run to his assistance too often. He must feel what it is like not to have me do so.

So, no more ... The waste appals me, so much energy expended on nothing. If only he would offer me more constructive thought I would feel less dammed up, physically and mentally. But perhaps it will pass. So many parents I know are anxious. Thank you again for writing to me so well and frankly. Love to you both and I'll write to Joe tomorrow.

Pamela.

A heartrending letter. One can see how Pamela didn't lack the motherly impulse. Just the opposite. It was so strong in her that she foolishly adopted Camillus against the firm advice of her closest friends, as Valerie Lawson recounts in her fine biography. Her friends well knew that Pamela didn't have the happy nappy nursery temperament for motherhood. That was no fault of Pamela's. The fault lay in her believing she had the mothering temperament and going ahead regardless. But then she had originally been an actress in Australia and was a highly imaginative writer. So it was understandable that, without a secure family background of her own, husbandless and loverless, she should invent a real family, as she had the fictional Banks family – a father for Camillus, an imagined husband and motherhood for herself. And if not actual motherhood, then she would be the magic nanny herself. If she had invented Mary Poppins, then she could be Mary Poppins. Why not? The victim in all this was Camillus. He wasn't a character in a fairy-tale.

On the other hand, had she not adopted Camillus he would likely have been sent off to the crowded, impoverished cottage in south Kilkenny with the other two, Geraldine and Antony. Would he have fared better there? Perhaps at least he would have known who his real parents and family were;

Pamela's not talking about this surely created a large part of his subsequent problems. Perhaps not. Pamela, with her undivided attention, love, patience, her imaginative responses to his problems, and her money, gave Camillus many practical and priceless things that he would never have had from the Hone family.

In any case Pamela was not to be denied in adopting Camillus. Despite her fantasy life and her mysticism among the stars and with Indian and other gurus, there was another side to her: Pamela was a steely, very controlling person. She got what she wanted.

It's interesting, too, how she says in the letter that Camillus's meeting Biddy would be 'the worst shock', and that Biddy would 'lie her way out of it all …' Presumably Pamela means that Biddy would pretend that she had nothing to do with abandoning us, that it was all Nat's doing.

I did go and see Pamela in her Chelsea house, and stayed there, the idea being that, in meeting me, Camillus would steady himself. I don't know that he did, or that I helped him any, for I saw very little of him in the two or three weeks I spent there up in a top bedroom. I was out in the day – that was my Harrods second-hand book department job – and he was out at night, on the town or in one or other of the private houses in Mayfair that catered for gambling then. I remember thinking, when I did see him, that he was very sophisticated, assured and intelligent, more so than me. And richer. Apart from his hundred-and-fifty-pound allowance he seemed to make quite a success of his gambling. I remember in the small hours one morning hearing a to-do in the hall. Looking down the stairwell I could just see the two of them, Camillus gesticulating, then saying to Pamela, 'You think I don't earn any money!' and then his throwing a snowfall of those old white five-pound notes up in the air.

On an evening, in the hope that Camillus would join us, Pamela and I sat in her first-floor drawing-room chatting rather warily, over drinks that she equally warily mixed from a cupboard on the landing: fifty-fifty, sweet and dry vermouth. Pamela was fluffy, grey-haired, laden with gold bangles and a lovely jade necklace – small and fragile, but very keen-eyed. She was a tough one. She was an artist. And she had the application. She lived to be ninety-six and left well over two million pounds.

I met her once more by chance, twenty years later, when we were both asked to the Kilkenny Arts Festival to speak in Kilkenny Castle; me about one of my novels, she to entertain a group of children about fairy tales and Mary Poppins, simultaneously so that neither of us heard the other talk. Needless to say she had an audience of hundreds and I about twenty. She gave me a lift back to Dublin in a huge limo that her publishers had laid on for her and, on parting at the Shelbourne Hotel where she was staying, I signed my novel for her on the roof of the limo: 'For Pamela, with love.' Looking at the inscription, then across at me, she said briskly, 'Love? You should never write that to someone unless you mean it.' Of course she was right. I didn't love her. But I learnt that from her – I never wrote the word 'love' again in any book dedication unless I meant it.

There is a final coda to my connection, or rather non-connection, with Pamela. Years on, when threatened with foreclosure on our cottage mortgage, which meant all of us would have been evicted from the place, I wrote to Pamela asking for a loan, two or three thousand pounds, which I would make a legal agreement to repay from my next royalties or from an advance payment on my next book. There was no reply, not a murmur, not even an old white five-pound note. As it turned out the day – and the cottage – was saved. Jacky rustled up some money of her own, and I had a good advance for my next novel from Sinclair-Stevenson and Pan Books. She was a tough one all right, that little old lady of Cherry Tree Lane.

Finally there are siblings to account for: Sheelagh and her twin Michael – born in Oxford in July 1941 (Michael died eighteen months later), and the last one, Patrick, born in February 1944, though I didn't learn of any of these names and dates until long afterwards. The story of these three is the toughest part of the Nat and Biddy story, and the most perplexing. First of all, as a child, I didn't know I had these two younger siblings, let alone three. They had never been mentioned, by my real parents, grandparents or the Butlers. They had been erased from the record. Until one morning in the summer of 1966, in my BBC office, I had a phone call. 'Hello, is that Joe Hone?' 'Yes.' 'Hello! I'm Sheelagh, your sister.'

A north country accent. I thought someone was playing a joke on me. But it was true. Sheelagh lived in Cheshire, she said, and would like to meet me. We made a lunch date at the BBC for the following week. I waited for her in the foyer of Broadcasting House, rather on tenterhooks. Eventually a tall, blonde young woman in a white summery dress and high heels came in, startlingly attractive, looking very like the movie star Kim Novak. All eyes followed her to the reception desk. It must be Kim Novak, I thought, coming in for a movie interview. But it wasn't. It was Sheelagh, for the receptionist pointed me out on the bench and she walked easily towards me, a fresh snowy dream of a woman, the never-known sister.

We talked over lunch, and at least some of the 'How on earth?' questions were answered then. She, and Michael before he died, and later Patrick, had been brought up in what I gathered was something of a baby farm in Wilmslow, Cheshire, by a Mrs Trevor, always a 'Mrs', though Sheelagh had never known any man in the house. Sheelagh was twenty-four when I first met her, married with one child. Mrs Trevor had told her that she, Michael and Patrick had been adopted as babies from parents in the slums of Manchester. Sheelagh, in her teens, had come to feel there was something phoney about Mrs Trevor's explanation of her background. Indeed, some months before she met me, this had been confirmed for her when, just like Camillus, she had found her old ration book in a drawer, with the name TREVOR–HONE on the cover. And, just like Camillus, she had asked her 'mother' who the Hone was. Mrs Trevor must have said that the Hones were the Manchester slum parents.

Sheelagh wasn't convinced; before this, she had overheard Mrs Trevor, with someone in the house, speaking of Ireland, and so she had the idea that there was something Irish about her. So she had rung directory enquiries from a friend's house and asked for the names of any Hones in the Irish telephone directory. There were only three, my grandparents' Dublin number, my uncle David's and my cousin Oliver Hone's. She picked Oliver and rang him up, speaking to his wife Muriel. Sheelagh asked if she might be part of the Dublin Hone family. 'Oh,' said Muriel, 'yes, you must be. But you should contact your older brother, Joe Hone, at the BBC. He'll tell you all about your family.'

So she rang me, and, when she came down to London, she told me something of herself, as I did of myself, or as much as we had time for, since

258

I was recording a programme that afternoon. Sheelagh came down again a few months later and stayed with Jacky and me for a night in our flat in Holborn. We all learnt some more but not much. It was a hurried visit, since we were preparing to leave for New York and the UN where I was to take up work as a producer in their radio and television department. We left early in 1967. I had Sheelagh's address. We'd be in touch.

When we came back from New York two years later I tried telephoning her. But Sheelagh had moved, I'd no idea where, and I lost touch with her for nearly forty years. It wasn't until writing this memoir in the summer of 2006 that I tried to get in touch with her again. So I wrote to my brother Antony's ex-wife, the actress Frances White, and struck lucky. Frances did know about Sheelagh, but not of her whereabouts now. She told me that she'd become good friends with Sheelagh ten years before, after her marriage with Antony had dissolved, though they hadn't been in touch for three or four years, not since Sheelagh had gone out to live in Spain. However, my writing to Frances prompted her to make enquiries, and within a week she came back to me saying she had traced her. Sheelagh had sold her house in Spain over a year before and had returned to England, and Frances had her new address and phone number for me. Sheelagh was living in the village of Lostock, outside Bolton in Lancashire. I phoned her. She was surprised, but calm.

Apart from the north country tones, her voice had exactly the same timbre as my sister Geraldine's. We made a date to meet and then I drove up to see her on a boiling July day. I surprised her at eleven o'clock. She was standing in the neat back garden of her new Barratt Homes maisonette, her skin bathed in golden light. She looked just like a taller version of Geraldine. Tousled blonde hair, bronzed, very trim in white tie-waisted cotton trousers and T-shirt, looking fifteen years younger than her sixty-five years. A dream again, such as I'd seen when I'd first met her in the foyer of Broadcasting House forty years before. An older Kim Novak? No, this was much better. This was my real sister, Sheelagh.

It's strange to look at a more-or-less complete stranger and know she is your sister. Absolute unreality, before she embraced me. Inside, in the neat living room, Sheelagh took up the talk at once, fluently, openly, as if we'd seen each other the week before and not forty years ago, talk of where and how she and I had been brought up, and what had happened to us later, talk way into the long hot afternoon.

She told me much more of her own upbringing, first of all of Mrs Trevor: 'a dog' as she said of her, and a liar, who had died in her mid-forties, of a brain tumour. 'In her mid-forties?' I asked. 'Surely she must have been older when she died? Mid-forties? That would have made her a teenager, when she took you over.' 'Yes, she was a teenager when she took me over. She was nineteen when I arrived on the scene.'

I was astonished. So Nat and Biddy had given Sheelagh – and her twin Michael, since he must have been with her, though Sheelagh doesn't remember him – to a teenager, and had followed them up by abandoning the last child Patrick to Mrs Trevor as well several years later: to some sort of baby farm run by a 'dog' and a liar.

There were still questions to be answered. First, how did Nat and Biddy meet the nineteen-year-old Mrs Trevor? There is no record of her in any of the Hone family letters, and Sheelagh doesn't know. Oxford, where the twins were born, is a long way from Wilmslow, in Cheshire. But Sheelagh remembered one clue. She had heard, somehow, that Nat had had a job in a Manchester department store early in the war, presumably with Biddy and the twins there as well. Did they meet Mrs Trevor then? In a pub? And unloaded the twins on her? This is possible, since it ties in with Mrs Trevor telling Sheelagh that she'd been adopted from a Manchester slum family. Was this slum family Nat and Biddy and the twins, penniless and possibly living in slum conditions? If so this gives a Dickensian twist to the tale, knowing what the Manchester slums must have been like in the early 1940s. But then, if one adds to this the death of Sheelagh's twin Michael, at eighteen months, we are moving into the rich melodrama of *East Lynne*, and the last despairing words there: 'Dead! And … never called me mother.'

But why and where did Michael die? And where is he buried? I suppose I could search through the Cheshire or Lancashire county records for a death certificate. But I don't feel inclined. I do feel inclined to say that the fate of these three children, at the hands of Nat and Biddy, is one of the most heartless things I've ever heard of.

Sheelagh had a child with her first husband, but they divorced and she remarried. She had three more children with her second husband before that marriage, too, ran out of steam. The man never paid for the family's keep, and not a penny for Sheelagh. So she saved up ten pounds, hid the notes under the living-room carpet and left early one morning with the three children back up north, to her homelands around Wilmslow and Manchester. The children have all done well. Jonathan, her first born, is a solicitor, and married with children, in Devon. Sheelagh's other three children, from her second marriage, have succeeded in their various ways, including her daughter Sally, a lovely girl whom I met later that day in Lostock, an IT consultant who lives just up the road from Sheelagh.

Sheelagh, having bought the house near Málaga, lived there for two years, but missed her family and friends and came back to Lostock and the bijou residence, where I met her. Despite the obvious emotional pain and the other material difficulties consequent on Nat and Biddy's abandoning her, Sheelagh is now a calm, balanced, beautiful woman.

There is still Patrick to account for, the last of the children to have been given away by Nat and Biddy, in February 1944, two-and-a-half years after Sheelagh and Michael had been unloaded on Mrs Trevor. But Patrick got on better with Mrs Trevor than Sheelagh did. When Sheelagh married her first husband in her early twenties, Myles Martin, whose father ran a garage, Patrick became absorbed in motor cars; to such an extent that, though he'd done little work at school, he decided in his late teens that he wanted to be an engineer, sat four 'A' Levels in nine months, got into Leeds University and took a good engineering degree.

In his early twenties, Patrick went to Norway on a holiday with three of his mates – flirting with delicious blonde girls no doubt. Patrick married one of them later, and went to live in Oslo and had children. Knowing of his Hone background by now, and hating everything he'd heard of it, he changed his name by deed poll to Trevor, with no Hone in it, wanting nothing to do with what he found out about his real family.

Subsequently, with the oil-drilling boom of the 1970s and 1980s, Patrick travelled the world, from North-Sea oil rigs to Far-Eastern jungles, earning a lot of money. But his marriage failed and he lives alone now, Sheelagh told me, as something of a recluse on a Norwegian fjord, in a cliff house filled with good furniture, silk tapestries and fine Japanese paintings.

I, and most of my brothers and sisters, have survived and done reasonably well in life. But we have not managed much emotional security, in ourselves or in our marriages. This can largely be laid at Nat and Biddy's door. Larkin's poem comes particularly to mind: it might have been written for me and my siblings: 'They fuck you up, your Mum and Dad ...' Of course millions of other children, whole continents of them, have had far worse upbringings. The point is that, given our backgrounds, none of us should have had these painful starts and difficult lives.

Are there any final conjectures I can make about our parents, which might explain why they abandoned all their seven children? Biddy came from a poor but loving Irish country cottage background. Her misfortune was that, like so many other young Irish women of similar background in those times (and later), she went to London in 1936 as a rural innocent, to train as a nurse; when she met Nat she was all too readily seduced by his good looks, charm and sophistication – and his money. Nat was clearly in charge at the beginning, and was a very different creature then; the confident but careless scion of a cultured and moneyed Dublin family. Naturally intelligent, he'd also had the best possible education, and when he was twenty-one a lot of money of his own, from his rich Hone cousin in Albany, Piccadilly. In short, Nat had every possible advantage. Except a crucial one: his parents, Old Joe and Vera, though with no lack of affection, concern and effort had, like many parents of that generation, no idea how to love him. Nat, wilful and spoilt, had not the temperament or good sense to settle for conventional parental affection. He needed a much fuller, unquestioned emotional connection.

As a result he remained a spoilt child, searching for a love he felt he'd been denied, but which Biddy readily supplied, becoming his very willing lover and camp follower. Their relationship became make do, with no real foundations, and the situation collapsed when TB struck Nat down in 1939, and he realized he wasn't going to be up to managing himself, let alone an increasing family. Minus half a lung, with the bacteria no doubt lurking in the other, he must have felt that death was waiting for him just round the corner, since there was no real cure for tuberculosis in those days.

So he lost all sense of responsibility and felt he might as well fling the sexual dice about before he died, in a further careless legacy of three more children. He forgot any ideas of sensible survival: his only survival lay in Biddy – his attachment at all costs to a woman who he knew loved him unconditionally and would therefore cater for him financially, emotionally, and sexually. From this came the irresponsibility of having three more children they knew they couldn't support. These children, like the earlier four, had to be thrown out as well. There was only room for one child in the family, and that was Nat.

Biddy, though, must have been at fault as well. Where was her maternal instinct? Quite lost, I think, in thrall to Nat, for how else could she have continued to conceive children she knew would soon have to be abandoned? The whole business wasn't about their not using contraceptives, or failing to keep to the monthly rhythm method of avoiding pregnancy. They could have used both methods. No, it was a total failure of conscience and imagination that set Nat and Biddy out on producing children they couldn't support, and in their not seeing the sad and difficult futures to which they were condemning us all. On the other hand, would it have been better if none of us had been born? Hardly. For most of us existence of any sort is surely better than non-existence.

For symmetry in this ending about my brothers and sisters, I considered visiting Patrick on his Norwegian fjord. But why extend the pain by reminding him again of the family unhappiness? Pain enough for him already. And for me as well. I've found something, in writing this last chapter and other parts of my story, in having to unearth and face the unhappy reality of what happened to us children. I've found something I've avoided facing in any detail all my life: the real pain of it all.

Well, I've faced it now, and I don't feel any the better for it. I wrote at the beginning of this memoir how, in my early seventies, I would surely be immune from any possible hurt I might suffer from unpleasant discoveries I might make in these letters, and through delving into my own past and that of my family. I was wrong. The wounds of my own abandonment, healed over happier years, have opened again. Though I acknowledge them now, they are no easier to bear. Rather the opposite: I've come to realize the full sadness of it all, for me and my siblings – and that makes the wounds more painful. So Patrick meanwhile must remain the brother I have never met, in a real family I never had.

Nearly every life, though, has its compensations, in the living and the luck of it, and I have had a great deal of both. There have been many happy things for me. So I'll see if I can get hold of the last survivor of my minders and mentors on the phone now, Kingsley Scott. He has a flat in Marrakesh; but he should be back in Dublin for the summer. Meanwhile I'll remember my fine fast schoolboy trips with him, winding up the Dublin mountains in his red MG, and our lamb chop and claret lunches in the Hibernian, and I will put on one of the Piaf tapes he gave me years ago, and smoke a Gitane.